PRESENT AND POWERFUL

PRESENT AND POWERFUL

A TESTIMONY OF GOD'S WORKING IN MEDICAL MISSIONS

Mary Broeckert, M.D.

XULON PRESS

Xulon Press
2301 Lucien Way #415
Maitland, FL 32751
407.339.4217
www.xulonpress.com

Paperback ISBN-13: 978-1-66283-359-5
Ebook ISBN-13: 978-1-66283-360-1

TABLE OF CONTENTS

Preface vii

PART 1: NORTH AMERICA 1

Chapter 1: Michigan 3
   Following the Cows 3
   Higher Education and Starting Missionary Service
   1971-1982 15

PART 2: AFRICA 19

Chapter 2: Mali 1982-1984 21
   Beyond Timbuktu 21
   Daily Life 27
   Ministry 36
   Family Times 44
   Moving from Mali to CAR 52

Chapter 3: Central African Republic 1985-1990 59
   Bangui 59
   Immanuel 70
   Patients and Staff 75
   Laird Memorial Project 84
   God's Care 96

Chapter 4: Central African Republic 1991-1995 111
   1991 Unrest 112
   1992 Serving as a Family 113

1993 Serving Other Towns in CAR. 118
1994 Serving Together. 128
1995 Increasing Trouble 134

PART 3: SOUTHEAST ASIA **137**

Chapter 5: Phnom Penh, Kingdom of Cambodia 2001-2003 . .139
Arrival Provisions 139
Medical Work in Phnom Penh 145
Water 151
Fire 153
Church Planting 154
Permission for Koh Kong work. .159

Chapter 6: Koh Kong 2004-2006 165
The Beginning of Koh Kong Baptist Church. 165
Starting at Koh Kong Hospital 169
In the Hands of Khmer Rouge 176
The Boat That Sank 180
Cham Yiem 187

Chapter 7: Koh Kong 2007-2011 191
The Growing Church. 191
Medical Work in Koh Kong. 205
Life in Koh Kong 225

Chapter 8 Koh Kong 2012 – 2016 .233
2012 Victories 233
2013 Rejoicing. 239
2014 Grateful. 246
2015 Peace 256
2016 Finishing in Cambodia 261

Preface

Declaring God's awesome deeds that we have seen Him do gives glory to His great name. From the Lord's loving care on the farm in Michigan, through His grace saving me, His calling me to be a missionary doctor, and the years of preparation He guided and enabled. He worked in lives in the hot Saharan sands of Mali, He provided care to the sick at the mission hospital of Ippy, Central African Republic, and then He displayed His deeds in a rainy province of southwest Cambodia. Truly, He is God, present and powerful, and we can joyfully entrust our lives to Him.

The information in this book was taken from daily journals I kept throughout the years, and from letters. Some names have been changed to protect privacy.

PART 1

NORTH AMERICA

Chapter 1

Michigan

You make known to me the path of life;
in your presence is fullness of joy.
Psalm 16:11

Following the Cows

Two old milk cows plodded up the pasture lane. Their narrow, well-worn path meandered beside the ditch and creek. A few tall sturdy trees lent shade. Spring trilliums and tadpoles beckoned. The cows' daily routine was simple. After grazing and resting all day, it was time to head into the stanchions for the evening milking. I followed the cows to the barn, occasionally prodding them to continue walking. Bringing in the cows was a fun chore. By the cow path was a large rock, a thinking place. One could climb up and sit on the bolder to just think, and talk to God. The Lord was so good. He had worked wonderfully. He had given me knowledge about Him through the lives and teaching of wonderful parents and a great church. He had blessed me with three older sisters, Peggy, Joan, and Sue, and two younger brothers, Tom and Mark. He had given the joy of working together on the farm. "Thank you, Lord, for what

You have done. Please guide my life to accomplish whatever You desire with it, for Your glory."

My mind recalled Dad's well-worn Bible, and the times seeing Mom (Betty Fuller Hovingh) on her knees before the Lord by the living room couch before sunrise, while Dad (Robert Hovingh) was out doing morning barn chores. Mom, an excellent storyteller, practiced her Sunday School lessons at home for teaching her class at church. After smoothing the beautiful flannelgraph backgrounds on the back of the sofa, she would carefully place each colorful figure while telling the story from her Bible. My siblings and I watched with rapt attention. Another day, it would be her Good News Club story that we listened to as she prepared it. Then, on the weekly day for the club, she would drive to pick up neighbor kids and bring them to our home to sing, learn verses, and hear the Bible story and missionary story. Later, the club moved to our public school after school hours. Our family never missed a service at church and sometimes classmates from school would go with us.

In the evening, when Dad got home from his millwork company in Grand Rapids, supper was ready in the dining room. There was happy, lively conversation and delicious food – most of it from our farm. We had to practice good manners, which included no bragging and no complaining. The siblings were very good at enforcing the rules with each other. At the end of the meal, Dad would read a chapter in the Bible, or help one of the children read it. After clearing off the dishes we all would head outside, happy to work together outside until bedtime. There were fences to fix for the hundred or so head of beef cattle, hay to be baled, chickens to butcher, and corn to harvest. Mom tucked each of us into bed and prayed with us. We could always tell Mom and Dad loved God, loved each other, and loved us.

Nicknames are usually fun, and it wasn't until my third sister started school that I discovered she had a name other than "Bug." So, we deduced that "Sue" was her school name. However, my nickname was less flattering, though more fitting, and fortunately, less used. It was "Fussyduck." I only remember two spankings from my dad (though I know there were more). One was for fussing at the dinner table, for I did want my own way and had a habit of complaining. Dad always gave one warning, and only one. When we persisted in doing wrong, he administered the consequences. We learned that sin needs to be punished. We learned that Dad spoke the truth. We learned to obey. The other spanking was for being noisy in church. We learned to respect the worship of God and not interfere with others hearing the Word of God.

I knew I was a sinner. I also understood from God's Word that the consequence of sin is death – separation from God – eternity in the lake of fire. God, who is merciful and loving, sent Jesus to die on the cross to take my sin and punishment. On the third day, He rose again. He invites people to "Believe in the Lord Jesus, and you will be saved" (Acts 16:31). So I sometimes prayed at night in bed, "Please save me, God. I don't want to go to hell." But saying a prayer did not save me.

Sunday night, December 4, 1960, there was a special speaker at church. After the message, he asked everyone to close their eyes, bow their heads and search their hearts. He said if we wanted to be saved, to raise our hand. I hesitated at first, but God's Spirit was working in my heart, and I raised my hand. After that everyone stood to sing an invitation hymn. The speaker said whoever had raised their hand should walk to the front and someone would talk with them. My old nature resisted, and I was embarrassed, but God was convicting me of my need and helped me walk to the front of the church.

My Sunday School teacher, Lois Zimmer, slipped away from the piano and led me into the prayer room. She took her Bible and said to put my name in John 3:16 in the place of "whosoever." She explained more, and I prayed, asking God to take away my sin and save me. That night I truly believed God, and He washed away my sin and came to live in my heart. He gave me such joy. From that time on I knew for certain God had given me salvation. "Because, if you confess with your mouth that Jesus is Lord and believe in your heart that God raised Him from the dead, you will be saved. For with the heart one believes and is justified, and with the mouth one confesses and is saved" (Romans 10:9-10). We used to sing a chorus, "A little child of seven, or even three or four, can enter into heaven, through Christ the open door." I was that child seven years old. God saved me and changed me. Later, Dad called me by a new nickname, "Sunshine."

Each Saturday morning, we six kids cleaned the church with Mom. As I dusted book racks on the back of pews, I asked God to please let me serve Him with my whole life in even bigger ways. He said to be faithful in small things first. Each of us children had responsibility for daily barn chores such as feeding and watering cows, cleaning pens, or gathering eggs. Chores had to be done before coming to supper. When we were old enough, Dad assigned tasks such as dragging a field, to prepare the soil after it is plowed. Dad would carefully explain and draw the pattern to follow with the tractor and drag. It gave a sense of accomplishment to finish what Dad assigned and do it well. It is the same with our heavenly Father. It gives us joy to accomplish the work God gives us (John 4:34).

On the big rock in the pasture lane, I talked to God about His will for my life. I knew He would show me, and that gave much peace. But in anticipation of having to choose courses in high school to prepare for a vocation, I asked the Lord, if it pleased him, to show me what to train for, to serve Him. Whatever direction He would take me, I needed to know his Word well. Daily in my devotions I studied the Bible. Books with questions to fill in helped me think more about passages. Memorizing verses gave joy, as did completing Sunday School lessons. The Scriptures were so precious.

As our family read letters from our aunt, Carolyn Hovingh, a missionary nurse in Liberia, West Africa, we learned of treks in the jungle, crossing swinging bridges, caring for leprosy patients, and people responding to the teaching of God's Word. We listened eagerly to missionaries at church or visiting our home, tell of faraway places like Timbuktu, or peoples of the Orient. We heard and read many missionary stories and biographies. The annual week-long missions conference at church was a highlight of the year. Posters and other projects were prepared. Often, I prayed, "Lord, please let me be a missionary overseas." Mission boards provided literature about opportunities. Being a teacher or nurse seemed like good options, but God's Spirit whispered, "Missionary doctor." Pictures of ugly tropical skin ulcers made me think I could not do that.

Summer camp was fun every year. Even though I always got homesick, the Bible lessons, games, meals, swimming lessons, and crafts were great. One year, when I was eleven, a special camp called "Jungle Jump Off Camp" was held, staffed by missionaries. My counselor was a missionary from New Guinea (who later gave her life for the Lord there in a landslide). The speaker was a missionary doctor. While I listened to him, God was working in my heart. After the meeting, I went directly to my bunk in the cabin, alone. God was saying, "You asked, and I am showing you that I want you to be a missionary doctor." I answered, "Lord, if that is Your will, take my life and make me a missionary doctor. I cannot do it, but You can." God gave great peace as I yielded to Him. After that I joyfully anticipated seeing God make me what He had chosen. "He who calls you is faithful; he will surely do it" (I Thessalonians 5:24).

Throughout the years of school studying to prepare for serving God overseas, He reassured me many times that this was His call. Frequently, missionaries gave an invitation at the end of their presentations. Anyone who felt God may be calling them to be a missionary and were willing to go anywhere and do anything for God, could walk to the front. The church was encouraged to pray for those who went forward. When I first responded to that invitation I was scared. Yes, I was willing to live or to die for Christ. But the path ahead was so unknown. On later occasions, when the same invitation was given, I felt no fear, only joy because I knew God could be trusted completely to take good care of His servants. "I delight to do your will, O my God" (Psalm 40:8).

Basketball was one of the ways God taught perseverance. From sixth grade through high school there were practices and games, with valuable lessons on sportsmanship and teamwork. During practice drills, my muscles would ache, but the coach would make us run yet more. It built endurance. Wednesday evenings required leaving practice early to go to prayer meeting at church, a priority. We had good teams and good coaches. Often when I got home after a game, Dad would ask how many points I made. I loved playing and appreciated my parents' encouragement.

Parental training also included handling money carefully, as God's stewards. Dad arranged jobs such as raising our own beef cows, or growing cucumbers for the pickle company. He worked up the ground for his corn field and measured off an acre near the house where I planted cucumber seeds. When the plants started producing, I had to pick them. Wow! An acre sure was big! The task seemed overwhelming, but Mom often helped me. She also drove me the twenty-five minutes to Zeeland to deliver them to the factory in keeping with my contract. The pickle field was so hot in the summer. I told the Lord, "If You take me as a missionary someday to a tropical country where it is hot all the time, You will have to make me able to bear the heat." He faithfully did.

While in high school, Dad gave me a Saturday morning job at his millwork company working on architectural plans, detailing doors. The drawings, measurements, lettering, and lists had to be exact. He patiently kept showing me how to improve. He taught me to detail other finished wood trim for Allendale School which I had attended. God was preparing me for when Ippy Hospital was building new buildings in the Central African Republic, and I needed to be familiar with architectural drawings. During college, Dad let me work as a receptionist and assist the bookkeeper, including doing payroll. God's intricate plans for our lives include many experiences in things we will need to use later. He also delights us with variety. Psalm 139:16 says, "In your book were written, every one of them, the days that were formed for me, when as yet there was none of them."

In my freshman year of high school, Mom had two seizures. After the second one, she was hospitalized and extensive testing began. One evening, after returning from the hospital, Dad gathered all of us children around the kitchen table. He gently recounted how God had been so good to us through the years. Now God was bringing a new situation into our family. It had been found that Mom had a malignant brain tumor and probably had only two and a half years left to live on earth. It was impossible to envision what the months ahead would be like, but we knew God would hold us all securely in His loving hands. Mom had brain surgery, radiation, and chemotherapy. That involved many trips to the hospital in Grand Rapids and in between she lay on the couch at home.

In the spring of 1968, Dad placed an order for a new pole barn to be constructed next to our big one-hundred-year-old barn. The materials for construction were scheduled to be delivered but got delayed a week. One late afternoon during that week, I came home from school and did my barn chores as usual. A little later, Tom went out to do his chores. He came running back out of the barn yelling, "The barn's on fire! The barn's on fire!" Joan phoned the fire department and they responded quickly.

Uncle Gene saw the smoke from his farm store in Allendale and arrived faster than the fire trucks. He began by hooking a tractor to the tall gas tank and pulling it away from the chicken coop, preventing an explosion. Firemen arrived and worked with him. Dad arrived home from the millwork a few minutes later. He ran to the back of the burning barn and opened the gates for the penned steers to run out.

The huge blaze could be seen from far away (the farm was on a hill), and cars lined both sides of 68th Avenue to watch. A police car guarded the end of our quarter-mile long driveway to keep people from coming up. Aunt Lois convinced the officer to allow her to enter to help care for Mom. She and others got Mom in her wheelchair to sit at the front door of the house and watch the action. Men were pulling machinery out of the tool shed on the west side before that building burst into flames. Firemen were spraying water on the corn crib and granary to try to preserve those. The fire rapidly leaped from the main barn to the big empty two-story chicken coop and in a short time to all ten buildings, including our three little empty playhouses.

God directed the wind so our house, a bit separate, was spared. Some of my siblings and I along with the neighbor boys were assigned the task of hiking to the woods and fields to round up the released steers into a fenced pasture. The smoldering ashes and stench of a couple carcasses of cows that had not escaped continued through the night and the next days. We counted our blessings from the Lord. No one was injured. The house was totally fine. The construction material for a new barn had not been delivered so it had not been consumed in the fire. Those would arrive in a few days. Very few animals had been lost. God had guarded our hearts in peace through it all. God was in control.

Men from church brought a bulldozer and cleaned up the site. Some men from Dad's office came and helped us sort ears of corn for many evenings – the usable from the ruined. The building crew arrived and put up the new pole barn and later a second, and eventually a third. God cared for us and provided.

The people of our church helped one another in many ways, one of which was adults leading the teen groups. The regular weekly youth group meetings were before or after the Sunday evening service. The young people themselves planned the program including skits or Bible drills or questions and answers – but always varied and aimed at studying the Word of God. Once a month were Saturday evening evangelistic outreaches, bringing unsaved friends. For one of those events, we elaborately decorated a platform in a corner of the fellowship room at church with a banner overhead, "What in the World are You Doing for Heaven's Sake?"

In my sophomore year, health problems brought Aunt Carolyn and Uncle Arthur Washburn back from Liberia where they had been serving God. (Aunt Carolyn had married just a couple of years before, and Uncle Art went to Liberia with her.) The Lord led them to start a church-plant in inner-city Muskegon. The rented old church building was prepared, invitations distributed around the neighborhood, and services began. My initial responsibility was as pianist each Sunday. Eventually, over the next five years, I drove the van to pick up children to come, and learned to teach Sunday

School under Aunt Carolyn's tutoring. She was a rich blessing from God, praying for me and mentoring me.

Peggy was married. Joan went off to college. When Sue entered nursing school, I was the oldest child at home. Peggy and ladies from the church came and took turns caring for Mom every day while Dad was at work and my younger brothers and I were at school. The ladies provided many meals, plus Dad cooked on weekends. He taught me a little about cooking. God lovingly cared for us all. At Joan and Ralph's wedding in December 1969, God gave Mom strength to attend in her wheelchair. She stood with assistance for the wedding photos.

But Mom was getting progressively weaker and had increased pain. Occasionally when the oral pain medication was not helping, we phoned our neighbor who was a nurse, to come give her an injectable pain med. I sat and talked with Mom sometimes, but I wish I had spent more time with her. Dad spent much time with her evenings and weekends. Peggy felt blessed to be her main care provider even though she was also caring for her own toddler, Bobby, and was pregnant for her second child, Valerie. She heard Mom's praying, so aware of the reality of the presence of Christ close to her. God gave Mom blessed anticipation of being in the Lord's presence in heaven. Yes, she felt sorry for her family who would be without her, but she knew God would care for them. She told Peggy the importance of the siblings praying for each other. Mom and Dad prayed for each of us children each day by their bed, which was now in the dining room, since Mom could no longer climb stairs.

The day arrived when Mom slipped into a coma. She remained on the living room couch which had been her place every day for so long. A couple days passed as she lay peacefully still. Then God took her to heaven. It was the beginning of her pain-free, joyous life in her Father's home. The message of hope at her memorial service gave glory to God for His grace and mercy. At the graveside, I was crying, yet so grateful for God's people there who comforted me. It seemed so final that Mom would no longer be there with us. Yet I knew someday I would go join her in heaven and sing praises together to God forever.

Just a month later, I was scheduled to leave for the Philippines as an exchange student. My sister Sue had enjoyed a summer in the Netherlands two years earlier with the school student exchange program. That inspired me to visit the other side of the world. God was guiding me during the months of anticipation, but now I was willing to cancel to stay with Dad. But Dad advised that I keep my commitment. So late June 1970 I was on a chartered plane with about 250 other teenage exchange students. It was so hard to say good-bye to Dad and my brothers, who saw me off. My ten weeks in Butuan City, southern Philippines, were special, in spite of being homesick. Dad's weekly letters to me were so encouraging.

Staying with a Filipino family was a great adventure. I visited the school, flew to other islands and other places on Mindanao island, savored lots of new foods and fruits, and sweated in the heat and humidity. Fellowship with God's people in churches was sweet. God gave opportunity at various times to witness to all seven people in the family I was staying with. There was a lot of free time, so I practiced basketball, read books, and memorized Psalm 139. Verses 9 and 10 were especially precious, "If I take the wings of the morning and dwell in the uttermost parts of the sea, even there your hand shall lead me, and your right hand shall hold me." God was faithful to me through my first overseas experience, and He would continue to be faithful all my life wherever He would take me.

October 1970 was Sue and Steve's wedding. They had beautiful fall colors for their theme. But there was no mother-of-the-bride. Our family seemed so small with just Dad, Tom, Mark, and

I at home. Mark was only ten years old. Since I had more responsibility now in caring for the family, I applied to the College right in our town of Allendale for pre-med studies after high school. That would allow me to stay at home, and I could work part-time at Dad's millwork company to finance my schooling. Dad's policy was that each of us kids pays for our own college education, but he helped provide ways for us to earn money. God got me accepted at Grand Valley State University which was located on property that formerly belonged to my great grandparents.

As the months went on, God brought Fran (Busman) Riemersma into Dad's life. He had known her and her first husband as neighbors nearly twenty-five years earlier. Now she was a widow with four children. Dad and Fran married in March 1971. Of their combined ten children, half were married and out of the house and half were still at home. God was blessing us with a loving, godly, second mother. She taught the Bible to toddlers at church and to elementary school children in Bible Club.

God continued to help me at school. I enjoyed studying and being with friends. Speech class led to being on the school debate team, competing against other schools. The Junior and Senior English classes traveled to Stratford, Ontario, to see Shakespeare plays we had studied. Advanced biology, studying human anatomy and physiology, was my favorite class. It would be useful in practicing medicine in the future. Because "the good hand of my God was upon me" (Nehemiah 2:8), Coopersville High School graduated me as co-valedictorian, which encouraged me to trust the Lord to keep enabling me in the years ahead. Next lay university.

HIGHER EDUCATION AND STARTING MISSIONARY SERVICE 1971-1982

University years were fun. The health science subjects for the pre-professional degree were so interesting. Knowing God's desire that the students and faculty on the secular campus learn of Christ, I prayed for opportunities to witness and rejoiced to see Him give those encounters. There were also Christian groups on campus where Christian friends could encourage each other. Driving from Allendale to Grand Rapids to work at the millwork each afternoon were profitable times to sing, pray, and enjoy the Lord.

The inner-city work in Muskegon with Aunt Carolyn and Uncle Art continued on Sundays. Other volunteers helped on Sundays or Thursdays. One of them, Frank Fitzgerald, told me about his friend Hubert Broeckert, whom he wanted me to meet. He told me Hubert was a student in seminary preparing for further service for the Lord.

The occasion arose when Hubert's car broke down, so he rode with Frank to prayer meeting at my church. Hubert wondered why he did not see me in prayer meeting. But after the service, I arrived from having led the youth group to minister at a nursing home. When I saw the visitor, Hubert, standing in the back of the church, we talked with each other briefly. In the ensuing weeks, we saw each other again at a party for my twentieth birthday, and when he and Frank stopped by the church where my cousin Donna and I were cleaning one Saturday. Hubert phoned later, asking me to play piano at the Mel Trotter Rescue Mission where he would be preaching. Afterward, Hubert invited me out for an ice cream float, the beginning of several months of getting to know each other.

Hubert was a man who loved God and His Word. Because he was from California, it was many years before I met any of his unsaved family. In fact, his parents both passed into eternity soon after Hubert and I met. God had brought Hubert to faith in Christ while he was a soldier in the US army. His roommates took him to church with them, and through the preaching of the Word and the witness of the lives of the people in the church, he saw he needed the Savior. While a brand-new Christian, the Lord took him into the war in Vietnam, working in radio and teletype. Upon discharge, he went to Bible School in Oregon followed by seminary in Grand Rapids, preparing to serve the Lord in full time ministry.

My parents were pleased with Hubert and with God's bringing us together to serve Him in missions. When Hubert asked Dad's permission for my hand in marriage, Dad consented. But he made sure Hubert agreed with my plans for many years of school ahead yet. Hubert shared the same goals, and we were following God's leading. I was honored that Hubert chose me to be his bride. Our lovely Christmas season wedding, December 21, 1973, was small by design, and ladies of our church served a chicken dinner wedding feast. Hubert carried me over the threshold into a mobile home, which we "house-sat" for a man in Florida for the winter. When he returned, we moved three times in the next year, the beginning of innumerable moves all over the world during our lives.

After marriage comes the baby carriage. In the middle of my senior year of pre-med and Hubert's senior year in the M.Div. program of seminary, God gave us our first child, Hannah. What a precious gift. The birth announcement was a little diploma. It was amazing to see God work out our schedules. I did independent study the school term Hannah was born. Grand Valley State University granted me a Bachelor's degree, with high honors, to the glory of God.

That summer, 1975, we moved to East Lansing, Michigan, to begin graduate school in physiology. My applications to medical schools had been declined. Yet God repeatedly had reaffirmed that He would make me a missionary doctor and use us on the foreign field. Obviously, it would be His achievement and not my own. God got me accepted the next year. The one year in the physiology masters program was a great help as some of the classes were applied to my course at Michigan State University College of Human Medicine, allowing me a lighter load in year one of medical school. God provided finances for school through Hubert's jobs, grants, and a small loan from my father which we repaid during the residency year. God wonderfully provided our every need.

In the second year of medical school, God gave us our second child, Cherith. I had been praying that God would give Hannah a sibling. Her birth announcement was a doctor's bag, like mine. In the third year, our third child, Davar, made his entrance. Hubert ministered as assistant superintendent of the Lansing City Rescue Mission and we both served in our local church. God again showed He was fulfilling His plan for our lives by working out our schedules for work and classes so that we seldom needed babysitters.

Taking the next step toward the foreign mission field, we prayed for God's guidance and chose a mission that established churches with the same doctrine as ours. We looked at which countries they were working in that could use church planters and medicine. In 1979 we were accepted for missionary service with Evangelical Baptist Mission. What a thrill to see God move us toward serving Him in Mali, West Africa. While I was doing my final year of medical school and during my one-year flexible residency (internship) at Spectrum Health Butterworth Hospital in Grand Rapids, our family spoke in many churches presenting the ministry in West Africa that God was leading us into. Grand Valley Baptist Church sent us out, even making us a beautiful memory quilt from the families in the church. God moved churches and individuals to be our support team, and we left to begin our first term of missionary service one week after residency was completed.

Linguistics training for two months in North Dakota was the first assignment. It included analyzing unwritten languages and learning skills for language acquisition. With that foundation, God took us to Sherbrooke, Quebec, for French language study. Other missionaries heading to French speaking countries struggled with us in getting the sounds and grammar correct. Our fourth-floor apartment provided a view of the distant hills, and exercise climbing steps while pregnant for our fourth child. Hans was born one week after our final exam for the course, God's perfect timing. We moved to Quebec City where Hubert pursued a summer French language course and I practiced French with neighbors while caring for our four precious little ones. By September 1982, we were off for West Africa! God had faithfully brought us through the years of preparation, showing clearly it was His accomplishment.

PART 2

AFRICA

CHAPTER 2

MALI 1982-1984

"You are my witnesses," declares the LORD, "and
my servant whom I have chosen, that you may
know and believe me and understand that I am he."
Isaiah 43:10

BEYOND TIMBUKTU

God's creation, the vast Sahara Desert, is sand as far as one can see. Stepping out of the plane, I felt a blast of hot air as if stepping into an oven. "Lord, You are sufficient," I prayed. "You have brought us here to Gao, Mali. We are counting on You to make us able to bear the heat and use us in any way You choose." Day after day the temperature hovered around 110° F, peaking at 126° F. Day after day God gave grace for it. And He did much more.

God showed us the beauty of the vast expanse of sand and sand dunes – it was like standing on the edge of the earth. The sun would fade in through the dust above the horizon each new morning and fade out in the evening. Shuffling down the sandy roads of the city, occasionally stopping to empty my sandals, I imagined walking with Jesus as He walked through the streets of Capernaum. Were those houses also mud brick with stairs on the outside going up to the flat roofs? Did He sometimes, like us, sleep on the flat roofs? And gaze at the gorgeous display of bright constellations in a cloudless sky that He had created? Surely, He was walking alongside us now. Sharing common experiences draws us closer to another person. God leads us in paths drawing us closer, to know Him better.

The camel caravans, which had traversed the desert in Abraham's time, still arrived in the livestock market in front of our house. Braying donkeys, frightened sheep, skinny cows, and frisky goats were grouped around sellers and buyers. Down the way were occasional small groups of little boys gathered in front of a Koranic teacher, writing on slates and memorizing Arabic prayers. This was all the schooling most would receive. Groups of men in robes and turbans bowed on mats or rugs in the streets to say Muslim prayers five times a day. How would God break through the stronghold of this religion to call out people for Himself? He had brought us there as His witnesses.

Being in the employment of the King of kings had started twenty-two years before when God made me His child. He had faithfully led and prepared us for this assignment in Africa. Leaving Michigan, we saw God get us to the New York airport on time in spite of car problems driving there. Three days in Dakar gave a little time to acclimate to the four-hour time change, the heat, the markets, dealing with the airport about our baggage, and trying to witness to Africans who spoke only a little English or French. God provided a mission guesthouse for us as we were in transit. The first night, we slept on the floor with lots of mosquitos buzzing around. The guesthouse was at the Atlantic Ocean, and a morning swim was a delightful gift from the Lord. Then came the time for our flight on to Mali.

Red dust covered our feet as we walked through the streets of Mali's capital city, Bamako. And all around were people. One man displayed his rows of brightly patterned cloth for sale. Another clutched several shiny watches in his hand. An old woman squatted by her pile of peanuts and called out to prospective buyers. A young lad supported a one-legged stand spread with candy and pens. A large tin pan of grapefruit balanced on the head of another vendor. A mother nursing her infant smiled and chatted next to her neat little piles of limes and tomatoes for sale. A tray of jewelry was stuffed in front of us for our inspection. A girl followed, persistently offering a sample of her caramel corn. A Tuareg nomad quietly guarded his place at my elbow, turning slowly the hand-fashioned sword he was selling. Amidst the push of the crowds, my mind mulled over the words "For God so loved the world...."

A deformed leprous face smiled and called out. A twisted body hobbled along with a cane – it could be polio. A severely hunch-backed woman – probably from tuberculosis – worked busily in the market. A child led a blind man through the mass of people. Mingling among the women over there was one lady with a large neck tumor. "For God so loved the world, that He gave his only Son..." (John 3:16). "Lord, I want to give these people that which they desperately need – the message that You gave Your only begotten Son so they can have life. Lord, these people are perishing. You love them."

Playful boys ran and jumped over the sewage ditch. Big brown eyes in a tiny black-haired head peeked around from the colorful cloth on his mother's back. A man in a wooden wagon urged his horse on. Several mechanics were covered with the grease of motor-cycles. A grandmother fanned the charcoal fire and turned her skewer of little meat chunks. "And oh, how You love us, Lord. Thank you for picking us up from another side of the globe and placing us over here in Your harvest field. We are watching You, Lord Jesus, to penetrate the sin-burdened hearts and give Your wonderful life everlasting to these people of Mali."

On the sixth day of being in Mali, Hubert, along with two other missionary men, boarded the riverboat with most of our baggage and supplies. They were in for a five-day overcrowded boat trip up the Niger River to Gao. God had provided from the Bamako markets cases of canned vegetables and powdered milk, a water filter, mosquito nets, a transformer, bottled gas, and many other supplies unavailable 750 miles to the northeast. The shipping office in Bamako told Hubert not to expect our barrels and crates from the States until after Christmas.

Meanwhile, I waited with our four children in Bamako. Malian ladies laughed at my five-month-old Hans cuddled close to me in a front baby carrier. How foolish this western lady was to not know that babies are carried on the mother's back with a cloth. Soon I bought some fabric and sewed a cloth for carrying my baby on my back, and sewed a matching African skirt. We fixed meals in the shared kitchen of the guesthouse. Seven-year-old Hannah helped me doing laundry by hand. We tried to do a little school with her and four-year-old Cherith. Three-year-old Davar fell in the open sewer ditch on the way home from church. We thanked God for a shower available back at the guesthouse. Some correspondence got written and I found Americans headed to the States to carry mail. Visiting the US Embassy medical clinic, a French rehabilitation center, and the Bamako hospital was informative. The hospital was very sparsely furnished and lacked cleanliness. God was encouraging me that He would use the medical skills He had given me.

One evening things were not going well. The oven wasn't working right, the meat for supper was spoiled, the gravy would not thicken, the children were fussy, and I missed Hubert terribly. But God whispered Zephaniah 3:17, "The Lord your God is in your midst, a mighty one who will save; he will rejoice over you with gladness; he will quiet you by his love; he will exult over you with loud singing." Seven days after Hubert had left, he sent me a telegram in French saying, "I love you." "Thank you, Lord, for word from him. He has arrived safely in Gao."

On October 21 the children and I along with two other missionary ladies and four more children boarded the seventeen-passenger Air Mali plane. Three of the children were seated on laps. Carry-on luggage was in the aisle and in front of the door. Even after the engines had been started, the door was reopened to admit another passenger, bumping off an earlier one. I sure did not trust that small plane, but I did trust God to get us safely to our destination. The plane stopped at Mopti, then Timbuktu airport, and finally Gao. How exciting to see Hubert there to greet us, although he sure looked different sporting a new beard and a cowboy hat for protection from the Sahara sun.

Arriving at our new mudbrick house that Don Carson, the veteran missionary, had found for us to rent, we discovered it wasn't completed enough to live in yet. Rather than stay with the two other families in the house by the church on the other side of town, we opted to camp in the yard of our new home. A high wall enclosed the house and sand which was the yard, like the other houses of Gao. There was a storeroom to put our things in, and a walled corner of the yard which was the outhouse. An open well supplied water which we drew with a long rope and a rubber bucket. Dan and Ann Zimmerman, retired missionaries, had left two trunks and two barrels for us of pots, plates, bowls, towels, sheets, etc. Hubert had purchased grass mats, a mattress, clay water pots, a charcoal burner, and a few other essentials for getting started. God had provided for all our needs.

Many neighbors came to welcome us. A Malian family was also living in our yard since they had been guarding the house during the months of construction and needed a few days to find a new home. We sat on grass mats in the shade of the walls, walked across town to market, and learned to cook on the single charcoal burner. It required a lot of fanning and creativity to prepare rice and side dishes. Sleeping on the roof on mats and a mattress at night was delightful. Toward four in the morning, it even got cool enough for a blanket to feel good.

However, God had prepared a special experience for us to walk through with Him next. It began on Sunday, day three of living in Gao. Hubert got sick. The next day it was Hannah. The following day Davar joined them lying on the mats and running across the yard to the outhouse with vomiting and diarrhea. At night, light from our flashlights chased the cockroaches away from the hole in the cement on the ground which was the commode. Hubert and Hannah started to improve, but Hans took his turn with the gastroenteritis followed by Cherith. God was so gracious in getting Hubert back on his feet to help me with going to the market for food, cooking on the charcoal fire, drawing water, doing laundry by hand, and caring for the sick ones.

Then Cherith became severely sick with fever, chills, and headache in addition to bloody diarrhea. Thursday morning at 9:40 she went into convulsions for five minutes and then became unresponsive. I felt helpless. I sat on the ground next to her limp body and prayed and prayed that God would restore her as Hubert ran across town to get help from the other missionaries. It normally took fifty-five minutes to walk there.

Don's truck had just started working – God's timing. Don came and took us to an African doctor at Gao hospital. He diagnosed her with dysentery and cerebral malaria. It was my first time seeing malaria, and this was life-threatening. The mosquitos back in Dakar, Senegal, our first night in Africa were probably the attackers that gave it to her in spite of our taking weekly chloroquine tablets to prevent malaria. She received quinine and phenobarbital injections and we were told to return each morning until the treatment was completed.

Our whole family moved in with our missionary co-workers for a couple days, where there was an electric fan to help cool her still, little body. They also had running water we used to sponge her down for her fever. At 10:30 pm Cherith woke up and started talking. We were so excited and relieved. Her coma had lasted about thirteen hours. God had answered prayer and spared her life. He was so merciful to us, and He was so present with us through it all. "That you may know and believe me and understand that I am He" (Isaiah 43:10). We had to be willing for whatever God chose and completely trust Him alone. He had taken care of us. We were in His hands and that is a safe place.

DAILY LIFE

Whose footprints were those pressed in the sand of our yard? Some were from workers finishing up construction on our house which we had moved into. Some were left by neighbors who stopped by to visit. Many times, Hubert sat down on straw mats with turbaned men and shared strong sugary Tuareg tea prepared in a tiny teapot on a tiny charcoal fire and served in tiny cups. Tuaregs are a people of the Sahara who often follow their cattle and camels. With those who spoke French we shared the message of Christ. With those who knew only their African languages, we at first only exchanged greetings and visited with few words. Often, they enjoyed playing with baby Hans or watching the children filling their sand pails or sifting the sand. Later we were able to converse more and more with those same guests.

Women came alone or in groups of two or three to sit and chat. Everyone seemed to have lots of time. Life for the Malians moved slowly. God taught us that taking time for people took priority over other jobs like sifting bugs out of the flour or finishing the peanuts we had started roasting, or language study. Yet, He wonderfully directed the busy flow of people so that the other work somehow got done too.

Over there were the footprints of a young mother who came asking for help for her sick baby. Near those a middle-aged man walked, seeking relief from the pain in his side. Another woman requested aspirin for her headache. A teenage boy needed a dressing for an ulcer on his foot. An old shepherd begged for some rice, and young girls asked for money.

During siesta one day, the plumber's daughter came to retrieve a tool. She said her father was sick, so I went with her to visit him. His home was very humble. They offered me a pillow on the ground to sit on. After giving treatment for his headache and dizziness, I shared the gospel with them. He said he had listened to it on the radio. Praise God for His Word getting into some homes that way. Weeks later, he responded to the Lord and received new life in Christ. When I left there, the next-door neighbor called me in to see his baby with marasmus (malnutrition) again. This time someone was there who could interpret into French. I demonstrated how to prepare treatment for the baby and prayed with them. One afternoon, a neighbor came asking me to come quickly and help a very sick woman. Although she lived close by and I went immediately, on arrival she had already entered eternity. What a reminder that many, many people are going into eternity without Christ. "Lord, please send more workers."

See the place there where the young Christian men from the church came over for fellowship. It was encouraging to hear how God lifted them from sin and filled them with the joy of Himself. The young people of the church looked forward to spending the first two weeks of September at camp in Timbuktu each year. We too really looked forward to being there with them and seeing the famous ancient city. Believers from Timbuktu, Diré, Niafunke, and Gao anticipated sports, food, studying God's Word, and enjoying being together. They stayed in African grass huts. It was always a time of real encouragement to these Christians who stood alone in their Muslim families all the rest of the year. God's people prayed for spiritual growth, safety, wisdom, and fun.

Various builders working on our roof and ceiling, and repairmen came to our house. One was a refrigerator repairman, Banjie. While he sat on a folding chair outside waiting to see if the frig would get cold, he listened to salvation being explained. He said he had been searching to know God. He prayed, asking Christ to save him! He promised to read the French New Testament I gave him. Later, he came to church.

These prints reflected an eager step. They were left by our Malian language helpers. The senior missionaries helped us in so many ways, among them orientation and language learning guidance. We were to concentrate mainly on bringing our French up to a level that we could use to teach. The hours of study were repaid as we saw God use us to witness in French to people we met. When Hubert could start preaching in French and I started teaching Bible lessons to children and ladies in French, these were victories from the Lord. But since many people did not speak French, and Songhai was the trade language of the country, we found helpers to work with on that language as well.

Then our footprints led out the gate again as we visited shops, homes, hospitals, schools, and talked with people we met in the street, to practice our new languages, repeating newly acquired phrases innumerable times. This developed friendships and opportunities to show forth Christ, and witness. Because our section of town was Tuareg people and all spoke Tamashek, it was important to learn to communicate with them too. God was amazing in helping us with the languages. So many Christians back in America and some in Mali were praying for that, and God graciously answered.

The story of Rachel drawing water was true to life for us. Pulling each heavy bucket of water up from the open well and then carrying it to the house was exhausting work in the heat. The thirty-three-foot well was too deep for a pump to pull the water up. No submersible pump could be found to put down in the well and push water up. After many revisions to the system, Hubert placed a barrel next to the well. In the early morning and late evening, he or a worker would draw the water up with a rope and rubber bucket and empty it into a barrel. Then he pushed a hand pump lever back and forth to pump the water through a hose to the house and up into an eighty-gallon tank about nine feet in the air. From there it ran into the bathroom and kitchen faucets of the house.

When our well water was infested with tiny larva, we poured bleach in the well to try to kill them, and then tried cooking oil. Eventually, the pests cleared. All our drinking water got filtered and stored in clay pots. Most wash water was saved for flushing the toilet or watering the little trees we planted. Two layers of covers were placed over the well to protect children from a mishap. Once when our helper was drawing water, his money dropped out of his pocket into the well. He agilely climbed down the straight walls and retrieved it. After months of drought in the region the well ran dry. But God kept on faithfully providing water. While a crew of men dug the well deeper, a friend brought three small barrels of water. That water lasted until the new well was finished. "God will supply every need of yours" (Philippians 4:19).

Although we had been told in Bamako our crates and barrels would not arrive until after Christmas, we asked people to pray for God to send them before Christmas. The children's schoolbooks were in the shipment and we needed them. On December 2, we were informed that our shipment of crates and barrels from the States would arrive at our house in Gao the next day! They did not actually get there until over two weeks later. It was a pretty exciting day, and God showed His power in getting them through the paperwork and up the Niger River, even when we thought the riverboats had stopped running for the season. God brought them before Christmas!

One of the crates contained a kerosene refrigerator. From a small hole in the top of the crate, a few bees emerged. As the crate was pried open, a whole swarm of bees swarmed out. People scattered. Hubert sprayed. Soon we were sweeping up a pile of lifeless bees (they could not have lived long in that climate). Once again, God was my shield. I am allergic to bees. No one was stung. Since city electricity was rare, the kerosene fridge was really appreciated. It worked great – as long as we could buy kerosene in town.

In one barrel was Great Aunt Margie's treadle sewing machine. However, a main piece had broken in transit. How would God meet this need? A short-term missionary, David Benzil, took a piece of wood and carved the needed piece. The machine worked beautifully, and many items were sewn or mended over the ensuing years.

Two Honda 70 motorcycles required reassembling after arriving in the crates. That was lots of fun for Hubert and David. Riding them was fun too. I found I had to wear shoes or sandals instead of flip flops to work the shift. Patches of loose sand and chickens, goats, and small children running into the streets required agility, quick reflexes, and prayer. We were grateful for God providing these motorcycles to carry us all over town. When the children and I walked down the sandy streets to go to church, village children would sometimes throw little stones at us or run up to feel the foreign children's blonde hair. God protected us. We were not seriously injured. He is a shield around us. The motorcycles made getting across town much easier. We could get all six of us on the two little cycles. Having wheels also allowed us to make excursions out of town for picnics. Those were rare, treasured family times relaxing away from our work.

Our library (about forty-two boxes) arrived in book-rate mailbags. Within six months of our arrival, all the bags had reached Gao! There were plenty of books for the children, all of Hubert's theological library, and my medical books. God provided these needed tools for His workers even in the Sahara.

Not many insects hung around in the desert, but scorpions thrived. They were the little brown ones which are the most dangerous to small children. God would sometimes make my eye catch sight of a little critter heading for the children's school desks and I would whack it with a flip flop. Or it would be hiding on the towel in the shower room, or next to the plates as we reached to set table. One evening right after supper I saw a scorpion sitting right in the doorway where Hubert was carrying sleeping, barefoot Davar. God carries us over danger many times. We began to mark the scorpion count on the calendar. In one month, we killed thirty. Not once in our term in Mali were we ever stung. Only God could do that!

The Niger was only deep enough for boats to run part of the year. When no mail came for six weeks, we knew trucks must not be moving much either. The surgeon was out of gloves and the bank copy machine was out of paper. The pharmacy was out of oral penicillin and the market was almost out of fruit and vegetables. The dried fruit from our home church sure was appreciated. I marveled at God's faithful provision for us. We had good meals three times a day, and romantic lantern light at night. We were grateful for little woven grass hand fans giving some relief for sweat trickling down our faces and backs. Other times of the year our skin stayed dry from the immediate evaporation of any sweat. Best of all, we enjoyed knowing the presence and joy of our wonderful Lord.

On a Wednesday afternoon in June, we had just left to walk to prayer meeting. We had walked about one block down the road, when a man speaking good French asked, "Are you going somewhere while the wind is coming?" We turned around and saw in the distance a gigantic mountain of brown sand billowing toward us. It was our first sandstorm. We quickly turned back home, and Hubert went on the roof to film it. I closed the metal window shutters. It rolled in fast and when it hit, all was pitch dark. Outside you could not see your hand in front of your face. Inside we could see our hand only if it was close to the lantern. The intense darkness lasted about thirty minutes. Then the air became deep red, then gradually brightened to orange. After about two hours it was possible to go outside. The big gate had blown open, and our laying hen behind the house was dead. The air cleared more during the night. The next day, sand blowing steadily again accumulated on the floor in a thick layer.

A little over a year later, while walking home from prayer meeting with the children, another memorable sandstorm approached us. A stranger called us to come into her home for shelter. We sat in a tiny room of her mud brick house, together with a couple of lambs and chickens, throughout the black sandstorm and the rain that followed. Toddler Hans was crying at first, but the lambs God provided made him content. We stayed more than an hour, praying the rain would lighten so we could walk home. It did, and we sloshed and waded home with two little flashlights. The lightning was beautiful breaking up the darkness.

Hubert had taken the motorcycle from church to visit a doctor's home. He left that house at the approach of the storm hoping to make it to our home, but got caught in the storm. He lost his way in the thick sand and darkness. Finally, he arrived home all wet from the rain, but did not have his key. He squeezed through the big gate and waited outside the house in the rain until we got home. The following day, the lady whose home had been our shelter, came and visited us. God used the sandstorm for us to meet her, and for her to hear about Christ.

Sandstorms rolled over us every two to three days from June to September, but most were not too thick nor long lasting. Only about three of them each year were "black sandstorms." Others were only various densities of brown. While at church one Wednesday a sandstorm hit followed by rain and wind. When we got home, we found our ham radio antenna had fallen across our bed on the roof, breaking the bed. We were so grateful to God that we were not in the bed when the antenna fell. August usually brought some rain. Sprinkles or rain following the blowing sand made mud. Sandstorms or rain in the middle of the night routed us from bed. We would toss the mattresses over the low roof wall to the porch below, then drag them inside. But it was too hot to sleep inside. When the rain stopped, we moved outside again. Even though sleep was interrupted, God's grace was so precious in the midst of the storms, and He gave strength for each day. Later we sewed plastic coverings for the beds so we could leave them on the roof even in the rain.

God supplied every need. Not only did He provide protection from storms and scorpions, supply food and water, give us use of the languages to communicate, but He also gave us many opportunities to meet people and be His witnesses.

Hubert teaching the Bible

Our well

MINISTRY

A gentle breeze blew through the little courtyard of the church.
About eight Malian Christians gathered for Wednesday afternoon
prayer meeting along with the three missionary families. One tree
shaded the benches a bit to bring a little relief from the desert heat.
Trying to ignore the sounds of goats, donkeys, and children on
the other side of the mud walls, we turned our attention to the
lifting of songs to the Lord and the preaching of the Word of God.
Uniting in prayer before the throne of grace we thanked God for
His church.

"Eglise Evangélique Baptiste" read the big rust-colored sign
firmly attached high on the cement plastered face of the church.
Its bright yellow letters announced the hours of services as if to call
"Come! Come!" There were people who faithfully came: a handful
of single men God had redeemed from the darkness, and some families. Some were teachers and one was a doctor. These came from
the southern part of Mali in government employment to serve for
a couple of years in the north. They spoke a number of languages.
Therefore, songs were sung in several languages. The sermons were
in French.

While Sunday morning services were going on inside the
building, the children's church outside was singing songs with
visuals, learning verses, and having a Bible lesson. The lessons were
in French, and the students were a mixture of Malian children and
missionary kids. Another missionary and I alternated teaching. The
teacher not giving the lesson was sometimes occupied outside the
metal wall at the end of the courtyard, trying to keep village children from banging on the wall making it impossible to hear. When
invited to come into the class, they refused. Hubert alternated with
another missionary leading the Bible study for the Sunday afternoon

prayer meeting. Friday afternoons were the ladies Bible studies. It was a joy to see God help me teach the Bible and health lessons such as "Cough," "Wound care," or "Fever."

Our requests to God were that He would 1) use us to introduce the lost to Jesus Christ and the salvation He offers, 2) build up believers in the knowledge of God's Word and in their walk with the Lord, 3) let us see the church growing, 4) provide a Malian pastor for the church, 5) provide a Malian Christian to take over teaching the children's class at church, 6) provide Christian wives for the single men in the church, 7) call Christians to be trained in Bible School to serve in Gao, and 8) help each of us as God's people to live victoriously that His name would be glorified.

Besides the ministries at the church, God used Hubert to teach a Bible study on the basics of the Christian life held in our yard Thursday afternoons. From one to several young people came each week, a mixture of Christians and unbelievers. Some were contacts he had made at the Bible bookstore he and the other missionaries ran.

As people would come into the store and browse, there were many opportunities to share the gospel with individuals. Books were ordered in French from Paris and a lending library was set up as well. One book in high demand was *The Bible and the Koran*. God worked in hearts and several people turned to Christ there. One day, a Muslim Tuareg high school student that had talked to Hubert at the bookstore came to our home after dark. He said he had been beaten before for reading the Bible. Hubert answered more of his questions and that night he asked Christ for salvation.

Zuda was a young Christian Tuareg man who was very faithful in Bible study. He felt God was leading him to go to Bible school in Niger. Many people were praying for a Christian wife for him as well as for the other single men in the church. What a tragedy if they would unite with unbelievers. Zuda witnessed to his cousin, Fatimatou, for a long time. She started coming to Bible study and discussed at length about what she was learning. However, she did not want to disobey her parents and risk being kicked out of the family. Finally, one Saturday she yielded to Christ and received Jesus as her Savior. She became faithful at church, memorizing and studying the Word. Then she followed the Lord in baptism. She was bubbling with joy and the love of Christ. She was the only Christian Tuareg girl we knew. She planned to leave a month later to attend college in Bamako. Cousins are the preferred choice for marriage in their culture. It appeared God had prepared a wife for Zuda. But before leaving for their respective schools, they planned to attend the church camp in Timbuktu in September. What an opportunity for feeding on God's Word and being encouraged by His people.

With the church singing songs in seven languages, Hubert saw a need for a single songbook containing the songs we used. He laboriously typed stencils (perforated sheets) for the book. When the twenty-nine-page songbook that we had put hours of labor and lots of francs into was ready to print, the mimeograph (copy) machine of the mission did not work. A couple guys from church found a fellow to print them on the school's machine, at an inflated price for labor. He did not really know enough about it and gave us back 1,500 pages of blotched ink and all the stencils ruined. We were back to the beginning needing new stencils.

But God had better plans. We waited a couple of weeks and then started typing all over again – this time on regular paper, new format, bigger and better – one hundred songs, seven languages with the one hundredth song in all seven languages. Mistakes correct much easier on regular paper. It looked terrific! We finished the whole manuscript. Next, a man from church said he would take it to a printer friend of his in Bamako. The church was able to get a beautiful product a few months later. God is able to do above and beyond what we plan.

In addition to the outreaches in Gao, we desired to reach further into the desert up north to carry the gospel there too. Missionaries were not allowed to have open air meetings unless they got a special permit for a special occasion. But we could have meetings in an individual's yard if invited. God led us to Mr. Batteri, a teacher in the town of Forgo, who was a Christian. He had a heart for his neighbors to hear of Christ and invited us to come hold services.

One Monday afternoon, four men from the Gao church along with some of the other missionaries and our family headed out the forty-five-minute drive to Forgo in Don's truck. It was hard to see where the road was as all the sand looked the same. We held a service in front of Mr. Batteri's house with singing and preaching in Songhai and French. Baby Hans would not sit still so I walked around town with him and visited with many people. Another missionary lady talked with Mrs. Batteri afterward. She had decided to follow Christ sometime in the past but then had gone back to saying Muslim prayers because of pressure from neighbors. On the way home, we had a flat tire. Flat tires were frequent from the trash in the streets in town or the thorns outside of town. We also got stuck in the sand twice. We all pushed to get unstuck. The trip was a fun new experience. We praised God for this opportunity and planned to return in two weeks.

But to continue to go regularly, we needed our own truck. When I stopped praying for a diesel truck, God gave us a gas two-wheel-drive little Peugeot pickup. The Lord provided an excellent exchange rate of dollars to francs right at that time so we could save up a little each month until we had the amount needed. We had a frame put on the back, covered by canvas. Then wooden benches were made so people could ride in the back protected from the sun.

Now that we had a truck, we headed out toward Forgo. But we only got half-way. The truck kept stalling. We crept eight miles back home in first gear, stalling every twenty-five feet or so. It may have been dirty gas (not unusual in Gao) clogging the fuel filter.

The nine guys and two children in the back of the pick-up had a sort-of service. I suggested singing but none of them were singing the same tunes or together. Hubert asked Reuben, our African assistant pastor, to give his testimony. Four of the passengers were high school youth that Hubert had met in the bookstore. Two others were also unsaved. For two hours the captive audience had a good discussion on Islam versus Christianity. God worked all things out for good, again. We prayed God would open their eyes to turn to Him.

The truck problem got fixed and in a couple of weeks we ventured out again. The route to Forgo was bumpy with many stretches of soft sand and numerous detours around the worst spots. This time we only got stuck once. As we entered the Batteri's sandy yard there were seven or so men seated on a bench in the shade of the mud brick house waiting for us. I started playing the accordion and a few more people assembled. We sang, then Hubert opened the Scriptures to them. Our purpose was two-fold: to feed and encourage the lone Christian family and to evangelize their neighbors. After the study, the men continued to question and discuss for almost two hours. God allowed me to teach a flannelgraph story to the women and children and help them learn the chorus of "Jesus Loves Me" – brand new to them. After drinking tea and promising to try to return in two weeks, we said farewell and headed back down the road rejoicing that this town could hear the gospel.

Other obstacles arose. On one trip out, we found Mr. Batteri's family was not there, so we could not have a regular service. But I taught the ladies and children. Coming home we got stuck twice and almost ran out of gas, but God got us home. Then for several months we could not use the truck because a different registration paper was required from Bamako. Finally, God made it come.

After one of the ladies meetings in Gao, I could not get the truck to start. The ladies prayed together, and God made it start. A couple of weeks later, it became normal to push the truck to start it until we bought a new battery. We suspected that when we bought the new truck, the dealer must have made a previous deal on the side and sold the new battery, replacing it with a used one.

When the supply of fuel in town got very low, Hubert had to stand in line at the Governor's office to get a ration slip to buy gas for the truck. Finally, he got a paper for twenty liters. Next, we went to the gas station. It gave us half a tank – enough to go to Forgo the next Sunday! When there was no gas in town – there were no trips to Forgo. Once, when fuel came to town again, we took the truck to the gas station and sat in line over five hours. It was rather fun talking with the children coming around. One evening we had good rain a couple days before going out Forgo. We wondered if the mud would hinder us. It did not, since things dry up so quickly, and we saw beautiful carpets of green where dormant seeds had sprouted. May the Lord make the seed of His Word grow in the hearts of listeners.

The truck was used around town too. One Sunday two neighbor girls, about twelve years old, squeezed into the big gate while we were getting into the truck. They wanted more tracts because they had finished reading the others I had given them before. I invited them to jump in and go with us to church. They did! They sat through the whole service and came home with us afterward.

When too many people were coming daily to the gate for medical consultations, I set regular "porch clinic" hours three afternoons per week. People respected it, and generally outside those hours were only emergencies. Later, I stopped giving medicine and only gave prescriptions. They could fill prescriptions at the local pharmacy, and it encouraged them to use the local medical system.

House calls were frequent and included rich homes and poor, missionaries and tent dwellers. Tuberculosis was rampant and a couple people came for daily streptomycin injections along with the oral medications. If they did not come, I went to their homes to ensure continuity of care. The public tuberculosis program was often out of meds and some people mistrusted and refused to use the government system. Visiting two elderly ladies at their tent one day, a crowd of people gathered around wanting medical help. My friend interpreted from Temasek as I sat on the ground for an unplanned open-air clinic. What a challenge to get a limited history and then write a prescription. Jesus was surrounded by multitudes and loved them. "Thank you, Lord for this experience with you."

Once a week I went to the maternity and the government hospital to learn more about the medical system and French medicines available. God helped us find the right people to get permission to practice medicine. The application process began soon after arrival. After talking to a doctor about the process, I went to the market and my wallet got stolen. There wasn't much money in it, but the name of the next doctor I was to meet for the application was in that wallet. Back to square one. But God worked and after several months the acceptance in the medical society was granted, which made it legal for me to work as a physician in Mali.

On a typical Wednesday, I went to the hospital about 8:30 am and joined the Malian general practice physician. We made rounds on the hospital patients, then saw about fifteen patients in consultations in the office. There were typhoid patients, patients with liver cancer, uterine cancer, depression, hypertension, malaria, tuberculosis, hyperemesis gravidarum (excessive vomiting in early pregnancy), pneumonia, cardiac enlargement, plus more. People with deformities from advanced leprosy were sad to see but we were grateful these patients could get specialized care in another city. One patient at the hospital had been bitten by a hippo. It was quite a reminder of God's protection of Hubert when he watched a hippo at the river showing off its humongous mouth.

God gave opportunities to witness at the thirty-bed hospital. The staff taught me and asked my advice on some cases. Occasionally, I worked with the surgeon, assisting in patient care. There were also opportunities at a private clinic. Once a week later became twice a week. They asked me to see patients on my own too. Sometimes medical students were with us, and it was fun to teach them. Doctors completed their couple of years of service in Gao and moved back to Bamako. New ones came. These professionals did not have strong ties with Muslims in the community. One of the clinic doctors mocked Christianity but others seemed genuinely interested. God allowed us to visit many of their homes, and to entertain them in ours.

God's joy overflowed as we thanked Him for letting us serve Him in Mali using the training He gave. It was so fun teaching Ruth to teach the children's church. Then a second lady started helping there too. God raised up deacons, a Malian assistant pastor, and at the end of our time there, a Malian senior pastor. It was great fellowship visiting in the homes of believers and studying the Bible together. Attendance at the church grew. Two men went off to Bible school. One of God's great works was the salvation of a man at Forgo. We prayed he would grow in the Word of God and stand firm in spite of the Muslim pressures. God answered the prayers of His people and gave tremendous opportunities to witness at the hospital and clinics to doctors and other staff. We praised him for the many people who heard the gospel, and for those God graciously saved. His Word does not return void.

Children's Sunday School

FAMILY TIMES

Lantern light flickered across the pages of my Bible in the early hours of a new day. Soon daylight dawned and the children shook their slumber. They ran to the back of the house to see who might spot an egg, and then cleaned and filled water cans and tossed millet to the chickens. When the market had no eggs to sell, or the only batch of eggs we found had more rotten ones than good ones, God provided chickens. Our children's Christmas present the first Christmas was eighteen soft, fuzzy, cheeping baby chicks. They were penned in the narrow space between the back of the house and the back wall. That area was shaded all day. Since corn was never seen in our parts, they were fed millet and table scraps. The heat was rough on them and not all survived. Over time they were replaced with other hens. After some of them went flying up on neighbors' roofs, we found new ways to keep them in. Little Cherith prayed that God would give us eggs from our chickens. When the "guaranteed hen" we purchased laid her first egg we gave special thanks to God. He had answered prayer. Eventually, we were getting about three eggs a day from seventeen hens.

The aroma of hot pancakes floated out the open window, calling the children in. A little later the sound of the Honda 70 was heard from the front yard, and Hubert was off to the market. I prepared the meat for dinner and slid it in the solar oven, turning the glass face to the full eastern sun.

School time! Everyone to your desk. Each morning the Broeckert house found three children standing at attention beside their little wooden school desks to recite the pledge to the American flag, listen to Scripture reading and begin their studies for the day. The teacher's manual from the correspondence school laid out each day's lesson plans. Hannah, in second grade, was working on fractions, reading lots of interesting stories, writing little compositions, and learning about gravity. Cherith thought kindergarten was lots of fun but wished she could still have Mrs. Brown back in Michigan for her teacher. Davar, being four, listened in and amused himself in his preschool workbooks Grandma and Grandpa sent him. Usually, Mommy was the teacher, but for a time David came over to teach. About the middle of reading lessons, Hubert returned with fresh vegetables, bread, and other necessities from the market. He then went back downtown to the Bible bookstore to discuss new life in Christ with teachers, students, storekeepers, travelers, and anyone else interested.

The noon sun was hot and bright when the rice was ready and the whole family sat down to dinner. After a short rest, Hubert delved into changing a flat tire on the motorcycle and then took off again for a French lesson. The girls took turns practicing their lessons on the toy piano while the boys made roads in the sand or played in the miniature Tuareg house, which our helper had built for their playhouse. It was dome shaped and made of grass mats. My friend Fatimatou stopped by for us to pray together before her dental appointment. She was asking God to allow her to witness to the dentist.

The continual blowing sand outside settled as a thick layer inside. Sand covered the bare cement floor, the wooden table, and the mats and Tuareg pillows which were our "couch." The little trees we had planted, dancing in ever changing directions as the wind played with them, were a refreshing green. They peeked through the fanciful, curved bars of the glassless windows. "Thank you, God, for the beauty around us, for our home, and for using our home to serve You and Your people."

Late in the afternoon, Beliel appeared. This day he brought two school friends with whom he had been sharing the gospel. When Hubert got home at 5:45 pm he answered questions and then was thrilled to watch the new birth of these two young men. Beliel suffered persecution from friends and family.

After supper was Winnie-the-Pooh story time with Daddy. When the little ones went to dreamland, Hubert studied his message for the next Sunday night and I wrote letters. Outside, the moonlight shone brightly but the prominent constellations still showed their steady path advancing across the sky, our night clock. Praise God for another day of life – in Christ – and in Africa.

African drums beat until after midnight when people were celebrating Mohamed's birthday. Another night, drums with a different, eerie, deep tone could be heard near us. They were sorcerers trying to cast out evil spirits. A regular night sound was packs of wild dogs running through the city howling. Thank you, Lord, for a nice high wall. One day as Hubert played softball with the children in our yard, he heard a riotous crowd of people outside the gate approach. They were beating up a woman. He ran out and stopped them from further injuring the woman. His words may have carried extra weight because his bat from the ballgame was still in his hand. God protected him.

"Epaphroditus...has been distressed because you heard that he was ill" (Philippians 2:25). Such was the state of Hubert at the end of August 1983. Lying there at home so sick, he felt he was going to die. Most of the rest of the family had fever and gastroenteritis at that same time, but his illness was more serious. We could only cry out to the Lord, "Please help us." During those long sleepless days and nights all normal activity was halted except to wait on the precious Comforter and Great Physician.

Reflecting on our first year in Africa, we knew God had been faithfully beside us, helping us and using us. We looked forward to what our Master and Enabler would do in the years ahead. We tried to get medical advice from the local doctors, but the testing needed was not available. Our fellow missionaries helped us in so many ways. They sent a telegram to a mission plane in Niamey, Niger, to come evacuate us to Ferkessédougou, Côte d'Ivoire (Ivory Coast), where there was a mission hospital. It took four days for the message to reach the pilot and get a response back.

Then the plane arrived the next day. God was already mercifully beginning to restore health and strength for us all. We had to overnight in Bamako to secure visas for Ivory Coast. Radio permission was given to enter Ivory Coast at a small district airport. We stood at the edge of the runway there and answered questions for the official to fill out his paperwork. In a few minutes, we were off to Ferkessédougou. Our plane buzzed the hospital twice, then landed on the rutted, old, overgrown airstrip by the mission hospital. We were grateful to God for a skilled missionary pilot. We were taken to a guesthouse for patients, and the doctor came there to see Hubert. Testing showed some things were back to normal function, but the infections were resistant to the antibiotics we had. Appropriate ones were begun. We thanked God for the loving ministry of mission hospitals.

When Hubert was discharged, we took a train down to Bouake, Ivory Coast. We were amazed to see electricity, piped running water, paved streets and streetlights, very little trash on the roads, cement, wood, and glass buildings, taxis, and an ice cream cart! Green grass, western foods available, horizons, and sunsets were so beautiful. They even had telephones, so we called our family back in the USA. Davar learned to roll a hoop and wished he could lose teeth like his sisters to get fifty francs. At the American church by the missionary kids' school, he burst out of kindergarten Sunday School exuberant over the story, cookies and Kool-Aid in class, and his handiwork. He long remembered the paper lady he made that was bent over until Jesus came and healed her. Gao children did not have paper crafts. They were not familiar with scissors or crayons.

After some time vacationing, we returned to the mission hospital for me to learn more about tropical medicine. It included some surgery cases, delivering babies, and participating in consultations and emergencies. One emergency was six villagers who arrived with poisoning. They had mixed a local brew in a log that had previously been used to mix insecticide. We used a lot of atropine to treat them. I felt like a medical student trudging at the elbows of these three, seasoned American missionary physicians, and they gave me many pearls of knowledge for which I was very grateful. Then an Ivory Coast mission plane flew us back to our home in Gao, Mali, with joyful anticipation of what God would do next.

How did we celebrate our second Christmas in Africa? It all began in the September mail delivery, which we got in October upon returning from Ivory Coast. There was a goodie box from a lady in Fruitport, Michigan. We tucked it away without the children seeing. We had purchased a couple of Christmas watches for the two girls in Ivory Coast. For decorations, the children cut out construction paper chains, bells, and other shapes and hung them in doorways and all around the house. A Christmas tree was constructed from a bamboo pole stuck in a can of sand. A metal barrel ring suspended from the top of the pole using "unrolled" bandages made a conical shape. We draped a green cloth over this frame and pinned on wrapped hard candies and bows. A popcorn chain and a doll made into an angel for the top completed the trimmings. The children were delighted. They made gifts for each other. We made candles and pajama bags for our missionary Christmas party.

One week before Christmas we baked cookies and made candy, then our family hopped in our truck. We caroled on the Rathbuns (surprise!). Then they jumped in, and we all went to Carsons and caroled. Don joined us to go to Zimmermans (a fourth family who had arrived) to sing. God gave joy! We thanked God for our coworkers. We had our family Christmas celebration on the 24th, opening presents. In the afternoon we helped an old lady move her belongings across town to her new home. She had never ridden in a truck and in fear covered her face and refused to look up. Then we took a trip out in the desert and ran up a sand dune. Two Malians went with us to search for little pieces of wood. The evening of the 24th was an evangelistic service at the church with a film, the choir, and preaching. I stayed home with the children because the previous year the Christmas eve service had lasted until after midnight. This year Hubert was home by 10 pm.

Christmas day was a Sunday and we all went to church, picking up riders as usual. There was a Christmas sermon and special music by the Ladies Bible Class. Afterward, everyone went next door to the Rathbun's house. There were two small roasted sheep, salad, bread, and singing. Toward 2 pm we had prayer meeting (usually held at 4 pm) and got home plenty early. I really felt like part of the church this year, with a bond of love in Christ, unlike being a new strange foreigner our first Christmas.

On December 26, we worked all day cooking and baking more Christmas treats for a missionary Christmas party that evening. It was at Carsons by their real artificial Christmas tree with lights! We had drawn names and made gifts to exchange. Hubert and I got smiley face pencil cans from three- and five-year-old Philip and Marc Zimmerman. Don made Davar a wall hanging with a poem, "Uncle Don's Desire for Davar." It urged Davar to always follow Christ, the Lord of his life. He kept it for many years. We sang and had another great evening. God answered the prayers of everyone who prayed we would have a nice Christmas. "Thank you, Lord, for happy memories made."

Other special family times enjoyed with other missionaries were once when we rode on camels and another time Davar rode a donkey. With our truck, we went looking for giraffes in a region some distance away that had scrub trees, but we did not spot any. For one picnic we took canoes across the Niger River to climb a big sand dune. It took an hour to cross the river as the drivers navigated through rice paddies on each bank. The annual conferences were special times when missionaries from Diré and Timbuktu flew in for a few days.

Short term visitors were also fun. One of the Malian men offered several camels as dowry to take one of the short-term young ladies as his wife. Hubert told him our custom required he talk directly with her father in the States, which he had no way of doing.

Hubert often tried to reach our church family back in Michigan via ham radio. With the time difference, it was the middle of the night for us when Larry Stanton or Cliff Cole were at their radios in Michigan. Our little generator seemed loud interrupting the quiet of the African night. Hubert was able to contact many people in distant parts of the world at different times. It was an encouraging touch with the bigger world outside Gao.

In May 1984 God again showed his triumph. When I became very weak from hemorrhaging due to a miscarriage, an emergency D & C procedure was performed at our little local hospital in Gao. It took quite a while to regain strength, but we thanked God He spared my life to serve Him longer on this earth. The Christians were so kind coming to pray with me and give comfort in the time of loss. The presence of the Lord was precious, and His people were also precious.

Soon after that was the beginning of Davar's rheumatic fever. His treatment included six weeks of rest in view of his new heart murmur. As a five-year-old he found he could make many things from dominos. Did you ever make Monopoly last five days and then get tired of five-hundreds and hotels so just counted up? Cherith won the coloring contest. Hannah read aloud to Davar with great expression. When I became ill, it became clear not even Hubert would be able to go to the two-week camp at Timbuktu when the group from Gao left in a few days via Land Rover. We would miss the fellowship, the ministry opportunity, and seeing the ancient prominent city of the former Mali Empire. Even in disappointments, we were grateful to God that he was working out His better plan.

MOVING FROM MALI TO CAR

God did great things in Mali during our term there. We loved the Malian people, the work God had given, and our fellow workers. The sand stretching to the horizons was beautiful. God had faithfully cared for us, and graciously used us as His witnesses there. But in August of 1983, God began showing us His plan to use us in a mission hospital. After the trip to Ivory Coast for Hubert's treatment, God confirmed He wanted us to move.

In October we wrote to the Baptist Mid-Missions' hospital in the Central African Republic (CAR). Five months later, in March 30, 1984, we received a reply from Dr. Rhodes, the missionary physician there, who was temporarily in the States. The following day we wrote to our home church asking their permission to change to the field of CAR, and a couple days later told our co-workers in Mali how God was leading. We were excited about the new venture, and it was hard waiting for word back from our church. We knew God would move them to understand the change if it was His will. When a positive comment finally arrived in a letter from my sister-in-law Tammy, our hopes soared. Lots of letters and telegrams traveled between Gao, CAR, and the USA. Missionaries in CAR invited us to visit for a month mid-October to mid-November before flying on to the States for furlough and working further on the field change. The Missionaries in Mali also helped, including Don Marshall working on getting CAR visas for us from Niamey, Niger, which took about six weeks.

Things got packed and ready to leave, but the sale of our truck kept falling through. The money from selling the truck was needed to buy tickets for the trip. Delay meant joyful continued service in Gao each day. Finally, in God's perfect time, our truck sold. Plans to go by road to Bamako fell through and in answer to Jan Carson's prayers, we flew. She knew flying was much safer.

On October 7, 1984, we were off from Gao! All twenty-eight checked suitcases and eight carry-ons got to the airport with us by 9:30 am. The charge for excess baggage was more than expected, but God worked out details, so we had just enough money for the whole trip. Takeoff was 11:30 am. One hour later was the arrival in Timbuktu! The itinerary had said the plane would go to Mopti before Bamako but did not mention a stop in Timbuktu on the way. But Jan had been praying we would get to see Timbuktu. After a few passengers exited and a few others boarded, the plane taxied out to the end of the runway. But then it aborted its plan to take off. Forty-two degrees Celsius (108° F) was too hot for takeoff. The plane had to wait until 6 pm when the air cooled a bit.

So, we went into town and found fellow missionaries, the Beckleys. They fixed us a nice meal of rice and gravy at 2 pm. Harold Beckley took Hubert and I for a tour of Timbuktu. We got a few pictures but ran out of film. We saw a walk-in well and walked down to see the green algae water. We saw the house where René Caillié stayed (the first European to make it to the city and back out alive). There were a couple other historic plaques over doors. Many doors were wood decorated with ornamental metal. Key-hole shaped window shutters were unique. The mud walls had artful decorations – pillars and designs – unlike Gao's lack thereof. We saw the only hotel in town. It was first class and thirty dollars a night at today's exchange rate.

We visited Pastor Noah and his wife Fati and their children. He was a faithful Malian pastor, whom God had guarded and enabled through many trials and many years. They gave us a decorated rope for leading camels, made of braided goat skin, a treasured gift. There were two old gas pumps which comprised the only gas station. The town was small compared to its historic glory and size. It was rather compact, with narrow winding streets, but cleaner and quieter than Gao. The kids opted out of the tour to plunge in Lori Beckley's swimming hole. God gave us something we had wanted for a long time – to see Timbuktu, even after it looked impossible. The Lord delights to give special perks to His children.

We got back to the airport and lifted off at 5:45 pm. It got dark. The plane landed in Mopti with flares (jerry cans of fuel with rags for wicks) to light the runway. All the passengers were taken to a guest house for the night, compliments of Air Mali. Supper was provided at 10 pm. Beds were wood with thin foam mattresses and short sheets. The guests shared a common bathroom. There were lots of mosquitos, but God answered prayer that we did not get bit up much during the night. Praise God we had insect repellent. Hannah prayed that we could leave in the morning and God answered prayer.

Breakfast was at the hotel – café au lait and bread, then on to the airport at 7:30 am. Everyone waited while the plane's flat tire was changed. It had blown during the landing last night. Praise God for protecting us. We arrived in Bamako about noon. It was fun traveling, even though four out of six of us got airsick the first hop but not after that. The kids behaved so well (somebody was praying) during all the waits in airports and late meals – but we never missed one. They played our little electric keyboard often when they got bored. Hubert walked all over town to get airline tickets to CAR, send telegrams, and figure out what to do with all the excess baggage (half of it hospital supplies) that we brought this far and now found could not go on the next flights with us. Finally, we had tickets on Air Ivoire to Abidjan, then Air Afrique to CAR and our excess baggage would be air freighted through Air Mali via Paris to CAR.

On October 14, 1984, after breakfast, the guest house missionary host in Bamako took us to the airport, and was a real help getting us through the lines and completing the forms. The Air Ivoire plane was overbooked so we were delayed while they hunted for the last person on the list to put them off. The plane stopped in Bouake to clear customs rather than going all the way to the capital, Abidjan. There they confiscated our passports because we did not have visas for Ivory Coast. The customs officials entrusted them to a flight attendant, who gave them to the police in Abidjan. We did not have Ivory Coast visas because we were only in transit, but they got all excited.

The police waited while we claimed our thirteen pieces of baggage as it was unloaded from the plane. Then they helped us move it all from the entrance of the terminal to the police office. That was a small, upstairs room swarming with uniformed men busy running around. They took Hubert in one room, out, in another, out, and back. We were both a bit stressed. Hans started crying for a banana, so I gave him one then gave some to the other three children. A policeman, nervous about a mess, quickly came and held a wastebasket for us to put the peelings in. Not too long after that they took us down to the transit waiting lounge and kept our passports until boarding time. Thus, we arrived exactly at the place where we wanted to go, and had help with our baggage, but quite an experience. God can even use a toddler crying.

The layover was only a couple hours, but the airlines said they did not have our reservations we had made and confirmed in Bamako a couple days before! They put us on standby. We prayed. Finally, after all the other passengers were lined up at the gate to board, they came and told us they had six seats, hurry, and board first! Families went out a special gate and normally were preboarded. Hubert ran back up to the police office and retrieved our passports while the plane proceeded with boarding. Our baggage was still sitting in a pile in the waiting room as we boarded. The agent assured us they would bring it. We watched from the plane windows, and at the last moment flight attendants came scurrying out with our bags on a little hand cart, spilling them halfway out, and then got them on our plane. It was a beautiful Air Afrique 727 and a lovely trip once we reached twenty-nine thousand feet. The clouds were gorgeous from above looking down on lightning. We landed in Lomé (Togo), Lagos (Nigeria), Douala (Cameroon), and then Bangui (CAR) at 12:20 am local time.

Dr. Rhodes and his son waved to us from the upstairs railing. Once inside, a uniformed official told us they were watching for us as the pastor had requested. He then brought Dr. Rhodes to us in the immigration formalities area as well as a missionary pastor who had special permission to help new missionaries arriving. He helped us fill out the arrival cards. We zipped through. Customs opened only one box (schoolbooks) and sent us on our way. This was quite unusual. The airport workers may have been eager to get home for the night. God had worked marvelously on our behalf. We were taken to a guest apartment on the Bangui mission station, rejoicing that God brought us to CAR to serve him there next. "You guide me with your counsel" (Psalm 73:24).

A month working with Dr. Rhodes up at Ippy Hospital was a great initiation into the Lord's work in CAR. He taught me bowel resections all with hand suturing for strangulated hernia repairs (removing a section of necrotic intestine and connecting the good ends of bowel), how to use the dermatome and do skin grafts, use and care of endoscopes (for looking in the stomach, in the colon, and in the bladder), and much more, as we cared for patients that had no other place to go for medical care. If the mission hospital didn't treat them, most would go home and die. Many of the patients had advanced disease and complications when finally coming for help. Truly I would need the presence of Christ with me in the work, and

His power to make a difference in lives. The next step was heading to the USA for furlough, reporting to our churches, and becoming a part of Baptist Mid-Missions.

CHAPTER 3

CENTRAL AFRICAN REPUBLIC 1985-1990

Behold, I am the LORD, the God of all flesh.
Is anything too hard for me?
Jeremiah 32:27

BANGUI

December 14, 1985, was a freezing, wintery white day in Michigan. Hubert handed me his heavy winter coat, put on a light spring jacket, and walked out to the plane. The runway had been plowed and he soared up and away into the sunny blue sky above the clouds. It was still windy and cold when he landed two hops further east. A bus ride from one airport to another gave him a brief tour of the giant New York metropolis. Then it was up, up again, into the night sky, to fly over the Atlantic.

Warm African air surrounded him as he emerged a couple of flights later in Bamako, Mali, about midnight. Unfortunately, his two suitcases did not arrive at the same time. Eventually, they reached him. At that time of year, the hot Sahara had so shrunken the Niger River that boats were not able to carry passengers and goods to Timbuktu and beyond. So, travel was by truck up to Gao and then back down with the remainder of our belongings. Hubert prayed a lot when he overheard robbers plotting to attack him when the truck reached the big open desert. God heard. A big uniformed policeman walked up, telling the driver he was going to ride up to Gao and plopping into the cab of the truck right beside Hubert. After bringing our belongings back to Bamako and arranging transportation for them to the Central African Republic (CAR), Hubert caught a flight to CAR.

Traveling from Michigan in early January with our new three-month-old baby Hadessah, our four other children, and a teacher for our children, Becky Kitchen, New York airport presented challenges when they required me to claim and recheck all twenty-three pieces of luggage. Doug and Irene Golike showed up right then and were a great help traveling with us for the rest of the trip. Hubert met us in Bangui, CAR. We were grateful that Hannah's schoolbooks were in a bag that arrived with us, not in one of the missing pieces that came later. When Becky's suitcase arrived, it had a square hole cut in the side of it, but nothing was missing. My late arrival bag was missing Hubert's Christmas watch. We thanked the Lord repeatedly for bringing us to CAR and for what He would do.

The first Sunday we walked to the church right on the Bangui mission station. It was amazing to see about four hundred Central Africans praising the Lord and listening to the Word of God in Sango for about two hours. We looked forward to when we could understand what they were saying. Sango language study began the next day. After the 8 am lesson time with Wilma Rosenau the children started their school classes with Becky.

Hubert and Mary Broeckert 1985 Hannah, Cherith, Hadessah, Davar, & Hans

Walking through the neighborhood we would repeat our few sentences with ladies by their mudbrick houses with cement floors and tin roofs. Or we met them by their wells, or in their little gardens of manioc. At times, many children followed us. One little girl cried with fright to see us. Being a language learner involved hours and months of work, times of joy and times of discouragement, humbling situations, and appreciation for our great God, and for people who were praying that the Lord would help us.

Fellowshipping in a smaller church the second Sunday, cracks in the hard dirt floor caught a heel of Becky's dress shoes. A little breeze reached us on the backless benches. After a short time, baby Hadessah and I joined the other mothers in "the nursery," sitting on stones under a tree outside. We could still hear Bruce Rosenau inside preaching. We so appreciated him and Wilma being our mentors while we were new to CAR.

There were more lessons to learn. We were grateful for an electric washing machine but frustrated when it quit. Perhaps it had something to do with the oil leaking out of the motor. One of our missionary coworkers found another washing machine for us. Another was our first traffic ticket for slowing down through an intersection. We learned an appeal in the office increases the fine. Then there were the dry season grass fires. They are yearly intentional burnings of the tall, dry elephant grass. One evening a large fire was getting closer and closer to our houses. I went to the bedroom and prayed. God gave peace, assuring me He would take care of it. Then the fire died down and quit advancing. We thanked the Lord in our missionary prayer meeting that evening. About the seventh week after Hubert had sent our baggage from Mali, and after a few phone calls from the post office, which was the only phone we knew of, we finally got word from a transporter in Bangui that the shipment was coming.

One of the privileges of living in the capital was an invitation from President Andre Kolingba for an evening with several evangelical pastors and a few missionaries. After the fancy meal, there was a choir, a sermon, and a prayer meeting. Our prayer was that God would bring many Central Africans to Himself, and bless the country.

One Sunday in mid-February we traveled through beautiful country, some of it home to pygmies, to a church twenty-two miles southeast of Bangui. The pastor there cared for seven churches. God helped Hubert and I give our testimonies in Sango for the first time in public. A couple months later just Hubert and Bruce went deeper into that territory and saw pygmy people wearing loincloths and leaves. For part of that trip Hubert walked, to make less weight for the car to get over stones in the road. Near that area cannibalism was still practiced.

In the afternoon, back on the station, a 5-foot 1-inch mamba, a fast-moving, aggressive, venomous snake brushed Bruce's foot. He and a guard speared it. We praised God for His protection. The following day, Hubert saw a viper jump from a tree in our yard. And the day after that, Hubert saw a six-foot-long snake within three feet of him, but it slid into its hole. Gasoline and digging failed to coax it out. Eight days later it was back, near our porch. The guards killed it and confirmed its identity as a Gaboon viper. Its fangs were impressive. I studied up again on treatment for snakebites. It was amazing to recall God's faithful protection of His servants from snakes throughout the years. Seeing snakes was not usually frequent and we were vigilant. Most of them in our region were poisonous.

In late February the process of getting authorization to practice medicine in CAR started. We were introduced to various officials and gathered a list of what was needed to submit with a request. But it was difficult to secure the proper form to complete. About a month later there was success in getting the needed form from the secretary of the Organization of Doctors. We praised the Lord for progress on the permission. Mid-May I picked up my professional identification card for the CAR doctors' organization. Now that I had received the card, I could submit a letter requesting authorization to work as a physician. I needed the mission field president to co-sign my letter. He arrived from another station two days later for other business and signed it. Then I turned in my request to the Ministry of Health. Eventually, the permission to practice medicine was granted. God accomplished it!

We were up before the sun one Sunday morning and out to the car by 6:15 am. Soon we saw the sign in front of the large cement block, tin-roof building: "Eglise Baptiste Ngou-Ciment." If you translated the Sango literally, you would read "Water-Cement Baptist Church." It was the name of that section of town. The choir was gathering under the shade of a Mango tree to practice before going in. The French service began promptly at 6:40 am. There was singing, a meditation on Psalm 100, long announcements, mail call, the choir accompanied by accordion, and then Hubert expounded the Word of God.

Following that Harold Dark took us to another church where he preached in the 9 o'clock Sango service. A man clanged the iron wheel rim which was the bell. Children, then women, then the men, recited with their group the verses they had been memorizing in Sunday School. The wood benches were getting pretty hard by 10:45 am when the service ended.

In the afternoon, I taught a Sunday School class in English for the missionary kids (MKs). Most of the time, our children were the only ones, but many other families made trips to the capital for supplies, truck repairs and other business, and their MKs would join in the class.

We were not entirely isolated from world events. Living near the airport, we noticed an increase in flights when Chad's war escalated, and French troops came through Bangui before heading north. Planes were constant and loud through the next morning headed on bombing missions. We were in no danger, but I prayed for the Chadian Christians and missionaries. Tensions between Libya and the USA led to the harassing of Americans in CAR as well as all over the world. But we were secure in God's care. Other issues in Bangui stirred student rioting and looting downtown. A military plane crashing into a Koranic school killing 122 people resulted in anti-white sentiment. We stayed close to the house for a time. Also in March, after getting up several nights only to find clouds, we finally saw Halley's comet!

There was no city water for several days and we were using our rainwater cistern while praying for God to keep the supply sufficient.

Then the sky turned dark, and rain fell so hard that the church services were cancelled. Our cistern was replenished, and we thanked God. Another night, strong wind arrived with rain and the tin roof was stressed and creaking. It had blown off once in the past and we prayed that would not happen again. God protected us and, in the morning, everything was still in place, with only some nails loose.

We were encouraged that our crates from the USA arrived in Bangui, but it took two weeks before they were released from the customs office and delivered to our house. With no forklift available a solution was found. A bunch of guys helped push them off the side of the truck onto the ground. The bottoms broke on both. Everything got packed away in the house and gradually transported to Ippy. While we were in Sango class, three-year-old Hans was riding his shiny new red tricycle that had come in the crates the previous day. A group of children came, lifted him off it, and carried off the trike, as well as Hans' flip flops and hat. Davar and a guard came running and succeeded in retrieving everything.

Our first container of hospital supplies could not be located (was lost) somewhere between the USA and Bangui – but eventually found. When it arrived in Ippy, getting a heavy twenty-foot container off the truck was accomplished by tying a cable and chain to the container and to a tree. The truck lurched forward, causing the container to fly off.

After three and a half months living in Bangui, we took a brief break from language study. The whole family loaded our pick-up with things from our crate shipment and visited the station and hospital staff we would soon be working with at Ippy. The trip sharpened our vision of life after language study.

But for the next months, the moving air of the oscillating fan helped relieve the heavy hot air a little as we sat in class each morning. "*Mo tene*: you speak," and we took turns around the table repeating phrases. Our teacher Wilma patiently corrected our pronunciation and tones. We said it again. She wrote on the board with a marker, and we wrote in our notebooks. "Now give me a nice sentence in Sango to say, 'We went to the meeting at the church to worship with God's people.'" Sometimes it took a few tries to formulate an acceptable sentence: word order, grammar, vocabulary, tones, and expressions. We listened to our African language helper, also at the table. He said it the right way and we repeated it. There was progress since the start of language study for which we thanked God. After class was study time at home. We listened to the cassettes, searched the books, wrote out sentences and memorized. In the afternoon, there was a class with just the African language helper. He read and we repeated phrase after phrase. He asked questions and we answered from the lesson.

Practicing was vital to gain speaking proficiency, so besides walking in the neighborhood, we found other creative ways. From our house we could see a mountain beckoning us. A family hike up the mountain gave practice using the language as several village children went with us. Another time Hubert took me for a dugout canoe ride on the Ubangi River, always watching for crocodiles. Bargaining with the owners required the use of Sango. Of course, in churches we practiced speaking Sango with the people. One of the churches we visited was near the Falls of Boali, one and a half hours outside of Bangui. The thundering falls were high and majestic. CAR's hydroelectric works were located below the falls. Another interaction was buying a baby mongoose, which we named Rikki and fed with a dropper.

Five months after Hubert's trip to Mali and getting two crates and some barrels on their way toward CAR, they arrived as air freight. All the things cleared customs duty free! What an answer to prayer after a huge customs bill for our crates from the USA the previous month. My accordion was in one of the barrels and was broken inside, but Hubert put the pieces back together and it made joyful music again. He also reassembled Great Aunt Margie's treadle sewing machine whose first project was making a mosquito net for eight-month-old Hadessah's crib. One of the barrels was a moldy mess from some spilled fluid.

Bangui had great trees for the children to climb. But unfortunately, eight-year-old Cherith fell. On the fourth day after her fall, she began to show signs of increased intracranial pressure (pressure on her brain), suggestive of possible swelling or bleeding inside her head. We made her lie very still and we prayed. One of our prayer warriors in the States was stirred to urgently pray that very day for our health, encouragement, and God's enabling. God answered prayer and healed Cherith. We received a letter from that prayer partner two months later, asking what had happened that day that God prompted her special intercession. What a wonderful God!

The six months living in Bangui sped by. We were grateful for the time for concentrated Sango language study before moving into the work at Ippy Hospital. We learned from various missionaries who came to the capital as they sat around our dinner table. It was good we were there for the three shipments that came in, our crates from the USA, the hospital container, and our goods from Mali. Getting licenses, vehicle registrations, and carte de séjours (residence permits) all had been accomplished in the capital. We were happy to be leaving the thievery of the city: Hans' cap had been stolen off his head again, this time while I was walking with him and holding his hand, but it was recovered. The mirror was stolen off our motorcycle downtown, a station storage building was broken into, visitors' valuables were grabbed from right next to them in vehicles, Davar was pick-pocketed, and more. It was affirmation that the people desperately needed Christ to change their hearts and give new life.

Mornings, on awakening, God put a song in my heart. He is so good. Several times God gave us fabulous lightning displays across the night sky. Falling to sleep at night to the steady little beeps of tiny hidden tree toads, the cadence of infant heart monitors, we thanked God for bringing us to CAR to serve Him.

Sunday, July 6, 1986, Hubert preached in a Bangui church to a crowd of nine hundred six people. It was our last day living in Bangui and I spent the afternoon in bed with malaria. The next morning, I continued to feel light-headed, and it seemed like an impossible mountain to finish stuffing all our accumulations into boxes by noon. Satan was buffeting as we planned to enter Ippy to live and work. God gave me the verse "Whatever you do, work heartily, as for the Lord" (Colossians 3:23). So I dug into the task for the Lord, His assignment for me that day. My head gradually improved throughout the morning, and God gave me strength. Hubert washed clothes and Wilma dried them. Then we hauled many things to a storeroom to bring up later and packed the pick-up to capacity leaving room for kids and two dogs in the back. We got all loaded by noon which was our goal and I marveled at God's great mercy to have accomplished the task.

Ahead were dirt roads which in the event of rain, would be closed by a pole across the road and military guards prohibiting travel until several hours after the rain stopped. Knute Orton arrived with rain barrier passes at 12:15 pm and we pulled out at 12:35 pm. We enjoyed peanut butter and jelly sandwiches and tomatoes during the three-hour trip to the mission station to the north, Sibut. They made room for us to spend the night even though they were already filled with guests. It rained all that night.

On Tuesday morning we waited to leave Sibut until about 9 am, two hours after the rain stopped. We had to use the rain-barrier passes we had just received. Praise God for perfect timing. Without the passes, it would have been a six hour wait. There were eleven barriers plus two police checks in the next four-hour leg of the journey. We bought bread and used the station short wave radio at Bambari mission station (they were like ham radios). While downtown, a bunch of rowdy kids gathered at the back of the truck. Becky guarded it until we pulled away, but at that point they broke the clasp on the back end. The two dogs would have ridden fine except that Taffy, the female, was in heat. Every stop we had to guard her from other dogs. The scenic ride through grasslands included beautiful hills, occasional small villages, and one monkey crossing the path.

Arriving at Ippy at 4:20 pm, Doug and Irene Golike (Doug was our mission pilot), June Stone, and Tom Dessoffy (nurses), welcomed us warmly. Unfortunately, Dr. Rhodes was not able to return to work in CAR, so I was the only physician at Ippy. The nurses had a patient with a broken arm waiting. The fracture had happened from her husband beating her the night before. I went down to the hospital to care for her.

On Wednesday morning, the nurses asked for help with only a few patients. They tried to give me time to unpack. We made good progress clearing boxes, barrels, and crates in the house. But at 3:45 pm, June drove up on her motorcycle. "I think we've got a cesarean section for you, Doctor." They had tried everything else first before calling me. While waiting for the nurses to set things up for surgery, I went over to Dr. Rhode's library. I found the book explaining the surgical technique for doing cesareans, read through it, and headed back to the hospital. The amazing work of God was that I quickly found that information the hour I needed it, whereas in April I had hunted several times for that book in the same library without success. And we had no cesarean cases in April. It was not urgent then. But God provided it exactly when needed. It was the first cesarean

I had done on my own. Hubert was praying for me at home and at the 4:15 pm prayer meeting at church. God was my help.

Leaving the operating room (OR), we stopped to check maternity. Two ladies were in labor. One had had a previous cesarean because of being too small – and needed one again. The staff said the arrival of doctors was always celebrated with lots of emergencies. They were glad not to have to transport these patients to the government hospital two hours away where patients did not do too well. I found out the next day that a third patient was on the way to us after six days of labor in a village, but she died before arriving.

IMMANUEL

It was the wee hours of the morning – Christmas morning. I was standing at the foot of the delivery table in maternity with our elderly African midwife, Justine, assisting a mother giving birth to her infant. The brand-new baby finally arrived, and we heard its beautiful first cry. It had been a difficult delivery. The night was hot and the mosquitoes thick. But as we saw that precious new baby that had just entered the world, Justine smiled at me. "Immanuel," she said. I was puzzled. Did she mean the baby's name? It is used as an African name, but names aren't given until a week after the birth. "God with us," she said. Then I grasped her meaning. God was with us – there – during that delivery, to enable our hands and minds to assist that mother and child. God was very present in the heat of the night, in the heart of Africa.

Yet, there was more to that sacred name. Being Christmas morning, we were celebrating the arrival of Jesus into the world. What better way to celebrate than to witness a birth! His birth was God becoming man. The Incarnate One, Immanuel, came to do the profound work of redemption – to buy us back from the kingdom of darkness to the kingdom of His glorious Son. Jesus lived a sinless life on this earth. He died on the cross to pay for our sins. He was buried. On the third day He rose from the dead. He invites all people to come, repent of their sin, and receove his free gift of forgiveness. Each person who believes in Jesus receives everlasting life. Christ comes to live in them.

A young man, Raymond, was very quiet as I visited his bedside at the hospital. Each day that I made rounds, going from bed to bed checking each patient and updating their treatment plans, I tried to get Raymond to interact. I had first met him on a busy clinic day. The waiting room was full of people standing, sitting, walking around, waiting their turn to see the African nurse for consultation, or for the lab, dental work, the doctor, or to receive their pills or injections.

Amidst the noise and crowd, friends carried a man, bleeding, and breathing with difficulty. He was dirty from the ride in the back of a pick-up truck over a dusty road. The story we learned was that he had attempted suicide with a shotgun. We took him immediately to the operating room and started the generator for power. It took several hours to reconstruct his lower face. His brain and eyes had not been injured. The pieces of his jaws had to be lined up and wired in place. Debris had to be cleaned out and skin sutured. In a later procedure, some cartilage was taken from his ear to reconstruct part of his nose that was missing.

Day by day, as he was in the hospital healing, he heard the preaching of the Word of God. He listened as we talked with him. "Raymond, God spared your life." We explained to him that God loved him and wanted to wash away all his sin and give him eternal life. The African staff and the missionaries prayed for Raymond. The medical evangelists several times patiently explained more.

71

Finally, one day, we heard the news: Raymond had decided to ask God to forgive his sins and enter his life. How we rejoiced! He was given a Gospel of John and the nurses taught him more and more, helping him grow in the knowledge of God and His Word. We contacted the pastor of the church near his village so he could continue to disciple him when he returned home. How Raymond radiated a new joy from his scarred face! God was with him.

As a wife, and mother of five, there were always many things to attend to in caring for my family. I tried to help my husband. I tried to train my children to walk with the Lord Jesus. On top of that was the challenge of making creative meals when it took so much time to sift the bugs out of the flour, wash the bugs out of the rice, use dirty sugar as it was, bake with only basics, plan the shopping list when canned vegetables were three hundred miles away, and staples came in cases or one-hundred-pound bags.

When the phone rang just in the middle of supper preparation, I turned it over to my daughters and buzzed back down to the hospital for a couple more hours. Paperwork for the hospital and mission stacked up, and classes needed to be prepared and taught for the African medical evangelist training program. God gently reminded me that He is Lord and I am His loved servant. He does not overload us. "Lord, show me what Your orders are for this moment and make me content to do only that, and leave the rest until later."

As I walked between the main hospital building and another building for private patients, I watched the Muslims carefully going through the rituals of their prayers. They knelt on the grass mats, facing east, rose, knelt again, chanting, and repeating the process, with foreheads to the ground. How they tried to work their way to heaven. What a thrill to recall various Muslims as well as animists who found Christ while at the hospital.

Weekends in villages were special. Most of the hospital staff went out to various towns to start churches, build up struggling churches, or to serve as pastors in well-established churches. Sometimes they preached in one of the three churches in our town of Ippy. We went Sunday after Sunday to Ndakala. It was about an hour's drive out. The elephant grass (taller than elephants) along the way, was interspersed with scraggly trees, beautiful streams with bamboo and vines, or small fields of manioc, corn, or cotton. Chairs were brought under a mango tree, the meeting place. When we first started going, they did not know any songs or have any Bibles. But oh, the joy, when God saved people. His church grew.

The old army field phone that connected the hospital and house awakened me at 3 am one morning. The hospital needed me for an urgent case. I dressed, pulled on my white coat, and hopped on my little motorcycle. As I puttered down the hill in the dark, balancing a flashlight on the handlebar (for lack of a working headlight right then), a song came to mind. "I'll Go Where You Want Me to Go, Dear Lord," and I added, "where and when. I made that promise many years before in church as a young girl and I still mean it. I told You I was willing to go anywhere in the world with You. And right now, if You want me out in the night at 3 am, Lord, I'm willing. Thank you for the privilege of serving You here and now." Then came the song, "Anywhere with Jesus I can Safely Go." I was headed down to this task with Jesus there too.

After the emergency surgery was over and I was returning home about 5 am, up the same hill, on the motorcycle, God spread out a brilliant display of color across the eastern sky. It was a fabulous sunrise. I said aloud, "Thank you, God, for bringing me outside to this spot, at this hour, so You could show this beauty to me." He gives so many expressions of His love.

A Saturday in April was relatively quiet, until 5 pm when the hospital became inundated with wounded people from a traffic accident. Several people filled the central waiting area of the wards. A bus had rolled over. People kept coming. Soon they overflowed into the hall in the surgery ward. We called in all the staff who could be found. Some triaged, sorting the people who were more seriously hurt from those who could wait a little longer. The head African nurse washed and sutured cuts. The missionary nurse supervised patients being carried to and from X-ray. The African X-ray tech kept shooting films and sending them back with the patients, trying to keep all the paperwork in order. Other staff found beds, registered patients, or applied bandages. When we finished at 9:15 pm, we had treated sixteen patients, one with a broken neck, another with pelvic fractures and internal bleeding needing blood transfusions, several other fractures, lacerations, and contusions. Two more came in the following Monday, making a total of eighteen.

One particular Easter, our family drove a day's trip out on Saturday, to a small town for a wedding to be celebrated on Sunday. We crossed the river on a ferry, then our pick-up crawled through ruts and holes in the road to arrive at the town of Daba. We were warmly received. A fine meal of goat, rice, manioc, gravy, pineapple, bread, and tea loaded with sugar and milk was served. A shelter made with leaves provided a place to wash up. A basin of heated water was provided. But I found it difficult to sleep that night. The truck bed was hard. The goats would run races, bleat to each other, run more races, and then rest intermittently throughout the night. A lone mosquito buzzed inside my mosquito net.

When light began to push aside the night sky, I climbed out of the back of the pick-up. All was so still. I saw no people emerging from their huts yet. No cooking fires had been lit yet. I walked quietly to the edge of the clearing around the little mud brick church.

I sat on a fallen tree trunk and opened my New Testament. Mark 16:1-2, "When the Sabbath was past, Mary Magdalene, Mary the mother of James, and Salome bought spices... And very early on the first day of the week, when the sun had risen, they went to the tomb." That moment too, was dawn. I was another Mary. The women were seeking Jesus. I was seeking fellowship with Jesus. And as they were running to tell the disciples about the angel and the empty tomb, Jesus met them on the path. What joy was theirs to be with Jesus again! Later He met Mary Magdalene alone. How happy she was! And then He met the disciples in a locked room and said, "Peace be with you" (John 20:21). What peace to have Jesus with them. They were once again in His presence. The children were beginning to awaken. I went to help them wash up, start more water filtering to drink, and try throughout the day to remember the presence of Immanuel.

PATIENTS AND STAFF

Drums, drums, drums, drums on and on through the dark African night. "Please Lord, help me sleep in spite of the drums." Then a ring awakened me. "Thank you, Lord, I must have fallen asleep." I grabbed my flashlight and shuffled to the old army field phone in the hallway. The voice from maternity came, "Madame, a lady has been in labor a long time and the baby is not coming. Would you please come?" Trying not to awaken the children, I headed to my little motorcycle waiting by the back door and drove down the hill toward maternity. What magnificent stars were displayed across the big sky! Each in their assigned place, following the course designed by their Creator. "Thank you, Lord, for Your course for my life." After the safe arrival of the new baby, God gave me sleep.

In the morning, I straightened the house, worked on meal preparations for company at noon and then prayed with the children to send them off to school at Becky's house. At the hospital were devotions for the staff and preaching services in the ward and clinic. Student medical evangelists joined me to do rounds on the hospital patients. There were patients recuperating from surgery, a man with a badly broken arm, a lady with multiple abscesses, a man with a bleeding ulcer, children with measles, others with parasites, and a man who had been bitten by a chimpanzee and then developed gangrene in his finger. There were several others as well, and each one God had allowed to come to receive care and hear His Word.

Prayer in an Old Ward

God was working in the hospital, the churches, the Bible conferences, the classes, yes, in the lives of individuals. We prayed for strength and health, for a teacher to come after Becky, for more churches to be established, for more pastors for Ippy region churches, and that we would be humble students before the Master who desires to teach us His ways. We asked God to help Hubert learning the Fulfulde language to reach nomadic Muslim herders. God surprised us on a trip to other dispensaries in CAR when we were given a Bible in the Fulfulde (Borolo) language, and an address where he sent for a course book and tapes to help study that language.

Friday, March 6, 1987, June was gone to Bangui. I got a call at 11:15 pm from Becky, helping the midwife at maternity. A mother was hemorrhaging after her delivery. I rushed down and saw her lying in a pool of blood. It was a Borolo woman (nomadic tribe) and her seventeenth baby. The baby was fine and healthy. Becky was like an angel. She helped get the kerosene lantern working. She got the African nurse from the hospital to help the midwife and me. She held flashlights, looked for instruments, held retractors, felt faint and white several times but kept on. We got IVs going, and got the bleeding stopped. The patient went into shock, but the Lord brought her through as IV fluids poured in. Becky went and got the lab tech, Abraham, to prepare for a blood transfusion. She got the blood typing serum from June's frig, then gave her own blood. When all was stable, I headed home and caught two hours of sleep before Saturday arrived. We thanked God for each of His servants, capable national staff handling most of the emergencies, and fellow missionaries, both short or long term.

A young lady arrived at maternity thinking she was nine months pregnant. She was not in labor and there was no heartbeat. At exploratory surgery, an ovarian tumor six kilograms (over thirteen pounds) and thirty-two centimeters diameter (twelve and a half inches across) was found. She made a beautiful recovery and turned from her Muslim religion to faith in Christ Jesus.

The faucet above the sink for scrubbing up for surgery could be turned on with a hand, but after the ten-minute scrub, it had to be turned off with the elbow to keep the hands clean. However, it was intermittently giving off shocks when touched! Hubert disconnected wire after wire in the web of old wires in the high attic while keeping power supplied where needed. Finally, he succeeded in stopping the shocks.

One Wednesday at about 4 pm, Sibut station radioed that a Bible School student had a painful abdomen, probably needing urgent surgery. They asked someone from Ippy to meet them at Bambari. Vernon Rosenau and Nurse Jean (John) transported the patient that far. Jim Buerer and Nurse Martin went from Ippy to Bambari. June and I listened for details on the station radio. We prayed for the patient and the team helping her during our evening missionary prayer meeting. Since they were not expected to arrive in Ippy until about midnight, I caught two hours of sleep, then went down to the hospital. It was a beautiful starry sky as I waited and prayed. The patient arrived at 12:50 am. Examining her, I suspected a ruptured ectopic pregnancy. At surgery, the belly was full of blood from her hemorrhaging. Praise God for helping us stop the bleeding and for His sparing her life. Praise Him for so many people helping in the time of crisis.

On July 12, 1987, an interesting patient arrived at Ippy after he had visited several clinics and hospitals. He carried with him his health record from Bangui showing a positive HIV (human immunodeficiency virus) test. That was the first person I had seen with that diagnosis, and quickly read more about it. The World Health Organization (WHO) provided criteria for making a clinical diagnosis of AIDS (acquired immunodeficiency syndrome) while waiting for confirmatory blood tests. We sent suspected cases to Bangui for testing. In the next ten months, we saw seven cases of AIDS, but that increased to one or two new cases each week. We procured HIV tests for the lab, wrote and printed Sango gospel tracts about AIDS, and thanked God for each opportunity to share the hope Christ offers. By the end of 1988, our AIDS registry showed we had hospitalized a cumulative total of seventeen cases and had seen many more in clinic. Graphing the number of cases and dates gave an exponential curve just as had been predicted.

The hospital lab provided vital information for caring for patients. One day the tube for the hemoglobinometer broke. How could we care for severely anemic children with chronic malaria, or hemorrhaging adults without being able to measure their blood levels? The same day, I opened some mail that had just arrived from a missionary in Bangassou. She had sent a booklet of blotting paper with a chart for reading hemoglobins! God gave it to us with perfect timing! It sufficed until we were able to get a new tube and later other methods to measure blood loss.

One afternoon, I saw a child with severe anemia from chronic malaria needing a blood transfusion. Our lab techs were out of town. I prayed that God would help me do the blood typing, collect the donor's blood, and do a "cut down" procedure on the child's vein to give him the blood – all skills I had never done before. June walked into the clinic while I was searching for instructions for doing blood typing, and she found some. God helped me find the cut down procedure in a medical Handbook. It turned out well and the child's life was saved. He returned to his happy and bouncy self. God did it again! God also brought Jim Johnson, a lab technician. His work for the Lord was greatly appreciated.

August 2, 1988, was a grand day of ceremony and celebrating. Martin and Adoum each received diplomas as Medical Evangelists. They had been training intermittently for eleven years in the hospital's five-year program. God gave us beautiful sunshine. We started scurrying around by 7 am. Food to prepare was carried down to African cooks. Tables and water were set out. Gifts were readied for the graduates. The children got the house set up for a reception. Hannah decorated cakes. Cherith made cookies and candies. Irene put lettering on diplomas. The *sous préfet* (head administrator for our region), mayor, and military leader arrived early.

The program went well – led by the four pastors on the medical committee. It was held at Center I church and included prayer, preaching, speeches, and presentation of the diplomas. The medical staff sang a beautiful special song. It all brought praise to God. Rosie Johnson organized the reception of cookies and Kool-Aid that followed. Jim drove the three officials back to town. Then we walked down to the new surgery building for a dinner. Irene was in charge of the mid-day dinner and the missionaries served. It included the graduates, spouses, visiting pastors, hospital staff, and missionaries.

At 4 pm we went to the nurses' village on the mission property for another program and another feast. Young people from the church choir were singing and playing accordions. The graduates gave their testimonies. A visiting pastor preached. There was much prayer offered for these two men. They heaped plates with rice and gravy with chunks of beef and roast goat. God had accomplished a great thing.

A particular Monday in October I saw God answer prayer over and over. First, He gave a delightful quiet time with Him in the early hours of the day. Meditating on a passage in the Song of Solomon, I prayed my love relationship with Christ would be strong and beautiful. Second, I asked the Lord to show us how to schedule the workers since one more was leaving for ten days. June and I worked on it early in the day and the schedule worked out fine. Third, I prayed that one of the head nurses would accept sweetly having to work some night shifts in the hospital – and he did! Fourth, I prayed for new workers we needed. A man showed up and we interviewed him – a very good candidate to present to the medical committee.

Fifth, my head cold was making me weary. In answer to prayer, God gave strength to keep going. Sixth, that day I had to discuss with several patients their serious illnesses. God enabled me. Seventh, I prayed for the Holy Spirit to lead and give opportunities to witness. He gave many! Eighth, I prayed I would get some correspondence done. God sent an emergency hernia surgery in the afternoon, but the staff did most of it and I got three letters written while sitting in the operating room overseeing them. It was wonderful that God had brought the head nurses so far in their training. Ninth, I prayed for God to bless our evening with company for supper. The Lord did and gave wonderful fellowship. Praise God for His loving working toward His beloved.

A French Catholic priest came to us with a cardiac problem (heart trouble). He and his superior asked us to assist in getting him to Paris for medical help, which I agreed was medically indicated. Doug, our pilot, was on furlough so the mission plane sitting right by our house could not be used to get him down to Bangui. Using the station radio, I asked Elmers in Bambari to talk to the Bambari Catholic mission that our patient worked for. That mission phoned Bangui and arranged for a French military evacuation helicopter. The message got mixed up and went to the American embassy, then the German embassy, and finally to the French embassy.

The next day we were watching for the helicopter all day. When we checked on the radio at 1 pm we were told the paperwork was done and the transport arranged. Finally, at 4:15 pm we heard that the helicopter had left Bangui at 4 pm and was expected at our airstrip at 5:30 pm. So the Catholic sisters brought the patient in their car at 5:20 pm and we went out to the airstrip to wait. Darkness rapidly approached, so I brought a portable generator and a light. Hubert brought our truck and parked it halfway up the runway shining its lights on the clearing.

The helicopter arrived at 6:15 pm. I stood on the near end of the runway and waved the light. Johnson's truck and the Catholic missionaries' car also shone their lights. The helicopter was huge! A crew of about twelve soldiers in green uniforms jumped out. They set up their radio. I gave a report to the army doctor that came, and he set up a cot for our patient in the copter. A crowd of people came to watch. The helicopter took off about 6:30 pm, lifting straight up resulting in a spray of dust and fine gravel on us below. It was an exciting night! I love the variety in the Lord's work. We were grateful to God that the patient was able to go where he could get the care he needed.

A man who had been gored by a buffalo was brought to the hospital. He had been gathering some wild honey when the angry animal charged into his chest. The long horns inflicted fourteen large cuts and collapsed his lung. That was the second case that year of trauma from the most dangerous animal in Africa, the Cape buffalo. The first man had his chest and lung pierced from the large horns as well as his knee laid open. Another trauma case that week was a sixteen-year-old boy who was having his manioc ground into flour by a machine. The grinding wheel broke and flew up lacerating and fracturing his jaw. A young lady received treatment when she came with gangrene in her hand from a human bite. She had been fighting with her rival – her husband's other wife. As we cared for patients, we tried to tell them of God's mercy. He had brought them to us through unfortunate circumstances, to hear of Christ.

Late July 1989, a kerosene powered refrigerator for the vaccination clinic arrived and our three men that were trained for the international program were able to start giving routine childhood immunizations. That ended the annual measles ward filled with children who had complications from measles. Twice a year God provided a visiting ophthalmologist. Many, many people with vision problems came. Many of those regained sight when their cataracts were removed.

When I went to the clinic at the usual time after rounds one morning, the head of the military for our region (CB) was waiting and asked why I had kept him waiting so long. I had not been informed that he was waiting. He wanted a consultation for his father. Then he asked about the death of the town butcher from hepatitis two days before at the hospital. I explained that his diagnosis was infectious hepatitis, which in our area was generally a viral illness. We saw many instances when patients died from that in a very short time. Later I asked a couple of our nurses about the case. The butcher had been accused of mishandling funds collected for a celebration. He had grabbed the flag in front of the major's office and swore that if he was lying, he should die. It was very soon after that he died. There were murder charges concerning his death and lots of accusations, including that we had not properly treated him. A little later, two police investigators came with questions about the hospital. God protected. We heard nothing more about the issue.

A two-day old infant had not passed any stool. After searching the books and doing a plain abdominal X-ray, we took him to surgery, where atresia of a section of the ileum was found. During embryonic development, a section of intestine had failed to develop a lumen, or channel for intestinal contents to pass through. The abnormal section was removed, and the good intestine was anastomosed (attached together). The child recovered well. God had been our help.

It was clearly God guiding our hands and minds caring for shotgun injuries (one man had 42 holes), reduction of femur fractures with traction, Burkitt lymphomas (a jaw tumor seen in children which improved nicely as long as methotrexate treatment was continued), osteomyelitis (chronic infection in bones, with drainage) and a myriad of other things that kept me praying and studying.

LAIRD MEMORIAL PROJECT

Missionary nurse Margaret Laird had been God's instrument to begin the medical work at Ippy. Seeing her clinic alone was not sufficient, she prayed and labored to see a hospital built for evangelism and for caring for the health of Christian workers. In the 1950s the first three resident missionary doctors arrived at Ippy and the hospital opened. In 1982 Dr. Charles Rhodes initiated the Laird Memorial Project to repair the termite-riddled hospital buildings and add new buildings and equipment. American churches, Sunday schools, children's clubs, youth groups, women's missionary groups, and individual donors contributed money for the project. Next, it was time to build.

Gleaning ideas from other mission hospitals in hot tropical countries, plans began to formulate. The need for skilled builders was made known and there was much prayer for God to guide every step and bring His chosen workers. My trip in April 1986 up to Ippy during language study included a project building committee meeting, detailing room sizes on the initial plans with missionary builder Jim Buerer and nurse June, and walking around the site to choose the best locations for the buildings.

Hospital plans were sent to the States for suggestions and approval. The group of missionaries composing the project building committee met again at Ippy in September. They worked together and the plans were reworked and revised. We were ready to start digging foundations. A request was sent for a Men For Missions group in the USA to load a container with doors, jams, wire, etc. to send out.

On June 18, 1986, Hubert and June staked out the surgical/classroom building and the inpatient ward building. They were to be aligned with two fairly new existing buildings, the clinic building and the central supply/office, making a center square with sidewalks connecting the buildings. Workers clutched their hatchets, climbed into a big old mango tree, and started chopping. It was right where the new operating rooms would be. There was a plethora of other mango trees old and new all over the property and lining the main road. Men with shovels began digging foundation trenches and hauling big stones and sand. Villagers dug sand from a small riverbed and piled it on the bank to dry. Hubert hauled it with our pickup to the construction site.

Ippy Hospital Construction

In early January 1987, Hubert left Ippy at 6:13 am, arriving in Bangui at 5 pm and picking up Marvin Nelson, a builder from the States, at the airport at 5:30 pm. God had orchestrated details to make it to the plane on time even with Hubert's trip including transporting a student family and their belongings to Bible School in Sibut. The men were not able to leave Bangui to return when planned because the store to buy pipe for the construction was closed and the truck battery was having trouble. But the following day he took Marvin to the market and then drove to Ippy.

Marvin dug into the work, adjusting the level of the foundation for the surgery building. Hubert left for a pastor's conference in Bambari and returned the next afternoon. After that Marvin and Hubert worked each day along with the African crew for the construction of the two buildings. People were excited to see the cement floor poured for the first new operating room. It took all morning mixing and pouring, then in the afternoon the top was smoothed with cement and water. Marvin worked on it until the generator was turned off at 9 pm. It was a little frustrating in the morning to see little air pockets from tiny green mangos that had gotten mixed into the cement. But a solution was found.

Two days later the floor of the second operating room got poured. There were some diversions, such as when a truck delivering bags of cement tipped into a ditch by the bridge at the carpenter shop. They got it out by jacking and putting stones under it. Another day Marvin and Doug responded to the police downtown who requested they hunt by the big river for a hippo that had become aggressive. When Marvin left to return to the States, his most vivid memory was monkey heads for sale in the Bangui market he had seen his second day in the country.

Wood and sheet metal were ordered from Zaire. But after six months, it still had not arrived. Jim Buerer finally said in prayer meeting, "Let's ask the Lord to send these items to us within two weeks." The Zaire order was canceled, and Hubert hunted again for wood and sheet metal in Bangui. This time he found some, bought it and got it loaded on a transport truck. It arrived about two weeks from the time Jim prayed for that. God delights to show His works.

In January 1988 the next shipping container from the States arrived. Unloading was again exciting. The strap and chain popped up several times. The corners of the forty-foot container kept getting caught on the side rails of the truck, but exactly four hours after the start of unloading, the truck left, job completed. It contained one hundred metal doors, door jambs, and other building supplies, plus air conditioners for the operating rooms! No more wiping sweat off the gowned doctor and nurses' faces while they did surgical operations.

Hammers continued swinging and saws buzzing. Wiring was going in and sand was sifted to use in plaster. We were watching the dreams laid out on paper now rising in the form of brick walls, plaster, paint, windows, doors, and shiny metal roofs. God graciously sent more American builders to work on the construction with the African workers. We prayed that God would bring about the construction of the rest of the buildings planned and give daily wisdom in the work for Him.

On April 1988 Jon and Patricia Wall arrived. It was God's perfect timing again right when we needed another builder. Jon was a pastor, but he also knew construction. Patricia was the schoolteacher for our children. Their prayer letter that month stated

> We have moved into our little house and are beginning to feel at home with the lizards, cockroaches, and bats. Life is full of surprises and our Lord does have a sense of humor, we remind ourselves as we step into the shower with a multi-legged creature, or reach for our glass of water, longing for a

refreshing drink, only to stare into the eyes of a winged creation.

We are learning. We are comfortable with being here because this is the will of the Lord. We praise and thank Him for this opportunity to serve.

In June 1988 the sterilizer exploded! As the heavy machine tumbled out the door in a mantel of black smoke, patients, who were in other sections of the old hospital building, fled in the opposite direction exiting by other doors. We thanked God that no one was injured. When the workman running the sterilizer had seen steam starting to escape from the boiler, he had gotten back out of the way. The water from the boiler put out the kerosene fire, which was the heat source. Investigations pointed to a blockage in the steam escape valve from a mud dauber's house. Such a small beetle builds mud houses in inconvenient places. The gages mistakenly read normal. The old boiler had been soldered many times. Just two months earlier the station had approved buying a new electric autoclave with an electric steam generator and we had requested that the order be placed. We were praying God would provide the finances for it and bring it to us quickly. Meanwhile, we had to find alternative methods to sterilize.

A large pressure cooker designed for home canning was used for the next year, with various heat sources including gas, charcoal, and a kerosene burner. Only a few surgical packs could be sterilized at a time. One Sunday morning as we began an emergency cesarean, we found the indicator strips in all the surgical packs read non-sterile. Fortunately, we had a few disposable gowns we used. Friday, July 15 we received a morning telegram that a boiler and a forty-eight-inch autoclave had been ordered. There appeared to be a mix up with the order, so Monday morning Hubert headed on his motorcycle to Bambari to phone the States.

Thursday, September 8, 1988, the missionary field executive committee met in the morning and discussed the building project and other issues, but I was not happy with their conclusions. As I prayed, I felt led by God to ask for the project committee to meet in the afternoon. They scheduled it for 2 pm. At 1:45 pm I finally broke away from my other duties and knelt in the bedroom. For fifteen minutes I pleaded with God for His overruling all our thoughts, ideas, and words at the meeting. I had a blank paper and pen. As I prayed God guided me concerning topics to write down for the meeting. At 2 pm I rose and went to the meeting – trusting God. The meeting was blessed with His presence. All who came were helpful, working to advance the project and much was accomplished. They even scheduled the second week of December for all the missionary men of the field to go work on the building. God does above and beyond!

In early 1989 we kept watching for that next container of building supplies to arrive. Without it, Jon could not make progress on the construction. He was busy with trips to visit churches and God used him in many ways. Besides supplies, that container contained the new (reconditioned) sterilizer and steam boiler. In April, we heard it had reached Bangui. Its estimated weight was listed as four thousand seven hundred pounds. How would we lift that off the truck when it arrived at Ippy? Hubert went down to Bangui trying to get the paperwork cleared on it and arrange for a truck to transport it the three hundred miles upcountry. Another missionary, a mechanic, planned to install it. We eagerly anticipated when we would be able to use it to sterilize all our surgical supplies. Building supplies in it for the Laird Memorial Project included ceiling materials, soffits and fascia, wiring, gutters, special plumbing supplies, and more. These, along with many purchases being made in Bangui, such as windows, screen, plumbing and electrical supplies, and plywood would hopefully bring the day of completion a little closer for the new surgery/administration unit, the ward building, and the nurses' duplex. We kept praying for more builders to come help. God "is able to do far more abundantly than all that we ask or think" (Ephesians 3:20).

A couple of months later, Hubert was continuing to make trips to Bangui to try to get the container released. On one of the trips, he loaded June's truck with forty sheets of plywood for partitions in the wards, three and a half toilets, florescent light fixtures and tubes, glass panes, and for our family: one hundred pounds of sugar, one hundred pounds of rice, one hundred pounds of flour, cans of margarine, powdered milk, gas bottles, fresh beans from the market, a new battery for the truck, and lots more to take up to Ippy, along with thirteen people. We hoped the repairs on our own truck would be done at Sibut so we could transfer everything to it and go on to Ippy.

For six months Hubert worked on getting that container released. On yet another trip to Bangui, he had to spend the night on the road when it got dark and his lights failed. He passed a week in Bangui, much of it sitting in offices, only to be told after waiting all day, to come back the next day. We were praying especially for him in staff devotions one day, when news came that he had managed to see some different officials and succeeded in getting a whole series of signatures! That cleared it through customs, and the papers were handed to a shipper to get the container on its way to Ippy! We praised God for that victory. Daily storage charges in Bangui had been accumulating. Finally, a transport truck started the ten-hour trip from Bangui up to Ippy carrying the long-awaited container. But for the next ten days there was no word on its whereabouts.

The truck kept breaking down. The afternoon of August 6, 1989, it pulled into the station, sixteen months after the station had ordered the sterilizer. The crate with the kerosene boiler alone weighed twenty-nine hundred pounds. All the contents of the container got unloaded with many men working together without any machines.

In a few days, one of our missionary mechanics came up to Ippy to install the autoclave in the new surgery building. However, some of the diagrams were missing, which took another three months to arrive. Then it was another two weeks before the mechanic was free to come up to Ippy again. He delved into the installation project again but had questions. We prayed that we could reach the sterilizer company on our ham radio. It would have to be God accomplishing it if He willed. I had only a novice license for amateur radio, and Hubert was not there to help. I tuned up at 7:30 pm. It was a good clear night. I got into a network calling Africa. They helped make connections in the States with the mechanic's questions about the sterilizer. We hoped for replies the following night, but it was three nights later before the answers came. By December 18, 1989, the sterilizer worked! We praised God for His victory!

It was so nice to be able to run full big loads of surgical instruments and supplies in the autoclave. The indicators inside the packages verified that they were fully sterilized. There was no more smoke from open fires under a sterilizing chamber (the old way). The boiler unit to generate steam was fully enclosed. It was a beautiful modern system that ran on electricity and kerosene. It needed electricity for the controls, and the generator was on only during surgery mornings and a couple of hours each evening.

Just after the autoclave was installed, Jon got a new distiller mounted and working. A letter to my parents on January 2, 1990, read,

I'm sitting here in the sterilizer room watching gauges on the autoclave. It's my first time running it alone. Two times before I did it with the mechanic right after he got it working. It's 6 pm. I called the children and told them to go ahead with supper and then join me here with some books (we're reading Mary Poppins).

We're gradually getting things into the new building. I had to borrow a chair from the classroom to bring into the sterilizer room. Across the hall is a bathroom. But I still haven't found a candy bar machine or drinking fountain with cold water. (But of course, such conveniences were nowhere in CAR, especially not way up in Ippy.) We now have filtered water. Jon hooked it up for the surgery scrub sink and the distiller. I've spent much of today working on making my first batch of intravenous (IV) solutions. It's taken a lot of running for the past few days to get all the paraphernalia together. There are still glitches to work out to make production smoother. It must be run in the autoclave immediately after mixing, which is why I'm here in the evening. Next time will be a training session for the African technician to learn to do it. I figured I should try to learn it before teaching it.

Soon, a routine was in place. Water got distilled in the morning, mixed and filtered in the afternoon, and sterilized when the generator came on again at 5:30 pm. Things ran fine for a time, until there was no water. And we were all out of IV solutions. The pump at the spring was working fairly well. Why was the reservoir tank empty? After the Sunday evening service, Hubert and Doug checked the water lines in the dark and found two breaks where all the reservoir water was running out on the ground. There was hope for water the next day. However, the following day was the start of men's retreat at another station. The plane left at 6:20 am with the other men of the station. Hubert stayed behind to fix the water line, start the generator to run the distiller, put kerosene in the sterilizer barrel and fix the telephone line. I was getting medicine orders for the dispensaries filled, and hospital papers together for him to take. He left at 9:20 am in our truck. Then I started rounds. Hubert's truck broke down on the way to the retreat, but the other men helped him out.

Emile, the African worker who did sterilization, learned to run the new autoclave and make IV solutions. While the men were still at the retreat, one hospital day was especially busy, plus company for supper and Wednesday evening prayer service. When it started to rain, the generator got turned off in anticipation of lightning and thunder. I jumped on my cycle and rode through the rain to the generator building and asked the worker to turn it back on so the nine liters of new IV bottles could complete their cycle, hopefully before lightning started. I was soaked. What a challenge it was to make IV solutions. But it saved the expense and handling of having them shipped from Europe. God was victorious in each hurdle of the autoclave and of making IVs. "No eye has seen a God besides you, who acts for those who wait for him" (Isaiah 64:4).

Construction of the new buildings continued, and Hubert kept on hauling dirt. One time when his truck got stuck, he spent four hours shoveling, jacking, and pushing to get out. There was no other working truck around to pull him out. Our children made ice cream with the hand cranked ice cream maker to enjoy when he got home – an encouraging reward. In late October, Hubert brought beds and cabinets into the new ward building. It was getting closer to being ready.

Meanwhile, did we thank God for patient overflow? When all the beds were full and patients lay on grass mats all over the hallway? On rounds, Paula Beckman and I squatted next to each one and juggled to keep the charts straight: No. 17a, No. 17b, No. 17c, and No. 17d. Number 17 was a pediatric crib in the hall. Sub letters were mats on the floor. Jon kept working away on the new buildings every day. When we started to use the classroom in the new administration building, we invited staff over and roasted a sheep to celebrate and thank God.

Having Pastor Jameson and Jim Starks in our home in January 1990 made many happy memories. God answered their prayers that they would be an encouragement. Pastor sang as he walked around, "Faith is just believing what God said He would do." Jim every once in a while popped up with the verse, "Think on things of good report." We made a video of them working and sent it to Mrs. Jameson as a present. The first thing on it was them putting up our new kitchen ceiling. That decreased the bats coming down from the attic. They fixed two of our termite-eaten doors. The video footage showed lots of their work accomplished on the hospital buildings to the point of being almost ready to move in.

Tile flooring in the two operating rooms was so much easier to clean than the old cement. Varnished plywood partitions in the wards shone. The indoor plumbing in the surgery building seemed so modern. More cabinets went in. Dr. and Mrs. Zemmer arrived to work at Ippy for six weeks. They helped with the move into the new buildings on February 5, 1990. "Where do we put these surgery table sheets?" "Now where did we put the plaster for casting this leg fracture?" Hadessah was the first patient in the new operating suite. Dr. Zemmer removed a chigger while I stood at her side. I wish we had pictures of the patients' excited faces as Hubert moved them into the beautiful new wards.

Ippy Hospital Buildings

"To God be the Glory!" was the theme of the service on March 3, 1990, for the official opening of the surgery/administration building and the ward building. Government officials, area pastors, and the hospital staff gathered for the celebration in the center square. A choir of our African nurses sang between short speeches. The history of the Laird Memorial Project was given, and a sermon of encouragement to workers in God's harvest field. The beautiful big blue ribbon across the surgery door was ceremonially cut by our *sous préfet*. The tour following led through the new OR suite, sterilization area, offices, wards, nurses' station, exam and supply rooms, two private rooms, and a physical therapy room. Also, a new African gazebo in front of the clinic to give more shaded waiting area was completed in time for the dedication. Of course, there was food and fellowship.

The *chef major* house for the head African medical evangelist was constructed three months later, using a local architect. A system of twelve-volt lights run on car batteries was added in the wards, and landscaping spruced up the center square. God had shown His power to complete the project.

GOD'S CARE

HANS' APPENDICITIS OCTOBER 1986

Little four-year-old Hans had a tummy ache. Late afternoon of the second day, when he developed tenderness in the right lower quadrant of his abdomen, appendicitis was diagnosed. Hubert and I took him down to the hospital and called the African surgical staff. His daddy held him while medicine put him to sleep. I scrubbed my hands and gowned to do the operation. We prayed continuously for God to guide my hands, decisions and thoughts, and to give healing to our son. The Lord's presence was close and strong. During the operation I found the appendix had already ruptured and by God's grace, infection had not spread. When the procedure was over and our special patient was waking up, we carried him home. Golikes had just returned from Bambari and had a prayer meeting at our home for Hans. Each day during Hans' recovery, Irene came and read him a story. When June got the news, she started back early from her vacation, but it took her three days to get back due to roads closed for rain.

A couple hours after surgery, through a series of relayed messages on ham radio via Ivory Coast and Liberia to Grand Rapids, Michigan, the news of Hans' surgery reached our parents. It was Wednesday afternoon there and they shared the request for prayer at the church prayer meeting that evening. A couple of days later we were able to get a message to them again that Hans was making a good recovery. Via ham radio we also made contact with a missionary physician in Tanzania who was on the radio with an internal medicine specialist, for another opinion about the antibiotic treatment. After that we were no longer able to make radio contact for a long time. God's hand controls the radio waves. And He answered the prayers of His people. When Hans had all his energy back, he took his toy dump truck down to the hospital construction site to again help his Daddy put in fill dirt for the new buildings.

CHERITH'S LEG PAIN NOVEMBER 1987

Poor Cherith limped from pain in her right leg. Seeking wisdom from the Lord and searching the books about the many possible diagnoses, it seemed most likely to be a transient synovitis (inflammation in the hip joint). Her X-ray appeared normal. I limited her activity and talked by ham radio to a doctor in the USA. He advised taking her back to the States to check for a slipped epiphysis, one of the more serious possible conditions and common at her age, ten years old. A couple other doctors felt she should have further testing and as her pain was increasing, we knew God was directing us to take her to an orthopedic specialist in the USA.

There was a flurry of activity to get the airline tickets, complete paperwork at government offices for exiting the country, get a visa for Cherith which she would need for reentering CAR, phone Dad and Mom in Michigan to let them know we were coming and complete some hospital business in the capital. Many people helped. I had mixed emotions about leaving. I cried when I thought about the separation from Hubert and the four children staying in CAR, but I tried not to think on it. I could feel God's strength in answer to so many people praying. I was happy to be going to hug Mom and Dad and see relatives during Christmas.

The stomach pains I had experienced the previous couple weeks got worse. God worked it out that I was able to get tested at a good lab in Bangui. We went back the same afternoon for the results, but the lab had closed. The lady who did the test drove in right then and volunteered to get the results. She had to go find a guard for a key and return; she knew I was leaving that night. It was positive for two parasites. I got the needed medicines and started taking them.

Cherith was wheeled out onto the tarmac, and we boarded a French plane, flying out of Bangui at 9:10 pm, November 25, 1987. Hubert and the other four children waited in the capital to be near a phone for contact with us and to get some much-needed rest. During the layover in Paris, Cherith was given a bed in a medical unit to sleep for four hours until time to check in. God was taking such good care of us. Pastor and Mrs. Gaines were on the same flight, but we only saw them briefly at the airport in Paris where he loaned me his suitcoat by the cold entry gate. The seven-and-a-half-hour flight seemed very long since I could not read or write due to nausea and stomach pain from the parasites and the treatment. Our flight from New York to Detroit was late due to Thanksgiving Holiday Rush. But the plane from Detroit to Grand Rapids waited for us because the flight attendants from our New York flight were scheduled to serve on the Detroit to Grand Rapids Flight too! Praise God for His working.

Our family in Michigan gave us a big welcome and we got to Dad and Mom's house at 11:45 pm. Cherith had crutches to use from that point on. Thanksgiving Dinner the next day and subsequent meals that first week provided wonderful foods we normally could not get in CAR, but I was too sick to eat them! Fortunately, I could still go places and get things done. We rejoiced to see God provide the money for the trip and even spending money. He took care of everything.

The doctors in Grand Rapids did exams, several X-rays, blood tests, a bone scan, and sent us to East Lansing for an MRI. They checked out several possible conditions. The final test results came back on Christmas eve. They felt it was a transient synovitis and should clear up with a few weeks of no weight bearing. During the month of testing, she got pretty speedy on crutches, and the Lord was healing her. Maybe the chocolate-covered raisins that her grandpa slipped her helped too. The leg became straight again, and the pain resolved. Between doctor appointments, supplies were purchased for Ippy hospital and items were collected from various people for a container of hospital equipment shipping from Detroit. And God provided funds to pay off the hospital debt!

On our fourteenth wedding anniversary, though separated by an ocean, Hubert surprised me with a sweet card and Le Jardin d'Amour perfume waiting for me at Mom and Dad's breakfast table. When we talked by trans-Atlantic phone at noon, God answered prayer for a good connection to hear each other.

The trip had been a delightful and refreshing time with Mom and Dad, lots of relatives (including helping deliver little nephew Jay, born December 13), seeing several of our churches and friends, enjoying Christmas gatherings, glistening snow, a variety of foods, and altogether a time away planned by the Lord, we gratefully received as a gift from Him. God had answered the prayers of His people in America and Africa.

Our flight leaving Grand Rapids on December 28, was delayed by a snowstorm, as was the Detroit flight, and the New York one. We were given a hotel for the night in New York, and another the next night in Paris, arriving in Bangui Thursday, December 31. Our ten pieces of luggage got messed up resulting in additional fees, and one suitcase was delayed in New York. It contained several Christmas presents. A few days later it arrived in Bangui, minus a few presents. It became clear why God had arranged the delays on our return trip. The Tuesday plane we were scheduled to be on, carried a CAR sports team returning to Bangui. They were met by masses of people in the airport and city. Some people were killed in the press of the mob. Arriving New Year's Eve, two days later, the city was quiet. God had guarded us. We had been gone thirty-seven days.

A couple months later, Cherith was "walking and leaping and praising God" like the man at the temple gate in Acts 3, without the use of crutches anymore. God gave complete healing for her hip. Her crutches then were used at the hospital by a man with a broken pelvis. He was riding on the back of a truck when it rolled over off the road and a heavy sack of manioc landed on him. After him, a man who had been in traction for a broken femur from a gunshot wound used the crutches. We prayed that those men would learn to know God and give Him praise.

FIRST KENYA CONFERENCE FEBRUARY 1988

It was an amazing two weeks of seeing God's victories over every obstacle as I attended a Christian Medical and Dental Association (CMDA) Continuing Medical Education (CME) conference. The day before leaving Ippy, both Hannah and Cherith were having health concerns. But God was caring for them. I said goodbye to Hubert and the children and climbed into our little mission plane. It landed at the little towns of Kembé, Bangassou, Rafai, and then Zemio to let off and pick up other passengers. The next morning it was another mission plane that carried me out of CAR. The missionary pilots skillfully dropped a package to a remote station in the Democratic Republic of the Congo (DR Congo, then Zaire) before landing in Bunia, eastern DR Congo. After a couple hours reprieve from airsickness, a couple other passengers joined us and we were back in the air, landing and taking off in Uganda before arriving in Nairobi, Kenya. Many surprises awaited me.

I found that no bank would exchange my bundle of Central African francs for shillings. I was a day too early to go to the conference center north of Nairobi, and I had no other reservations. I did not know if my second cousin, Alan Hovingh, lived far or near Nairobi, but I knew my cousin and his wife, Lee and Marcia Hovingh, lived far away. I was cast upon God to take care of me in a strange country with no place to go and no money.

The missionary pilot loaned me about $30 in Kenyan shillings and took me to a convent hostel. It was clean and meals were included with the low price for the room. Other guest houses were full, and hotels were expensive. Although the phone booth had long lines of people waiting to use it, eventually I managed to reach Cousin Lee by phone. He told me Alan was in Nairobi and had planned to meet my plane but wasn't expecting me until the next day. My flights had been moved up a day and I had no way from Ippy to let them know. Lee also told me people to contact to reach Alan, since Alan did not have a phone.

At the hostel were three other lady doctors who were headed for the conference. They had come through immigration just after me and the immigration agent told them I had not paid for my visa. It was the Lord's working that he hadn't asked me for money since I had no negotiable currency then. Americans were given free visas to Kenya. Only certain countries were charged and perhaps after my leaving, he thought since I had come from CAR, it meant I should have paid?

The next morning, God helped me reach Alan and soon I was whisked away by this relative who had planned out a weekend of touring for me. He was between mission assignments, so he "happened" to be in the capital and have some free time. He took me to his mission office, and they arranged a loan of shillings to me to be repaid by a transfer of funds from my mission to theirs in the States. Praise God for His provision.

As we drove north, the hillsides covered with bright green tea bushes, banana plants, coffee bushes, and gardens were gorgeous. The tropical heat of the city gave way to the ideal warmth of the mountains. I saw the high school Alan had started years before. Its flowers were spread out in a myriad of colors. Helpful information was gleaned while touring a hospital run by one missionary nurse and her staff. In the afternoon we drove through the wide grassy plains of Nairobi National Park spotting giraffes, zebras, hartebeests, elands, a vulture, guinea fowl, a mama rhino with her baby, two other black rhinos, an impala, ostriches, and water bucks. God gave a fun day and was working everything out. The following day was Sunday and the services at the large churches, in English, were a great blessing. Seeing many points of interest around Nairobi and its cultural center programs helped me learn more about the country. There was also time to relax and be alone with the Lord, and time to miss Hubert on Valentine's Day.

That Monday Alan drove me up to check in for the medical conference. Conference sessions began that evening with an excellent Bible teacher. The subsequent days were filled with medical lectures from experts who had overseas experience, asking other doctors questions about some of my patients at Ippy, fellowship in God's Word, hikes in the mountains, and passion fruit juice at tea time. It was especially helpful to learn more about AIDS which was just starting to show up in our area, about hospital administration, and about surgical procedures. I brushed up on CPR (cardiopulmonary resuscitation) and passed the tests for recertification. It was a lot of sitting for someone used to being on my feet most of the time.

For the weekend in the middle of the conference, Lee and Marcia came and took me to see Rift Valley Academy where their children attended. Their mission's hospital was also there. The decision was made to go on up to Lee and Marcia's place of ministry, Kapsabet Bible School, and ride back with someone returning on Tuesday. Marcia graciously loaned me clothes, since mine were back at the conference center. The Rift Valley was stunning! We drove down into the dry brown valley and during the hours crossing it passed two giraffes in the wild, lots of pink flamingos, and tall Masai herdsmen in colorful reds. Once at the Bible School, evergreen trees and green lawns were beautiful to see. And we toured yet another hospital, this one a government one. As at the others, I got samples of their charting forms and ideas to consider for our hospital. The time with extended family was such an encouragement.

During the last days of the conference, it was difficult reaching Alan, but God worked, and I was finally able to contact him about my return. On the way to the airport hangar about 6:30 am on Friday, Alan's car broke down, but one of the missionary pilots got it working. However, the plane had to wait for permission for the flight to CAR. We finally loaded. I was the only passenger in a six-seater plane, but there were two pilots, and they packed the rest of the space with baggage and mail, and we were off just before 10 am.

Three and a half hours of airsickness later we touched down in Bunia, Zaire. I sat in a Land Rover to wait while the pilots flew to another place to change planes and deliver their cargo. They told the missionaries to plan on us for the night if permission to fly into CAR did not come through on the radio within an hour. The permission came. God knew what lay ahead at Zemio, CAR. As we were boarding, some of the ground people said, "You sure look better than when you got off that last plane." The afternoon flight was another three hours of nausea and sleep from the anti-motion-sickness tablet, but we entered CAR! It felt like home to hear the Sango language again.

Soon after arrival, the missionary nurse asked me to see a lady from their church that had come the day before. They thought she might have a ruptured ectopic pregnancy, but their doctor was away at another station. He covered three hospitals plus visited many other locations. After checking the patient, I concurred with the nurse's diagnosis. Immediate surgery was necessary to save the mother's life. The staff was called in and the room prepared. We did indeed find her abdomen was full of blood, and got the bleeding stopped. No transfusion was available. We thanked the Lord for placing me right at that place at that time. God answered prayer and the patient recovered well.

The next plane wasn't until Monday. I was surprised with a call on the ham radio from Hubert on my birthday. His news included that God had healed Hannah and Cherith the day after I left and our new schoolteacher was arriving in one week. The ladies of Zemio station surprised me with a lovely birthday supper, a decorated cake with candles, cards and a present. I really did not expect it since I was a "stranger" there. It was a real treat from the Lord. I thanked God for all the people who prayed for my trip, for the churches giving to cover my expenses, and for the many details daily that God performed to show His control and loving care.

MOTORCYCLE FIRE JUNE 9, 1988

After doing business in the capital, Hubert's motorcycle was heavily loaded as he rode back home to Ippy. During the long hours of riding, Hubert prayed for God to show him more of Himself and

His works. His meditation and travel were suddenly interrupted by fire coming from the front end of his motorcycle! The manifold cover had fallen off allowing cloth mailbags to touch hot pipes. They ignited! He jumped off and looked for something to quench the flames before they ignited the gas tank. The bike fell as he tried to untie the mailbags. As the bike lay burning, a truck came up behind and men jumped out with a fire extinguisher! They quickly put out the fire. That truck was the only traffic he had seen on that road the whole day! He picked up the cycle and was able to ride it home! God had answered prayer and shown His powerful working.

Hubert's birthday present of a burgundy money pouch was synthetic material that melted quickly in the fire. Much of the money was burned up, but I regretted the loss of the pouch more because it was special from my trip to the States the previous December. The mail bags were cloth and burned more slowly. The fire burned holes and the mail fell on the ground. We did not know how much mail was lost since mail irregularly got through. Some letters were scorched. The motorcycle papers and his ID papers were spared. Some of his clothes were burned up. Two saddle bags were destroyed, but not his best and main one. We praised God for safety for Hubert. In the following days he ruined a few shirts with mud splattering up on him since he no longer had a fender. But a new fender was soon on its way.

STRUCK BY LIGHTNING SEPTEMBER 2, 1989

The heavens declare the glory of God and that includes thunder and lightning. Nearly every day in Ippy we could hear thunder, and most nights in the rainy season the lightning displays were gorgeous. One Saturday afternoon when the sudden tropical storm blew rain in the windows, I hurried to close them. Reaching up to shut the metal frame of the louvered windows in the library, a sudden crack of light with a crash of thunder sent pain down my outstretched arm. My upper arm hurt and my whole body felt like it was blown up like a balloon, especially my thumb. It then felt like it deflated leaving tingling all over. Having been struck by lightning that had probably hit the whole house, I was relieved to discover that I was still alive and standing. Walking into the dining room to rejoin the others, Cherith described me as white, shaking, and holding my painful arm.

As the whole family and our dog sat together, another strike made us all feel static electricity. With some other hits we saw sparks come out of the outlets. The several ground rods by the house were insufficient for the powerful hits. Way down at the station generator building, the voltage regulator on the generator blew out. The generator was not even running. The fuse in the ham radio blew out and the casing around it. The phone wires from the hospital to our house snapped in two places.

My feet and hands kept tingling and my arm hurt for about thirty minutes, and then I was fine. The storm passed on. It made me think. How wonderful God is! He wants to show His power to protect us. He preserved me to go on serving Him here in this world. Months later a letter came from my sister Joan. She said she had been burdened to pray especially for us on September 2, 1989. What had happened? That was the day God protected us through the lightning.

ANTS September 9, 1989

Our dog's barking awakened us in the night and Hubert went to investigate. Shining the flashlight around revealed nothing amiss. But then he felt bites on his feet. He shone the light down and found ants covering the ground as far as he could see. He untied the dog who took off running away from the tiny biting invaders.

The army ants were advancing as a mass and entering the house. Soon they covered the floor of the office, library, hall, kitchen, pantry, and back room. We sprayed in all the rooms where we saw them until we ran out of insecticide, while praying that God would turn them back. Then we went back to bed. In the morning, nothing moved on the floor. Dead ants lay everywhere we had sprayed. They had not entered any of the bedrooms nor touched the sleeping children. Outside, the ants were gone. God had protected us.

HOSPITAL FLOAT OCTOBER 14, 1989

For a regional holiday, we were informed that Ippy hospital must be represented by having a float in Bambari. The President of CAR, ambassadors of various countries, and lots of officials would be present. Hubert and the actors for the float drove on Saturday afternoon to Bambari. In the dry season, it was a two-hour trip. But this was the rainy season and getting unstuck from a mud hole stretched the trip into five hours.

The next morning, sheets were draped around the pick-up truck and an operating suite set up. Hannah, Cherith and a delegation from the hospital, dressed in surgical gowns and masks, made up the surgical team surrounding a "patient" on an "operating table." A blood transfusion was simulated by red water in a hanging IV bag. The float had to wait over five hours in the morning to line up for the parade. Finally, the truck could move through the crowds of people and pass in front of President Kolingba. The protocol men were hurrying the parade along until they saw such a unique entry. They instructed Hubert to drive very slowly.

Returning to Ippy that evening, they got stuck in a mud hole again. Further down the road, they heard "clunks" and the truck came to a halt. The universal joint had fallen off. It looked like they would have to spend the night in the truck and wait for morning light. They prayed. Then with little cheap flashlights they began searching the muddy ground. They found all the pins and parts of the universal joint, except, one bolt was still lacking.

An old African man ambled up from a lone grass-roofed hut and asked the problem. Hubert told him they were missing a bolt. The man replied that he had a bolt. He went back to his hut and brought out a small cardboard box of junk. Among the treasures was an old bolt. It was metric, but it fit the Dodge truck and secured the universal joint. They got home just before midnight. God had met the need.

Good-Bye, July 1990

It was raining the morning of July 29, 1990. Hadessah took the last paperclip off the chain that was counting the days until we were to leave for furlough. She asked how many paperclips it would be until we came back to Ippy. Several people came to say farewell, including the whole African medical staff, who were ready to start surgery, and the missionary family. It was truly touching.

Reflecting on the past term, various scenes of Ippy came to mind. Over there were two little children clutching a water bucket between them and skipping up the dusty Ippy road. A man chugged by on his little motorbike headed to work. Another man with withered legs dragged himself slowly down the dirt road on his hands and knees. A strong young man pushing a cart with two plastic water jugs approached. He stopped, helped the crippled man onto his cart and smiled. The empty water jugs got carried in his hand.

A woman balanced a large pot of water on her head with a trickle occasionally spilling down her back. A child marched by with his slate for school. Next to the road a woman set out her pan of peanuts and a tin cup to measure out sales. She sorted out the bad ones. Her black hair displayed an intricate pattern of closely woven braids. A mother walked by with her baby securely wrapped with a cloth on her back. A mechanic in a greasy coverall clutched a handful of tools. A policeman walked with tall posture and a smart, clean, gray uniform. A family gathered around some boiled manioc they ate with their hands. Christ became man and dwelt among men. He descended from the splendor of His celestial abode to bring redemption to all men, because God so loved the world. Oh, that God's immense love might flow through us to people all around us. Oh, that more people would know and love our wonderful God.

Chapter 4

Central African Republic 1991-1995

At the works of your hands I sing for joy. Psalm 92:4

In the wee hours of the morning, my little red Honda 110 motorcycle coasted to a stop at the back door of our house. I sat there for a few minutes. The moon had not yet risen, and stars were spangled magnificently across the African sky. As I gazed at the beautiful constellations, I said, "God, you are great! Thank you for helping me with that emergency surgery. Thank you for letting that patient hear the gospel of Jesus Christ tonight. Please work in his heart to receive you as Savior while he is here in the hospital. Thank you, Lord, for letting me be a missionary doctor back in CAR again. It's an exciting life – seeing all kinds of tropical diseases and snake bites and baboon bites and spear wounds from hunting accidents.... People try so many useless traditional healing methods such as charms, which fail. Just as they try nonexistent false gods. Yet, Lord, please help me keep focused on my purpose in life, that I might know You. Philippians 3:10, 'That I may know him and the power of his resurrection, and may share his sufferings, becoming like him in his death.' Please draw me near to Yourself to accomplish the work You have for me to do."

"I think of when Jesus was here on earth. He kept in view the work You had for Him to carry out. He said in John 4:34, 'My food is to do the will of Him who sent me and to accomplish his work.' You have placed in my hands the tasks of caring for my family, of making disciples following You, of treating patients who come to the hospital and clinic, of teaching medical classes, of administration at a mission hospital and more. I want my life to be spent doing exactly what You have purposed for me."

"Then, as I function each day in the tasks of your choosing, and the joyful times come – as assisting in the delivery of a healthy new baby, or the dislocated shoulder of a strong man slips back into place and is fully functional again, or standing and silently praying at a bedside as one of the national medical evangelists leads a patient to Christ, or when the times of 'sharing in your sufferings' come – as when I see one of Your children that I have taught Your Word fall into sin, or I am summoned to court repeatedly for labor-management problems, or malaria lays me flat in bed and my body is aching – may they serve as lessons in trusting You, knowing You better, and bonding me closer to You."

1991 UNREST

The decade of the 1990s saw much unrest in CAR. Government employees did not get their salaries for many months. Strikes and demonstrations ensued. Anti-French and Anti-American sentiment brewed. Baptist Mid-Mission's mission station in Bangui was attacked and destroyed. We were finishing furlough in 1991 and wanted to return to CAR and the work at Ippy. But the mission, concerned for safety, advised families not to enter the unsettled situation. So, God took us to the West African country of Togo for five months. The Lord used Hubert in building up a Togolese church and encouraging missionaries. God gave me the joy of serving in a mission hospital there. When CAR was calm enough, we went on to Ippy. The hospital staff had been holding special Sunday afternoon prayer meetings in the nurses' village praying for the return of our family and for each of our children by name. Ippy hospital carried on without any doctor for four months. As for the mission station in the capital, which had been wiped out, in December 1993 God provided a beautiful new complex, well-suited for ministry and with a wall for security.

1992 SERVING AS A FAMILY

All efforts to revive our old red truck failed. One of our churches in Michigan designated a fifth Sunday of the month for a special offering for a new vehicle. Anyone wishing to participate was encouraged to give ninety percent of their weekly salary instead of ten percent that day. Most of the cost of our vehicle came in that one day. There was much rejoicing in seeing God do it. We sent a letter to Amsterdam ordering a Land Cruiser and waited for word that they had received our order. A month later there was news the vehicle had arrived in the port of Douala, Cameroon, along with medicines for the hospital. Prayer continued for it to make it to Bangui. But a couple months later we learned that the order had just finally reached Amsterdam. The monetary exchange rate had dropped so much that the price was too high. So, a hold was put on the order.

A Sunday in August Hubert took me on his motorcycle out to Zoubingi, a half hour away. We got out of the local French service near our house at 7:15 am and exchanged our French Bibles for Sango Bibles and songbooks. We grabbed our helmets and sun-glasses, and Hubert kicked the starter into action. The next challenge was climbing on behind him. The bike was high for me. That accomplished, the cycle jerked into gear (it stalled if not jerked), and we lurched forward, ducking under the tree branches, across the drive and through the ditch up onto the road (there was no bridge left there). It wasn't far down the road before I wondered if I had chosen well to go along with Hubert. Often, he had an African pastor go with him while I went to Center One Church with the children. We hit a bump especially hard and my footrest, a metal rod, met firmly with the top of my foot, making a red streak and pain. A few other bumps kept me shifting position and holding on tightly.

Once settled, I was enjoying the wide-open spaces of out-doors, trees, fields, nature, and occasional village houses, when all of a sudden nature got too close! I felt a sting on my leg. My hand quickly went to the site of attack but found nothing – the attacker had already escaped in the wind. I kept rubbing the pain, wondering what to do if I had an allergic reaction. I looked at my watch and noted the time – only fifteen minutes out. We could get back fine if I started breaking out in hives. Fortunately, I had had only one allergic reaction to bees, and that was twenty-five years before. I decided to turn everything over to the Lord and trust Him. He was continually in control of the universe and all His work, and He would take care of me. For the rest of the trip, I enjoyed praying and going over the verses I was memorizing in Sango.

When we arrived at the town, there were partial walls, with framework for a roof and weeds growing up inside and outside the "building." For living beings, six large cows stood under six old mango trees. We climbed off the motorcycle, pried off the helmets, and stood around. After a while, a man came over. Hubert asked if people were coming for the service and he said, "No." No one had been coming to preach for two months so the believers quit meeting. There was no drum to beat nor wheel rim to clang to call people to come, so he walked off to search for other people.

We waited and chairs were brought and then three benches were carried to the space between the "church building" and the mango trees. The cows were shooed off. When four people had joined us, we started to sing. By halfway through the service, there were ten gathered. Hubert preached. He asked me to give a testimony about parents teaching their children to follow the Lord. At the end of the service, Hubert suggested he return on Wednesday and Saturday for door to door witnessing and then plan on him preaching at a service the next Sunday. They figured out a time people would be coming back from their fields and were very encouraged that Hubert would come help. Christians in the States prayed for God to help them re-establish meeting, worshiping, and learning God's Word.

Four months later, going to that church on a Wednesday afternoon, we saw two ladies walking along the road, carrying bricks on their heads. What a way to improve posture. But these bricks were the size of cement blocks, and each woman had three of them stacked on their head! When we arrived at the meeting place, we saw that the women of the church had cut and gathered thirty-two large bundles of long grass for making a new roof for the church building. This was half of the total needed. They were waiting for the men to climb up and tie them with bark onto the sticks which formed the frame for the roof.

Under the mango trees, Hubert gave a devotional on Mary's song of praise to God in Luke 1. Praise and prayer requests were shared, and then we had a blessed time together before the throne of grace. Over the next months, the group grew. Construction of their building was completed. They elected deacons. Eventually, God provided a national lay pastor. The Lord builds His church!

One Saturday in Ippy, the station water tank ran out of water about noon. The rain barrel outside our house was only one-fourth full. We used that. By late afternoon God sent abundant rain showers. We had all the water we needed. The children thought using water from rain barrels was more exciting than running water from faucets.

Hans was our happy gardener. Instead of having the chickens in the chicken yard, a nice, fenced area behind the chicken house, his garden was in that yard. Golikes' chickens ran loose. The fence kept them out of the garden quite well. When one broody hen got in and sat on her nest there, Doug and Irene told Hans he could keep the hen and her eggs. Eight chicks hatched. He put his chickens in the coup and his garden of lettuce, carrots, tomatoes, and pineapple plants continued growing. Climbing the outside of the fence were passion fruit vines with their delicate flowers representing the passion of Christ. Doug and Irene were greatly missed when they moved to Bangui to replace other missionaries there for a year.

Hadessah, then six-years-old, wanted to go with me when I taught the midwives one afternoon. Clutching a paper, a pen, a coloring book, and crayons, she took a place at a student desk with the ladies. Carefully, she copied the French word, "anesthésie" off the board, then put her head down and fell asleep.

Another day she came to the clinic with me. There were Bible story pictures in my white coat pocket for giving to children in the hospital. She and I played a game with them reviewing the stories in between patients. After lunch, I was at home working on an exam for the midwives' class. I got a note from the hospital about a man with a lacerated hand. Helper Hadessah and I went down and took him to surgery to repair his tendons on all four fingers of his right hand. He had been drinking and in a fight. The other guy pulled a knife, and it looked like this man grabbed it. The other children brought us a flashlight after it got dark, and we went home about 8:30 pm. My special assistant for the day was a happy, tired girl. There was fresh bread waiting and she took her sandwich to her bed while I tucked in the boys. When I checked her, she was fast asleep, still dressed, lying on top of the sheets.

One of the ways Cherith helped at the hospital during her summer break from school was assisting patients with physical therapy, trying to restore motion in joints that had limited range of motion. When the electricity was on in the evenings, she worked with some needing the whirlpool. She wrote her grandparents about her work and added,

> There are several "big shots" at the hospital now. They are either diamond collectors, or their husbands are. That means they have big money. They have private rooms, and beautiful Persian rugs all over the floor. Also, they have gorgeous sheets, pillows, and clothes. They are awfully nice though, and need the Lord too.

There were some days in missionary life that seemed hectic. One Saturday I was trying to can some pineapple on the charcoal fire, and the heat was too hot and burned the handles of the pressure cooker. Other times it was too cool, so the pressure gauge would not rock. At the same time, there was short notice company and I needed to come up with a nice meal and tidy up the house. The hospital called saying a patient had just arrived with a broken leg. I had promised to help Cherith with her Latin class (even though it had been twenty-five years since I had it in high school, so I had to relearn it with her). Lessons were not yet prepared to teach the medical class the following day. Maternity called with a problem delivery. Immediate action was required.

Hannah and Cherith took over watching the canner and preparing for the company. The studies had to wait. Walking quickly down the hill from the house to the maternity, I prayed for God to give wisdom to provide the best care possible for the lady in labor, and to teach the midwife on duty also. The patient with a broken leg was seen right after maternity. God worked out every detail again in a busy day. And before crawling into bed at night, I thanked the Lord for enabling to do the work He had given for that day.

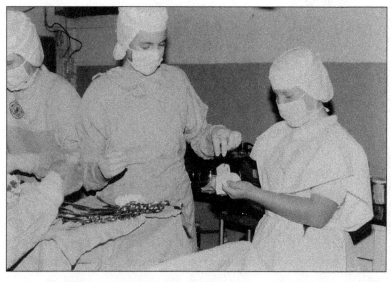

Hannah and Cherith Assisting Dr. Mary in Surgery

1993 SERVING OTHER TOWNS IN CAR

On January 18, 1993, Hubert and Davar loaded the motorcycle with an extra can or gas and overnight supplies, then traveled five hours to a small church. Their visit brought much joy to the believers.

God worked and there were decisions for salvation! Returning on the dirt path through grasslands, the cycle stalled. As they kept an eye on the dry season grass fires that had been burning both sides of the way, suddenly they saw flames were behind and in front of them as well! They were encircled with fire! But God rescued them. The motor started and they gunned it through the ring of fire, continuing on until safely home.

Travel the seventy miles to Bambari was sometimes eventful. Expecting a two-hour trip, we did not leave home one day until 9:30 am. Since our truck was not working, we counted on our one undependable motorcycle. It was old and worn out, waiting for spare parts delayed in a container shipment. The third time the engine quit, I could not push it fast enough to get it started. Hubert and I were alone between towns. We parked to the side of the road, and Hubert walked back to look for oil. He figured that was the problem. He had recently changed the oil.

I sat on a log under a mango tree's nice shade, enjoying the breeze, the fellowship of the Lord, and a book on Galatians, as I prepared for Sunday School class. An hour later Hubert returned on the back of the motorcycle of a Frenchman and carrying some oil. Praise God the engine wasn't ruined. Praise God the previous town had someone to help and had oil. Praise God we got to Bambari in time. We arrived at 1:30 pm and our classes to teach started at 2:30 pm. That gave time for lunch (Teachouts had waited for us) and showers (we were covered with red dust). Hubert taught the pastors' seminar on the theology of the cross, and I taught on AIDS and other related diseases.

God blessed the MK teen retreats. Young people from all over CAR studied God's Word together and had fun, including the bucket of water thrown through the screen onto the guys sleeping on the porch, the sunburns, the late hour Pit games, and evenings of special music and testimonies. Cherith wrote

> On Friday afternoon of teen retreat, we drove to the river and jumped in for a swim. Even my dad. While everyone was in the water, I was carrying some stuff to a rock, and suddenly saw a hippo come out of the bush and jump into the water. Praise the Lord, there was a slight wall of rocks separating the water he jumped into and where everyone was swimming. It was rather a spooky experience for me. Most of the teens swam down the river with the strong current, being careful to stay out of the middle strongest current. All the while we were watching out for hippos and crocodiles.

Hadessah and Hans could hardly wait to be teenagers, so they could participate instead of just watching. Hubert loved working with youth.

God displayed His power on our surgery trips to the southeast corner of CAR. Most of that area had no doctor. The mission dispensaries let patients know when we would be coming. Surgical instruments, gowns, drapes, IV supplies, medicines and our small personal suitcases were weighed and packed carefully into the five-passenger mission plane. In the operating room there was a twelve-volt car battery with wires to a lightbulb over the operating table. Hernia repairs and hysterectomies were the most frequent procedures done in the distant locations.

One village leader came to the guest house on Sunday afternoon. He brought us two live chickens, bananas, and beautiful pineapples. He had been flown to Ippy the year before and we had plated his fractured femur (put a metal plate and screws on the bone). He was so grateful for complete healing. The missionaries of his town told us that he was a changed man. Before he had been antagonistic to the mission work. Now he faithfully attended church and helped them whenever he could.

Hannah and Cherith were such good assistants for surgeries in the dispensaries. They would take vital signs, start IVs, place catheters, scrub abdomens, prepare instruments, and assist at the operating table. But the day watching Hannah leave on a DC-10 from Zemio's grass airstrip was very difficult. Saying goodbye to a child leaving home to start college on another side of the world was so hard. I did not expect to see her for the next two years. May 27, 1993, 8:10 am I wrote to Hannah,

> I am asking God to enfold you, Hannah, in His arms, and comfort and strengthen you. I am asking God for the same for us too. Cherith and I cried on each other's shoulders on the airstrip. The people around us here have been so encouraging and are bearing our burden with us. God is good to give us friends. I am glad Jewells, Aunt Edie, and Lynette are with you as you travel. It is raining hard here with thunder and lightning and thick fog. Uncle Doug was going out to the Bangassou airstrip at 6:45 am to come take us to Rafai, but he may be sitting and waiting, as we are blocked in here. I love a change of plans, especially delays. They are bonus time.

8:30 pm: Uncle Doug got to Zemio about 10:50 am. It took quite a while to unload cargo, put the airplane seats back in and reload. The sun was shining brightly when we left but the clouds got thick and low as we approached Rafai. I think Uncle Doug was hunting for the airstrip for a while, but I did not ask. He found it. When we landed, Christine (a missionary nurse) met us. Bisse (a Central African medical assistant) went back and forth taking us on the motorcycle. Three wheelbarrows took all the luggage. It was quite a way to the mission. They have no truck at the present. After dinner I did consults until after 5 pm and then we did the first OR case. God is blessing His work and His children.

We were grateful to God to be able to travel and minister in various towns. But patients came to us at Ippy from all over CAR too. About three weeks after that trip to the southeast CAR, I had a patient at Ippy with a dislocated jaw. A gang in Bangui had boxed him pretty hard. He was unable to get care at Bangui or Bambari because of the hospitals being on strike. God helped us get his jaw back in alignment and functioning well.

After church one Sunday morning at Ippy, one of the hospital workers, who was a deacon there, asked me if I recognized the man standing before me. He told me I had cared for him in the hospital back about 1988, when a hunting accident left a spear wound in his chest. During his stay in the hospital, he had received Christ as Savior. After that, he had taken new believers' classes, been baptized, and joined the church. He was faithful and active in the church and praying for his wife's salvation. God uses medical missions to draw people to Himself.

Davar and Hans enjoyed working with Hubert during their summer break from school. They shoveled gravel and dirt where new out-houses were being constructed at the hospital. They dug holes and transplanted little teak trees along the one edge of the property. They anticipated the day when the trees would provide abundant shade along the driveway there. Their leaves were so large that we called them elephant ears. Davar, along with his friends, chopped rock for the low stone wall the station was putting up. Most of the stones were delivered in wooden-wheel carts pulled by two cows each. There were lots of free-range cows and pigs in the neighborhood, and the wall was for keeping them out. Goats easily jumped over.

The distance we could travel to go out and minister was limited with no vehicle, not even a working motorcycle for a time. June 12, 1993, word came that our new truck had arrived at Douala, Cameroon! Two other hospital containers were also at the coast. Getting a transporter to bring things from the coast to landlocked CAR was problematic. Clearing all the paperwork in the Bangui offices was complicated by offices being on strike. And at times travel in Bangui was hampered by demonstrations.

An order of medicines we had been waiting and praying for finally arrived in Bangui. Two containers with hospital supplies were still en route. We needed God to get them through the miles of red tape in the offices that held them up. Things that are impossible for us to accomplish are opportunities to see God bring it to pass. Psalm 46:10, "Be still, and know that I am God. I will be exalted among the nations." June 23 brought word that our tuck and meds from The Netherlands were unloaded from the container at Bangui! We waited for customs papers to be completed. Getting registration papers, license plates, and other paperwork usually took about two months. In August, the new Land Cruiser with "Centre Médical d'Ippy" painted on the front doors finally drove into Ippy. God had gotten it through to us after waiting one and a half years.

August 17, 1993, "Dear Hannah, Guess what I have snuggling under my left arm? Something with curved claws, a long dragging tail, beady eyes that keep opening and closing right now, and an intermittent peep-peep-peep. This baby mongoose has been named August." Two months later, August killed his first snake, which is what mongooses were made to do well.

> September 14, 1993. Dear Hannah, Hans is in the next room listening to exciting Bible story cassettes borrowed from the Sullivans. The little red accordion that arrived in a container is enjoyed by many in the family. Hans taught Hadessah what he had just learned on it. Cherith and I share it the most. We were quite a while without one, so appreciate this one the more (our previous one was given to one of the medical evangelists). It is so helpful in village churches too. Hadessah and Hans really like school and their teacher, Aunt Barb Sullivan. She is doing an excellent job. Their school extra materials have not arrived yet, but the basic books have. Aunt Barb added a Bible course for them, plus music each Wednesday, and crafts on Thursdays. Uncle Dennis Sullivan wants to teach French to the sixth graders. They really enjoy having other children in the same grades (the three Sullivan girls). Cherith and Davar are waiting for their high school books to come.

We thanked God for sending Dr. and Mrs. Sullivan in August 1993 to serve Him at Ippy. It was great to have another physician, and he was a trained surgeon besides.

One of the afternoon thunderstorms started as distant thunder and lightning. Suddenly, one big clap of thunder hit close, just after Cherith had finished doing the 3:30 pm station radio broadcast. She saw sparks come out of the end of the antenna cord she had just unplugged. Hans and Davar were in the rafters of the ward building laying plastic. They saw the whole wiring system there light up and a ball of fire come out of the circuit box by Davar. Hadessah and Joy Sullivan were walking outside. They had just come through the metal gate by June's house. They saw it strike the ground in front of them and heard a snap in the metal fence behind. They hit the ground, then ran to June's house. I had just left the office room in our house and heard a snap there. God protected us all again.

On October 25, 1993, the sun shone brightly in Bangassou after the on and off showers of the day. We had come for Bible school graduation. I walked down to the cemetery where Mr. Hass' grave and three other graves were tucked on the hillside. God had used Mr. Haas to found Baptist Mid-Missions in 1920. The path cut through a gorgeous tropical forest displaying a variety of trees as well as pineapple plants. The palm branches were so pretty – almost like royal decorations for King Jesus – and the drops of rain hanging at the ends of broken branches sparkled like diamonds. The variety of insect calls and bird songs were sounds of praise. Back at the guest room was a view of the majestic, broad Mbomou River gently flowing through the thick green forested valley. A canoe in the distance moved silently and slowly, watching for crocodiles. The fragrance of two pink roses I had just picked filled the room. At night the baby-like cry of bush babies (galagoes) was heard, rising in pitch with each cry as they moved through the trees. The tropical regions of Africa were so beautiful. We enjoyed the fellowship of several other missionaries there.

Two of the graduates from Ippy that had just completed four years at Bangassou Bible School were Timothy and Marie Mananga. They had sharper skills now for preaching and church planting (He later became the head medical evangelist and hospital administrator at Ippy.). Their pastor gave them a wooden suitcase he had made "for the children's clothing." Another couple were the oldest students in their class. He had worked as a chauffeur for the government in Bangui for years. He felt called to the ministry, but the government refused to grant him leave from his job. The retirement age was fifty-six, so as soon as he qualified for retirement, he and his wife entered Bible school for four years. His wife could read but not write. It was a major work of God for her to learn to form letters and be able to accomplish her work as a student. They were so humble and sweet, loved and respected. The church was packed and overflowing for the graduation. The students had beautiful music and the congregational song lifted praise to God. The graduates' testimonies were stories of God's grace in calling people in various ways, giving victory over hurdles, and providing every need. It challenged others to full-time service for God.

There was one young man who wanted to serve the Lord, who was in medical school at Bangui when it was running. Because the government lacked money, the schools operated a cumulative total of six months the previous three years and again did not start classes in 1993. This man worked at Ippy Hospital and took the classes we were giving our nurses. He loved the Lord. We hoped God would lead him to someday serve the Lord at Ippy as a doctor. But all of our various efforts to get a Christian Central African doctor for Ippy Hospital were unsuccessful. God continued to use medical evangelists trained at Ippy Hospital.

God worked in the Womens Bible Conference held in Bria. About two hundred ladies representing fifteen churches came, many of them walking many miles. They slept on mats on the cement floor of the church and in an empty house. Their mats were folded up so tidy and small in the daytime. Cherith did schoolwork in a room we were camping in while children peeped through the windows and giggled. She also sold literature along with two African ladies. A journalist asked a few questions to report to Bangui radio. Candlelight was so pretty in the evenings. Sitting and talking informally with these sisters in Christ was a blessing. God provided water, food, and all our needs, especially wisdom to open His Word to His people.

The Lord gave me much joy teaching a set of ten lessons on the attributes of God. We prayed lives would be changed as ladies applied the truths. They were so attentive and responsive. Their enthusiastic skits for some of the Bible stories illustrated main points such as Saul's conversion to introduce the subject of grace. A chart of attributes, definitions, basic truths about them, Bible references, and applications was posted so ladies could copy it to take home for teaching or studying further (we had no copy machine). About two hundred women participated. Their testimonies of God's presence and power in their lives were moving. They could see that God was sufficient for their needs. June taught Colossians, hygiene and other lessons on Monday and Tuesday, and Rosie taught on the last two days. Two pastor's wives spoke for two afternoon sessions. It was great to see God use His servants to feed His sheep.

Meanwhile, we were still waiting for schoolbooks. Packages lost in the mail complicated the school schedule. After ordering the first semester high school books a second time, and having someone coming from the States bring them, Davar and Cherith had to work double speed to catch up for starting the 1993-94 school year in December. God's people also prayed for second semester lost books to arrive. God answered prayers and brought them through. Dr. Sullivan taught computers to Davar. Mark Stanley taught Hans about the plane engine as he worked on it. Hubert taught Hans and Davar some electrical wiring as they wired the hospital buildings.

1994 SERVING TOGETHER

God answered prayer, and an elbow that had been dislocated for six weeks went back in place! That patient was from Bria. The plane brought two patients from Alindao and took two others back to Sibut. A couple days later a man arrived from Pipi with burns over seventy percent of his body from a gasoline fire catching on his clothes two weeks previously. About a week after, a twelve-year-old boy and a Muslim lady received Christ. God was showing His power to work in lives daily.

At that time, June handled many administrative details, but when she was gone, it became my responsibility. Psalm 55:22, "Cast your burden on the Lord, and He will sustain you." Wednesday, January 26, 1994, in my journal I listed a dozen loads cast on me that day including a staff problem, pressure from the work inspector, hospital wheelbarrows and shovels being stolen, a complication with a container shipment, patients and staff being beaten up when they tried to get water from the spring, seeing young known thieves watching our house, needing to prepare for teaching the refresher course next month and for my trip to Kenya the next week, and more. I said, "Lord, why do You let so many things fall on my head at once? I'm trying to roll each burden onto You." He answered, "I want you to walk on top of the waves. Fix your eyes on Me and don't look at the billows." And then He flooded me with joy. What a blessed place to be, walking on top of the stormy water, by faith, regarding Jesus, and Him holding our hand, (Matthew 14:22 – 33).

Dry season was the only time Hubert could get through to towns by the Chad and Sudan borders. When he set off in the Land Cruiser, usually we had no news until he returned sometimes three weeks later. During one trip, some of the hospital staff heard that bandits destroyed a couple of bridges on the road he was on to prevent the military from moving there. During a six-hour period Hubert changed three flats and had to fix the tire pump. In places, grass and branches on both sides of the trail brushed against the vehicle. He worked his way between and around trees and maneuvered with the truck tilted precariously to the side. The pastor accompanying him walked in front and guided his wheels on the logs that were a bridge over a deep ravine. He brought back from Birao ten delicious watermelons, grown in the hot and sandy sub-Sahara, a gift from the Christians.

God opened hearts as the gospel was preached in town after town. Many people made decisions for Christ. Churches were encouraged. Many hours were spent giving Scriptural counsel. He challenged Christians to witness and evangelize. A pastor who spoke Arabic accompanied him to Arabic speaking Muslim regions. Another trip, he filled the truck with pastors and went to a regional church conference. Still another trip was to help one specific church with a problem. Even though he heard of a kidnapping and two abductions of foreigners that had recently happened in Bria, which he had to pass through, he went to serve God and God's people. Some April rains had started by the time of that trip, and he got to ford some deep waterholes. After weeks of sleeping in the vehicle or huts and eating lots of manioc, God brought them safely back. We prayed God would continue to change lives as people thought about His Word they had heard.

Hubert Talking with a Pastor

Ippy's two missionary nurses taught the 6:30 am medical refresher courses, and the two doctors taught in the afternoons. Eight national medical evangelists had come for two weeks. These men ran dispensaries throughout the middle and eastern regions of CAR plus a couple of them worked at Ippy hospital. We were grateful for godly men who were willing to be used by the Lord giving out the gospel in medical ministries. Some of the courses were essential medicines to keep on hand, handling administrative problems, using storytelling for health education, what's new in treatment and what is the research that led to changes in ways things were treated compared to fifteen years before, helpful ideas for running dispensaries, local anesthesia techniques for minor surgery, a Bible class, and lots of mingling in the work at the hospital to exchange ideas. The fellowship was great. Their reports about what God was doing in their regions invigorated us to press forward with training more medical evangelists.

In 1994 the CAR currency was devalued by one hundred percent. That made our costs for purchasing drugs double, and people had only half as much buying power as before. But we raised the wages of all the hospital staff and prayed for God to supply.

"Could we taste some *gozo* (manioc)?" "How do you say, 'I sympathize with your hurting,' in Sango?" "What do you do when you see a scorpion in your room?" It was great to have two successive teams of students and their nursing professors that summer serving God with us at Ippy. And one of the team members was our daughter Hannah! It was a gift from the Lord to have her back and see how God had taken care of her. She delved into the work, caring for patients, interpreting, cooking, and helping in so many ways.

The hospital ward and the clinic were overflowing with very sick patients from many places. It was partly due to the lack of medical supplies throughout CAR. The surgery schedule was overfull, and we kept seeking wisdom from the Lord to know what He wanted done. In the whirlwind, God's blessings also were overflowing. He was always beside us. We started running both operating rooms for a time, Dr. Sullivan in one, and myself in the other. However, there was not quite enough help, even with the visiting student nurses, so one Tuesday Cherith was called from her home schooling, and she scrubbed in to help. Visiting professors with the teams taught on fluid and electrolyte balance and other topics, with interpretation into French.

A Saturday morning, I was awakened at 4:45 am to the sound of a vehicle arriving at the back door. Vernon had brought another student wife from Sibut with belly pain. Vernon and Sam Rosenau had driven through the night. After delivering the patient, they turned around and went back to Sibut. I woke Cinnamon, one of the nursing students who was staying with us and went to the hospital to check the young lady. Besides this patient from Sibut, another patient had a ten-day-old knife wound that needed debridement. Her hemoglobin was four grams (very low). Dr. Sullivan did one of the surgeries and I did the other.

I got home late morning. The visiting nursing team was helping with various jobs at the house. After lunch we packed a picnic for supper, and our family and the team went to Baidou River. We hiked through the tall elephant grass for one hour and saw ten large hippopotamuses in the river close by us. Then we found a spot with less grass and ate sandwiches.

The second summer team's advisor was a professor in community health nursing. She found it fascinating seeing how strategic her expertise was in CAR. For example, I examined a seven-year-old girl at the clinic who was vomiting blood and had bloody diarrhea. She also had a high fever. The bleeding in her gastrointestinal tract may have been from schistosomiasis, a parasite that can be avoided by having clean water. The fever appeared to be from malaria, which was prevalent. There would have been less malaria if mosquito control and bed nets (mosquito nets) were used more. The staff really appreciated the professors' teaching.

Hubert made multiple trips to the capital for visitors and getting supplies, plus processing official papers in offices there. He bought foam for mattresses for the hospital and had a tailor cover them with plastic so they would be washable. God blessed so richly each day, giving wisdom and meeting needs.

God's people prayed as Hubert worked on writing a commentary on the book of Romans in the Sango language. He submitted it to the missionary language committee the summer of 1994 hoping it would be completed before our furlough. After they had looked at it, Hubert worked on revisions. He had several Africans read through it and mark changes. He also prepared a Sango commentary on Matthew and wrote out in Sango some outlines of various books of the Bible. National pastors and leaders could use these materials in teaching the Word of God. He turned over his teaching and administrative responsibilities at the Ippy Preparatory Bible School to area pastors after coaching them for a time.

Hubert was frequently called to transport patients to or from the hospital, or asked to fix the operating lights, or the twelve-volt lighting system, or the pipes under the surgery scrub sink, or the ward building doors, or the maternity wiring, or the operating table, and on and on. Sometimes repairs required a 300-mile trip to Bangui to hunt all over the capital searching for the right parts. Often, they could not be found. The Lord gave Hubert the opportunity to show three Moody Science Films in the public school. He also taught block courses at Sibut Bible School. His teen boys' class on our front porch continued and God changed the lives of several of the young men.

God allowed our children to cheerfully serve Him in many ways. Sunday afternoons, Cherith taught the junior high MK Sunday School class. Davar taught the primary MK Sunday School class. Then I taught the teen MK class. Hans helped the new pilot, Mark Stanley, pour a cement floor in the airplane hangar. Davar was involved with the local church choir and witnessed to his fellow soccer players. Hans, Hadessah, and I were able to watch one of Davar's soccer game downtown on a Tuesday afternoon. About a year before that he had dropped off the soccer team because the coach required all players to wear good luck charms. We thanked God that requirement got dropped. On Easter Sunday afternoon, Cherith had a closing program for the music seminar she had taught the youth of area churches. Hadessah faithfully practiced her piano lessons before running to play with her friends.

When we found we were expecting a new child, we called him Jacob and were very excited. But four months into the pregnancy, I had a miscarriage and grieved the loss. The theme of the approaching missionary conference was "Learning to Lean on Jesus." It is an expression of dependance on God, and confidence in Him. God keeps giving us lessons to help us learn from Him.

1995 Increasing Trouble

There were many more lessons on leaning on the Lord as unrest increased all over the country during 1994 and 1995. Hubert had to cancel a trip up north. Bandits were too active up there. Trucks were only allowed through with military escorts. Once he used a military escort to get to a church. The vehicle going through after his was attacked.

We heard rumors that Ippy missionaries were being targeted along the road to injure and possibly kill them. There were threats to make Ippy station another Gobongo (destroyed and burned mission station in Bangui). The mission field president said to keep a male missionary on the station at all times. For a few weeks, I was warned that my life was threatened even to walk to the hospital for an emergency at night. Hubert escorted me during that time. When he was gone once, sixteen-year-old Davar walked with me. God used such experiences to help me know Him more and hold fast to Him. He sheltered and protected us. A couple of the missionary ladies and I prayed and shared verses from Scripture together several times as different rumors came.

We prayed for our African brothers and sisters facing stress. We wanted to be Christ-like examples before them. We were willing to live or die for Christ. Ruth reported her houseboy had been taken to jail for two hours and beaten. He was accused of working for "the doctor." Bangui missionaries were facing increasing demands for money for processing paperwork and had to show their paperwork proving the mission had a legal presence in the country. There was an increase in attempted break-ins in homes. Close to our house, gangs of little boys threw stones at our little MK girls and stole things out of their playhouse. Psalm 57 was very special to me throughout those troubled times.

An encouraging moment during the upheaval was at the time of missionary Bob Golike's (then in the USA) completing his work on earth and being promoted to heaven. Several African nurses and two Bible school students came to our house for an hour in the evening and led a memorial service in his memory. They wanted to express to all the missionaries that they shared our grief and appreciated God's servants.

Labor-management problems were stirred up at the hospital by outsiders agitating all over CAR. Multiple lawsuits were filed against missionaries and the hospital. It was so sad to see the pressure on God's people who wanted to do right. God was teaching some special lessons through those times. Lots of people were praying. Over and over, I was called down to the office of the chief of police over false charges. Repeatedly, I had to answer summons to the work inspector's office seventy miles away. Twice I stood in court before judges. God gave strength, and throughout the days, gave His joy. Many people were praying.

Many of those unplanned trips were during the three-month period when Dr. Sullivan was taking an ophthalmology course in Nigeria, so I was once again the only physician in the region. Fellow missionaries were very involved with the issues as well. Throughout each day I had to come to the Lord – alone on my knees – and say, "Master, You are the Lord. I am Your servant. Show me what You want me to do in the next few hours." And always I had to seek to accomplish the goal of knowing Him better and helping others to know Him.

Halfway through her senior year, some of Cherith's schoolbooks had not yet arrived (like the previous year). But then God brought them through. By God's enabling she completed her studies on time – before our leaving for furlough. Her high school graduation on April 1, 1995, was special. The brief ceremony included "Pomp and Circumstance," as Cherith walked into the living room wearing a white cap and gown. In front of all our guests she was presented a "temporary" diploma (Her real one was mailed from the independent study high school to our address in the States.). Hubert made a little speech, and Cherith's piano students provided special music. Refreshments followed. Graduations were always very special times.

While we were in the USA on furlough mid-1995 to mid-1996, the turbulence in CAR became open fighting from rebel groups, and all foreigners had to evacuate. The hospital was turned over to the African medical evangelist staff and thus "graduated." They have been helped by God to continue to run the hospital, provide medical care, train others, and give the gospel, through years of intermittent war. "The men of Judah prevailed because they relied on the Lord" (2 Chronicles 13:18).

The Lord had worked in many lives in the grasslands of Central Africa. He was victorious! His Word was powerful! Churches and Bible schools were carrying on. The hospital had new buildings. More people had been trained to serve the Master. They continued to serve well, relying on God, who was always present with them. The Lord next led our family out of Africa and into the Orient.

PART 3

SOUTHEAST ASIA

CHAPTER 5

PHNOM PENH, KINGDOM OF CAMBODIA 2001-2003

To make known...your mighty deeds. Psalm 145:12

ARRIVAL PROVISIONS

The Khmer Rouge led by Pol Pot brutally massacred between two and three million Cambodian people in the years 1975-1979 and left survivors with horrid memories of executions, torture, starvation, and attempts to flee through minefields. Vietnam helped overcome the Khmer Rouge in 1979 but factions and fighting continued in Cambodia for the next twenty years. In the late 1990s, as communist rule relented, missionaries started to reenter.

It was to this Kingdom of Cambodia in Southeast Asia in August 2001 that God brought us to watch Him work for the next fifteen years. Everyone we met who was over twenty-five years old had stories of barely surviving on watery rice soup as they worked long hours in labor camps and watched atrocities. Many members of their families had been killed. They had seen evil, despair, and death. The Cambodian people needed to hear of hope and life in Christ.

Entering the capital city of Phnom Penh with only suitcases and a few plastic trunks we joyfully anticipated seeing how God would provide everything needed. First, He was with us. Secondly, he provided co-workers, the Michael Freeze family, who had arrived ten months before us. They opened their home to us and lovingly helped us get settled. After purchasing a bicycle, we enrolled in language school. Hubert walked thirty minutes to the school; I biked, and Hadessah diligently studied her home-schooling high school courses at home. Learning to speak the Cambodian language, Khmer, was a priority in order to share the gospel, start churches, and care for the sick, the work God had called us to do.

By the third week, God had given us a house to rent within view of the Tuol Sleng Genocide Museum. During the Khmer Rouge time it was an execution center known for torture and sending victims by truckloads to the killing fields (places of executions and mass graves) outside of town. Rent prices were a little lower near the museum due to the locals' fear of spirits of the dead hovering nearby. Lacking furniture, we used one trunk for a table and two others to sit next to it. Enjoying our first meal in our new home – peanut butter sandwiches – we thanked God. Freezes loaned us mattresses and a stove. Temporary pillows were made from clothes stuffed in pillowcases, but in spite of the appreciated provisions, we were awakened several times by our malfunctioning doorbell. The next day Hubert figured out a way to disconnect it.

Obstacles piled up. What was God going to do? The cash we had brought was almost gone and the bank was taking a long time to clear the check we had deposited with them. Our arrival visas were only good for one month and needed renewing. The first language school bill was due. The landlord needed to be paid for some items he put in the house for us. Hubert had purchased a motorcycle and the licensing office kept asking for additional papers. To get our shipment from our previous place of service, a creative access country, the customs office required a fancier letterhead and a stamp on our paperwork. The phone company accepted our reference letter and agreed to put a phone line to the house but needed $330 for installation. The doorbell needed a repairman. Scrubbing the kitchen floor feeling hot and sweaty I knew we needed a part-time house helper. Then the Lord blessed us in the Wednesday evening prayer meeting with Mike, Michelle, and little Abby Freeze, praising God together. We were reassured that God would triumph.

In the morning, sitting on our flat roof enjoying His Word, the breeze, and the colors of the sunrise, God gave His peace and joy. A Cambodian lady from one of the churches came to help me with housework. She took over doing the laundry that I had started by hand. When I got home from language class, she had the whole first floor shining. Hubert was able to get the shipping form stamped and the company picked the paper up at our house. The realtor worked on the motorcycle papers and planned to come the next day. We found a "phone booth" in the neighborhood. Individuals put up a sign, then loaned the customer a mobile phone and collected a small fee.

Throughout that fourth week we saw God bring the license plate for the new motorcycle so we could start driving it. Our check cleared at the bank to pay for visas, language school, a house phone, the landlord's bill, and the doorbell repair. We bought a refrigerator, beds, pillows, a table, and chairs. Our electric piano and medical books (at least the ones that had survived a flood there) arrived from the shipper. Hadessah could once again do her piano practice after her school lessons, and we would have accompaniment later on when a church was started. It was exciting to see God overcome each challenge.

September 11, 2001, will long be remembered in America. Since Cambodia is eleven hours ahead of Eastern Daylight Time, I was sitting at a small table in my morning Khmer language class on the twelfth. When my Khmer teacher told me about the attacks in New York and Washington D.C. I could not believe it. Her English was very limited and my Khmer language even more limited. Surely this could not be true. But when Hubert arrived for his class the next hour, he confirmed that he had just been listening to reports of the attacks on Hadessah's tiny portable shortwave radio. It was many months before we saw any photos of the event. We prayed God would use it to turn people to Himself.

God was already giving opportunity for people in Phnom Penh to hear of Christ. Our landlord spoke French and listened as the truths of God's Word were shared with him. A salesman in the rattan shop asked about the Bible. The realtor who helped us find a house to rent and his assistant spoke English, allowing us to communicate with them about the Lord. We did house to house tract distribution with Khmer Christians from another church and to the crowds that came to the capital for the water festival and boat races. What joy to be again in a land that was open to missionaries teaching God's Word.

Then God started putting us in contact with Cambodians working in medicine. While house hunting, the Freezes met a pediatric surgeon. That doctor gave me the names of some of the hospital directors. We met more medical staff at various hospitals when missionaries had Cambodian friends admitted as patients and they wanted me to see them as well. God was opening the way to build friendships and share with many Cambodian doctors and nurses the message of salvation in Jesus Christ alone.

God had blessed the Freeze's time in Phnom Penh. They saw some people turn to Christ and continue in discipleship classes with them. By December 2001 they were ready to start holding church services. There was much preparation for the big day. The first floor of their house was arranged for the meeting place. A separate room was for the children's church. Permission from local authorities was obtained for meeting as a church. A name was chosen to indicate the location – Santor Mok Baptist Church (SMBC). Plastic stacking chairs and a speaker's stand were purchased. We hunted around town for an electric keyboard and found a used one. Mike prepared messages in Khmer. Michelle prepared a lesson for the children. Since our command of the language with just three months of study was still poor, it was a challenge even to try to sing in Khmer. Hadessah and I practiced playing the Khmer melodies on the keyboard. Hubert bought us Khmer Bibles to use. We met and prayed together many times for God to build this church. Many friends in the States were praying.

A missionary from a church in another part of town sent flowers for the opening service. Attendance that first Sunday was eight people, which included the two missionary families plus one Khmer man. The preaching was a blessing to me, even with understanding only part of the Khmer vocabulary Mike used. God was present and was glorified.

People prayed for our language acquisition and God answered as we concentrated our first year on studying Khmer. We practiced it with neighbors and when we went to the market. Sometimes heavy tropical rains would flood the streets making it hard to get home. God kept our motorcycle and bicycles going through the water. Raincoats and plastic bags were always kept on the cycles, and we wore plastic flip flops. It was an advantage to not have a car since they were often stuck in the traffic jams caused by flooded intersections and stalled vehicles.

A washing machine was a wonderful gift from the Lord, so we did not have to do laundry by hand any longer. Another example of His bounty was when we asked for about twenty hymnbooks in English for use when missionaries gathered together to sing praises to God. Two different churches, one in Toronto and the other our home church in the USA sent books – and they were the same edition! There were enough books to share some with other missionaries who were delighted to get them.

During our first year in Cambodia, our daughter Cherith and son-in-law Jonathan (and the other missionaries) had to evacuate the Central African Republic (CAR), due to fighting there. Our son Davar, in Israel witnessed interception of a terror attack on his kibbutz. Our other son, Hans, and his fiancé Thuy worked on their wedding plans between USA and Hanoi. Our daughter Hannah and our son-in-law Kevin were serving the Lord in their church and workplaces in Ohio. Our children, scattered around the world, were all safe in God's strong care.

Visitors from the USA led to many new contacts with Cambodian people especially at hospitals, for us to strengthen relationships and share Christ. A medical student and his physician assistant wife, a student nurse, and many others came. An engineer friend came from Virginia and lectured in a high-level Asian engineering conference and taught classes. His wife taught cooking classes in our home, and we talked of God's Word as food cooked or baked. Friends from Vietnam, Singapore, Thailand, and several other countries came. God brought visitors to serve Him with us, to multiply our outreach, and to encourage. He orchestrates His workers in His work all over the world.

Sunday routine developed, helping Freezes at Santor Mok Baptist Church (SMBC) in the morning, followed by going to a church planted by Filipinos, Preah Yeasu Baptist Church (PYBC), where Hubert preached in their English service while the missionary pastor was on furlough. Then, in the early afternoons, we went to another sister church where Hadessah played piano. Late afternoon was teaching a Sunday School class for Hadessah and other MKs her age. It was a rich time digging into God's Word with these special students. We had excellent Sunday School materials provided free from the States and sent to us each quarter. The MKs prepared their lessons ahead and participated so well. I prayed God would hold them close to Himself and use their lives for His glory. Sunday evenings we went back to SMBC for their evening service.

Attendance at SMBC doubled (from seven to fourteen), then tripled, then kept growing. They wrote out a doctrinal statement and constitution in Khmer, had their first baptismal service, and organized as a church. One Sunday morning after the service at SMBC, three of their members took Hadessah and I to see the mother of one of them at her home. We had visited her at the hospital the week before, right after her stroke. The family had been witnessing to her and she had said that today she wanted to become a Christian. A big kitchen knife was found. The patient held out the rope spirit charm around her waist and one of the Christians cut it off. She was forsaking her trust in false ways. Then she prayed to ask the Lord Jesus Christ to be her Savior from sin! What a privilege to witness her new birth, another mighty deed of our great God.

MEDICAL WORK IN PHNOM PENH

What a privilege and joy to fulfill our calling from God to make disciples and care for medical needs of people. Neighbors, Cambodian Christians, Cambodians whom Christians were reaching out to, missionaries from various countries serving in Cambodia, and others, requested help. Many, many times, God used medicine to open doors to share the gospel, or encourage Christians, or serve God's servants. "Jesus went...teaching...proclaiming the gospel...and healing every disease" (Matthew 9:35).

An urgent call came from the home of a missionary stating his eighteen-month-old child had reached up to a pot of scalding hot water and pulled it over on himself. An American medical student and his wife serving with us for a month joined me as we dashed to the home of the child. Burns covered a large percent of his body. Praise God for helping these students and me as we cared for the child. Debridements and dressing changes followed. The father, who was a nurse, was giving very good nursing care. The family preferred not to return to the Philippines for treatment, as it would interrupt the great work they were doing in three church plants. Certain concerning signs developed on the patient. I pleaded with God for wisdom and felt very certain God was directing that they get to a place with more advanced care available. The patient seemed to improve a little the day before they traveled, but they did fly out. When I next saw them a long time later back in Phnom Penh, they were thanking God for taking them out to the Philippines. The child had been treated there with a special skin substitute rather than usual skin grafts and by God's grace got a beautiful result. We all praised God for giving guidance and healing.

One of the patients I escorted to Bangkok, Thailand, for care was an infant of missionaries, along with her parents. The baby had no complications during the fifty-minute flight. By the time she was admitted to the hospital and I got to a hotel, it was after midnight. I got up at 6 am and after devotions crossed the street to the hospital. I was able to give the baby her morning bottle and talk with her doctor when she came. I left a note for the parents and walked to a bank at nine. I exchanged some money, then bought phone cards. My attempts to call the airlines and Hubert from the hotel room were unsuccessful. I fared no better trying to use the public phones with the phone cards. Finally, I asked the nurse at the nurses' station, and she got through to the airport. I had forty minutes to catch the next flight. I met the baby's father, checked out of my hotel, and jumped in a taxi. The driver learned I was a doctor, so he shared with me many of his geriatric symptoms including his heart condition, and told me of a previous accident he had had – all of which kept me praying for a safe trip to the airport! We arrived safely and caught the flight. The baby got the care she needed and returned home with her parents a few days later.

A Khmer pastor's wife came to the house for treatment of her rheumatoid arthritis. She had received care in the local hospitals but was no longer getting good results. What a privilege to serve her, starting a stronger medicine that gave her relief. Some of the other medical challenges seen included typhoid, abscesses requiring draining, and trauma from falls – once even casting a child's broken arm at my kitchen table. Her father was carrying her X-ray with them. One missionary brought a man from his church who was on treatment for cardiomegaly (enlarged heart) and pericardial fluid (fluid around the heart). He had been treated for several years for heart failure from previous rheumatic fever. A South African man who had recently returned to Cambodia came for a consult. His symptoms suggested AIDS and when I questioned him directly, he told me he already knew he had it. He had come to know Christ as his Savior. One of his comments was, "I hope there is a purpose for all this." Explaining God's great purposes, sovereignty, power, and love brought hope.

Another patient came regularly for dressing changes. It was fun to see his spiritual growth. He never wanted me to forget to pray after each visit. For a time, a neighbor girl who attended our church services needed dressing changes. We had a Bible study together each time.

Finding good medical care available if our family would need it was a pursuit soon after our arrival in Cambodia. One clinic we visited, Raffles, was Singaporean owned, with Singaporean, Rwandan, and Cambodian physicians. Soon after, the director visited our home to recruit me to work for them. I was asked to help teach some of the younger physicians, as well as do consultations. Some of the patients were Cambodian, while others were from many foreign countries. Most worked for businesses or embassies. Raffles had its clinic in a hotel, next to the Tonle Sap River. That river was noted for reversing the direction of its current twice a year. The river flowed into the Tonlé Sap, Southeast Asia's largest freshwater lake, which swelled to seven times its size during rainy season. It shrank again in dry season, flowing out via the Tonle Sap River to meet the mighty Mekong River.

It appeared God was giving me a place with equipment and supplies to provide better care for missionaries. The clinic was the size of a private physicians' office in the United States and equipped quite similarly. I worked three mornings a week there for about a year while studying language. We saw patients with a variety of problems including tropical parasites, pneumonia, anemia, traffic accidents, etc. After working a couple months at Raffles Clinic, I asked the Lord to please bring more missionary patients, because that was one of the reasons I worked there. That day – all morning – the office was full of missionaries. One family with six children plus a couple helpers came from the province. A short-term missionary from New Zealand came with friends. He needed urgent care in a well-equipped facility. Wow, did God ever give a clear answer!

Another day was a special blessing. A short-term nurse and three visiting newly graduated Singaporean Christian doctors went with me to the clinic. Because of the New Year holiday, and the Khmer staff having off, the main Singaporean doctor was there all morning with us. She toured the four visitors around. Meanwhile, I was able to talk with the new Japanese receptionist. She said she wanted to come with us to the English service at church the next Sunday! Later in the morning, in answer to prayer, God gave the opportunity to talk with the main doctor alone about the Lord. In the afternoon at our house, discussion with the visitors focused on medical missions and opportunities, sharing some of what God had done in the past. After supper, we walked to the home of another missionary and watched a video on the work of a medical missionary in North Africa. It was a passionate challenge for medical missions. Oh, that God's people would yield their whole lives for God to use anywhere He chooses.

One rainy day, there were many people coming and going all day long, but God makes the clouds His chariots. He was near. He orchestrated the timing of the many visitors and house calls so marvelously! He gave peace and joy. He showed He was using us, and He would accomplish His work, using helpless instruments. For it is not our strength or ability, but God. I was also encouraged as I thought about one of our churches making us a focus of prayer that month. The Sunday following, the message at church was on God enabling for what He commands us to do. The strength does not come from ourselves – the very thing God had been showing me all week.

Drawing blood on a patient at the clinic one day I accidentally poked myself. There were only a few drops of blood from the patient but quite a lot of bleeding from my skin. I washed it well with Hibiclens and a brush. Then I asked the lab to test the patient's blood for HIV. The next day I got the result. The patient was HIV positive. I reported the incident to the head doctor. She asked if I wanted prophylactic meds. I declined because I was afraid the risks of the meds available might be higher than the risk of getting HIV from that poke. I told Hubert about the needlestick. Then I had my blood tested to show HIV negativity. While waiting to repeat the test in three months I thought about being fully surrendered to God and accept whatever He brought into my life, including if the test result was positive. He is a loving God, who has a purpose for everything He allows in our lives. Praise the Lord my repeat HIV tests remained negative.

For two weeks, I visited a Christian AIDS patient to give her palliative care and pray with her. At one visit I was surprised by a birthday party there for me! The patient, her two daughters, her elderly mother with a shaved head, along with an Australian missionary friend helping them, all sang Happy Birthday to me, in English! They had been practicing the previous couple days. They presented me a beautifully wrapped gift. It was a walnut apple cake my missionary friend had made. We all ate it together. It was thrilling to see their joy in giving to me. Surely, I received more from them than all the help I gave to them. One week later the patient went to heaven.

On Thursday, January 29, 2004, God was working mightily again. What a terrific day! The morning time with the Lord was rich. Reading the Bible with our helper was delightful. Next, I headed to the medical school with my letter of request for permission for a Christian American dental student who planned to come work with us the following summer. The medical, dental, and pharmacy schools were under one director. Hubert and I had met him several times previously and had built a friendship. As we sat in the director's conference room that day, God opened the way to clearly share the gospel with him.

After the visit with the director was a visit to the medical school library to give them my latest medical journal that I had finished reading. The librarian invited me to have coffee with her. She had read the tract that I had given her before. This day she was open to talking even more about the Lord. However, she felt that because her family had always been Buddhist, she could not change her religion. In the school lobby, I met a young doctor that we had gotten to know through the visit of other short-termers last year. I again invited him to church. In the afternoon I visited the general hospital to talk with the HIV program director. That evening a Filipina missionary and a Cambodian Christian stopped by for medical consultations. It was such a joy to serve God's people. Day by day God showed His working as He brought people to us and us to people that He loves.

WATER

Surprise! The sound of gushing water greeted me when I awoke at 5:15 am. A hose had disconnected in the first-floor bathroom and the entire first floor was flooded with water. Hubert got the connection fixed and for two hours we pushed water out the front door and mopped up with a towel and rags. I thanked God for tile floors, for my helper arriving to help finish cleaning up the watery mess in the bottom kitchen cupboards, for strength, for a happy spirit throughout the time, for the family to help, for no serious damage, for a washing machine to spin out all the wet rugs and that our three guests upstairs missed most of the excitement.

Our visiting American Filipina nurse and I visited several hospitals that day interacting with the staff. Some nurses and doctors gave us tours of their departments. God worked that some sat and listened to the gospel. Some people accepted tracts, and we invited people to church. God was working to help us connect with people who needed the Lord.

The next day, Sunday, it was Hubert who got up at 5:15 am and found the first floor flooded again! He woke me and together we fixed the hose again and mopped up water. My attitude was not as joyful as the previous day, and my joints ached. Lord, please give me strength for the task and a dry floor tomorrow. It took only one and a half hours to clean it up this time. We managed to catch two *cyclos* (bicycle taxis) and be on our way to church on time. Attendance was twenty-one people there! After Santor Mok church we went to Preah Yeasu Baptist Church for the English service. The new Japanese receptionist who worked at Raffles Clinic with me came to the service!

In the MK Sunday School at our house, the visiting nurse gave her testimony. It was so touching to hear how God had clearly led her, blessed her, and used her. We were so privileged to have her and her sister and friend from the Philippines ministering with us and to us those couple weeks.

Praise God it was several months before I woke to the sound of water spraying downstairs again. This time it was 3:45 am and again we had guests. A sprayer next to the toilet had cracked open and things were very wet in the bathroom, but the drain kept up with the leak and the flood was confined to that one room. God was gracious to us. I got a bit wet getting the hose clamped off and cleaning up the water. Several baby centipedes on the floor met their demise in the process as well. We grew to expect water challenges when we had company and God was always our help.

FIRE

One day our helper saw fire and smoke billowing up one block away. From the flat roof of our three-story townhouse, we watched flames leaping up from the wood houses packed closely together. Our street, lined with mostly brick houses, swelled with people carrying their belongings and fleeing the fire. Hubert went out and invited people into our front patio for a place of shelter for them and their goods. I packed a couple things including a change of clothes and passports to take with us if we would have to flee. The wind was moving the fire toward the north, but I knew it could shift to bring it eastward toward us. Our electricity went off. I made more rice on the gas stove to feed our new guests. I prayed that God would make the fire go out and protect us and the neighborhood. Soon after, God answered prayer and firemen got the fire out. Many homes had been destroyed.

Throughout the afternoon, people came and went from our patio. Only about three people ate the food we offered. A few accepted clothing. Talking with a group of four garment factory workers who were sitting and waiting on our patio was a profitable time. About 6 pm, only the last of the stuff remained: a mattress, pillow, and mat. A young couple asked if we could store those for ten days while they went to their relatives in the province. They came back for them a couple weeks later and sat and visited. We thanked God for His protection from the fire. Remembering hell's unquenchable fire is a motivation to urge people to call on God for salvation.

CHURCH PLANTING

God worked in the hearts of people to listen as we visited neighbors, gave tracts, and shared the gospel. Hubert started an English class for the neighborhood young people and then began a Sunday evening church service in English at our home. Students from his English class came as well as other people. Some were new believers, others had not yet embraced the Savior. As they sang together or played games afterward, we talked to individuals about what they were understanding concerning Christ.

After about three months, two people turned to Christ for salvation. A week later another girl received new life. She had good questions about forsaking all other gods. As God brought people to Himself, discipleship classes were begun, to train them in His Word. Some had converted from Islam but most from Buddhism. Several times some of the youth went to church with us across town at Santor Mok. One Sunday, seven neighbors went with us. One of them was a young lady who had heard the gospel before but rejected it. Though wanting to learn more about God and salvation, she did not dare receive Christ because of the pressure of the Buddhist society around her and their opposition to Christianity. Finally, she did. Praise God for His grace to her.

The children of our neighborhood needed to hear about Jesus. I hesitated starting a children's class, because I was so busy. But God kept bringing it to mind. At one point I thought of the excuse, "But I don't have crayons for the children to color pictures for handiwork." A short time later a new Singaporean doctor, who was a Christian, came to work at Raffles Clinic. He asked if I could use crayons and colored pencils he had brought for use in the Lord's work. It was a confirmation to me that God was directing to begin a children's class.

Sunday at 3 pm the first children's Bible class for our neighborhood was held. Michelle Freeze knew songs in Khmer and led them. A short-termer and Hadessah helped. Even the Singaporean doctor came. God was enabling us. We sat on the tiled court area between the house and the open gates to the street. There were only two children at the beginning, but several more came throughout the hour. Flash cards of the creation story were affixed on a tile wall as the story was related. The children used the colored pencils for coloring Bible story pictures. We prayed God would give fruit.

God worked wonderfully. By a few weeks later the number had risen to sixteen kids who came right on time, sat attentively through the whole story, and were orderly through the handiwork time too. They painted Styrofoam airplanes that had come in the mail that Friday from a church in the USA. More kids came and watched at the gate, so I told the Bible story again. The children were learning the songs too.

God works in response to the prayers of His saints. Wednesday night prayer meeting was begun for the Christians coming to the Sunday evening services in our home. Then the first Sunday morning worship service was started at our house instead of taking the Christians across town to SMBC. Hubert preached in Khmer on the garden of Eden. What a blessed relationship Adam and Eve had with God in the garden. A short Sunday School on the triumphal entry followed the service. The children in Children's Bible Class at 3 pm listened well and enjoyed molding with playdough the things in Pharaoh's dreams.

As the evening service grew to seventeen, we thought we might need to buy more plastic stacking chairs. One of the young ladies, Tida, who was already a Christian before she started meeting with us, brought a friend who wanted to receive Christ. She seemed to have been taught well already. That same Christian girl taught the children's class when I was away on a trip to Bangladesh. What joy to see God use Khmer Christians to bring others and teach His Word.

Just before the children's class one Sunday afternoon, down the street, a little three-year-old neighbor child was struck by a car and killed. It was sobering. I joined the family and neighbors that gathered in the evening. A tent had been set up in the street and food was being served. What a contrast to our joyful news the day before of our new grandchild, Katie, arriving to Hannah and Kevin. God gives to us so richly, though we have no more merit of our own than our neighbors.

When a new Bible School opened to teach the Bible and train people to serve the Lord, we were delighted. Hubert taught some Bible courses, and I taught a health and first aid course. The students learned what to do for fevers, diarrhea, snakebites, disease prevention, trauma, and several other practical topics. We used a big doll as a patient and practiced many scenarios. A couple years later some of the students taught the same health lessons, along with Bible lessons to parents of children they were reaching. Through that outreach, someone turned to Christ for salvation. What joy to hear of God using people we have taught.

There was much preparation for a youth party to be held at the Bible School. Four churches participated. Two days before, some of the young people helped us make lots of lemon squares. Then the night before the event, we learned there may be sixty instead of forty coming. That called for making more lemon squares. Hubert and one of the young men went to the market at 7 am to get chicken and other ingredients to make chicken curry. One young lady from our church was in charge of food preparation but had never cooked for so many people before. When my regular house helper saw the big project, she offered to assist. She was God's provision. She helped cut up ingredients and borrowed two more big pots. From noon until 5:30 pm we were making chicken curry. One big pot was on our small gas stove in the kitchen and another over charcoal in front of the house. Several young people worked together. Hubert loaded the food in cyclos and took it to the meeting place. Nearly eighty showed up for the event. Ten of those were Christians from our church. Songs, testimonies, games, and fellowship permeated the evening. Plenty of food and even leftovers showed God had provided abundantly.

Sunday morning worship services, evening evangelistic services, discipleship classes, baptismal classes, children's Bible classes and week-day English classes continued in our home. Prayer meeting was well attended, and the new believers were eager to learn. Four of them enrolled in the Bible school. One Wednesday afternoon there were eight in prayer meeting. Five stayed for supper. The menu I had planned for our family was only a loaf of fresh bread from the bread maker. But various things were added to make a meal for eight within minutes. Impromptu company for meals was common and welcomed. God gave profitable conversations.

There was little Christian literature in the Khmer language. God helped Hubert write a simplified English version of a two-volume discipleship book, and work with translators to put it into Khmer. He found printers to print it. It was revised and reprinted several times and used throughout the years in Cambodia. Hubert started teaching Articles of Faith in anticipation of forming into a church. A couple of the youth came daily to help translate and type those into the computer.

Fancy invitations were printed and handed out by the new believers to their friends and family for the first baptismal service. The facilities of a sister church were used, and the service was held on a Saturday evening. The first person arrived at our house at 5 pm and others gradually came. We needed to show everyone the way to the other church as addresses were rather lacking. Hubert left about 5:20 pm to go to the church. One of the girls led a group on motorcycles and bicycles about 5:30 pm, and I took the last group at 6:45 pm. One motorcycle in our group got lost but showed up about five minutes later at the church. Traffic was heavy and it was dark.

When I arrived, the people were already singing, and Hubert and the first candidate were in the baptismal. The six believers who received baptism did great giving their testimonies and answering Hubert's questions about the assurance of salvation and the meaning of baptism. There were about fifty people present, mostly unsaved friends and relatives of those receiving baptism. Some students from the Bible school came, and a few people from the hosting church were there to help. Hubert gave a challenge and invitation. After we came back to our house and most of the people went home, one of the young men and his sister and mother stayed to discuss more about Christ.

April 18, 2004, the alarm went off at 4:30 am to get up and prepare for an excursion to the coast. Fourteen young people left with us soon after 6 am. In the van we ate, sang, quoted verses, and talked. Hadessah was used of God all day in leading activities pointing to the Lord. At the ocean, we took a boat about thirty minutes to a deserted island. The water was so calm. We did a little snorkeling, swimming, games on the beach, shell collecting, picnicking, making a pyramid on the sand and then Hubert gave a devotional. We got lots of sun. Something just under the sand in the water stung several of us near the end of the time. But there was lots of fun. When we returned to the mainland, we ate at a restaurant overlooking the Bay. The sunset was gorgeous as we headed back to Phnom Penh. We prayed God would use that outing to build unity and strengthen the believers. Three were unbelievers who were able to see the love Christians have for one another and the joy of being together.

PERMISSION FOR KOH KONG WORK

The provinces were generally considered unsafe for foreigners to live and work in when we first arrived in Cambodia. So, the majority of missionaries were in the Phnom Penh area. But as banditry lessened and the residual Khmer Rouge melted into the general society, it was time to move out into unreached areas with the gospel. While doing language study we prayed and sought where God would have us move out to.

After talking with other missionaries and looking at surveys which had been done, in March 2003 we rented a van to go look at Kampot and Kaeb provinces in the south and get a couple days of vacation. Having dinner with a missionary family in Kampot, we were told that Koh Kong over in the southwest was one of the neediest places in Cambodia. However, the road there was impassable. People usually took a boat from Kampot to get to Koh Kong. They said the prison for political prisoners was there. They also mentioned there were still Khmer Rouge there.

In Kaeb, we saw ruins of old European houses full of bullet holes from the Khmer Rouge attacks back in the 1970s. We took a boat out to an island and walked four miles around the perimeter of it. Some places were rocky and challenging to get across. At one point on the beach the only place to pass had three menacing, growling dogs that stopped us. We could not go back because the tide had come in. We prayed and waited. After a while a boy came out from a small house carrying a dish of food to occupy the dogs while we hurried by.

Later that afternoon, back on the mainland, we took off on another hike. We went through roads of the ghost town part of Kaeb, then up through gardens near small mountainside homes. Going deeper into the woods we discovered there was no longer any path. So, we turned around. But we could not find the way back. We kept hunting and several times found we were looking down the edge of a cliff. We prayed together and asked the Lord to show us the way down. A short time later we found the way we had come, and safely returned. People along the trail greeted us. At the guest house, our van driver, Sothea, had just pulled out to look for us. We remembered all the warnings about not getting off paths in Cambodia, due to so many landmines still in the country. We thanked God for protection and for showing us the way back.

Returning to Phnom Penh, Sothea took us to a town a little off the main highway to visit his brother. They had cattle and chickens under their house on stilts, and coconut trees and banana palms in the yard. They climbed the tree and cut down fresh green coconuts for us and served us watermelon as well. As we walked through a little of the town, God let us talk with three teen girls about the Lord. One had been listening to Christian radio and was happy to hear more about Christ. I had used up my tracts, but Hadessah had one to give her. God directs our paths.

A few days later, in Phnom Penh, Sothea phoned to ask if we'd like to visit his wife and new baby at the maternity hospital. It was reasonably clean. A small firepot under the new mother's bed, along with her coverings kept her sweating as was the custom after childbirth. We had a good talk with Sothea, his wife, and his mother. I think God was working in his heart. His uncle had just died, and he had attended the funeral. He said his uncle went to hell. We had asked people to pray for Sothea and we talked with him several times.

The path to Koh Kong through mountains and woods had been worked on and upgraded to a road when we were ready to visit there. It was muddy and rough with washboard ruts. The jostling of the van produced motion sickness for our co-worker accompanying

Hubert, Hadessah and I on another survey trip, in October 2003. At least the ten-hour trip was broken up by four ferry crossings, allowing us to walk and stretch. We stood on the ferry as it crossed the wide rivers. Each successive river valley was more beautiful than the previous one. The mountains grew higher. Since it was rainy season, the forest was a verdant green. And at each of the towns I said to the Lord, "You've created a beautiful place here. Is this the place You have chosen for us?" Finally, we arrived at the end of the road – Koh Kong – a town isolated by the ocean and mountains, formerly accessible only by sea. It was known for its prison, prostitutes, and drugs.

Koh Kong did not match the beauty of the previous river valleys. A couple of its streets had broken pavement. The others were dirt with lots of holes. Litter was strewn around most of the houses and a noisy little carnival played next to one of the little hotels we inquired at. Even at mid-day, on a street of cheap little unkempt guesthouses, I saw a temptress lying on a bed under a red light. My thoughts were, "I hope God doesn't call us here."

But the Lord says, "For my thoughts are not your thoughts, neither are your ways my ways, declares the Lord. For as the heavens are higher than the earth, so are my ways higher than your ways and my thoughts than your thoughts" (Is. 55:8-9). Hubert saw the need of the people in Koh Kong for deliverance from sin. Dark places need the light – Jesus Christ. We are simply servants of the Lord Jesus Christ, commissioned by Him to carry the light of the gospel. We talked with directors at the Koh Kong Hospital and the Provincial Health Department (PHD). They said we would not be allowed to work in any of the towns along the road we had traveled because "the government could not guarantee our safety." But we were welcome to settle in the town of Koh Kong.

Over the next months I wrote letters to the Koh Kong hospital, to the PHD, and to the Cambodian Ministry of Health (MOH) in the capital, Phnom Penh. We wrote letters to Christians in America asking them to pray. Hubert made several trips to Koh Kong. I made many trips to many different offices in Phnom Penh as directed by the MOH. But we kept hitting roadblocks. We knew very certainly that if God wanted us to enter Koh Kong to work, it would clearly be His hand getting the permission, not our efforts. I was content waiting. If God did not want us down in that corner of the country, He would show us to continue where we were in Phnom Penh, with a fruitful and active ministry, or take us to another province.

"Ask, and it will be given to you; seek, and you will find; knock, and it will be opened to you" (Matthew 7:7). On yet another of Hubert's trips to Koh Kong, he pleaded with God to make his journey successful to get the needed signatures. God worked mightily! The hospital vice director saw Hubert on the hospital porch and asked if he could help. When the request was explained, he happily signed the needed paper in the absence of the director. Taking it next to the PHD, the vice director there was very helpful and in the absence of the director, put his signature on the document. God had placed the right people in the right places and guided their decisions. We submitted the required papers to the MOH in Phnom Penh. But they were not satisfied and kept asking for additional items. We duly submitted them. The secretary seemed to be irritated with our request.

On Friday, April 2, we were invited to the wedding feast of our neighbor. Seated at our table was a stranger that we found out was the Inspector General of the Ministry of Health. The music was too loud to speak with him much, but Hubert was able to explain to him what we had done in medicine in Africa and what we hoped to do in Koh Kong. He finished eating, excused himself to go home and walked away. His wife got up to follow him, so I quickly handed her my business card and asked her to give it to her husband. We wondered if God would use this contact to help process our papers. Less than four days later, Tuesday, April 6, 2004, the MOH phoned and said I could pick up my approval paper. I went right in. The secretary was very nice to me, wished me success in Koh Kong and said she'd miss me. I wanted to speak more with this person I had interacted with so many times, but she left the room. We praised the Lord for giving us the needed permission! It was confirmation that God wanted us in Koh Kong and truly God who had soared over all the hurdles.

CHAPTER 6

KOH KONG 2004-2006

I will build my church. Matthew 16:18

THE BEGINNING OF KOH KONG BAPTIST CHURCH

Almost three years of ministry in Phnom Penh drew to a close and many friends saw Hadessah and I off at the airport on May 17, 2004. Hadessah needed to return to the States to enter Bible College. Hubert stayed in Cambodia to continue the work, move our goods down to Koh Kong, and prepare the house for my return when I would bring a short-term missionary. Cambodia is on the opposite side of the world from Michigan, and it worked well to stop over in the beautiful Alps of Albertville, France, to visit Cherith, Jonathan and baby Adrianna. Davar, just finishing eighteen months serving the Lord in Zambia, met us there. Since none of Hadessah's and my luggage arrived with us, we joked about my wearing the same outfit for most of the visit, but the airline got the suitcases to us in time to leave on our next leg of the trip.

The six weeks in Michigan were a whirlwind of seeing lots of family and friends, giving reports to our churches who prayed, settling two of our kids into new jobs, multiple vehicle breakdowns, getting items to take back to Cambodia, and making a memory book page for my mother's 80ᵗʰ birthday. When visiting our churches in Lansing and attending a wedding, we stayed in a hotel overlooking a little lake. The afternoon sunlight skipped across the surface of the water creating jillions of sparkles. The Lord reminded me that the new work He was moving us into down in the province of Koh Kong was His work and He was going to show us His blessings as innumerable as those sparkles on the water.

Assured God watches over His own, we tearfully said goodbyes in Grand Rapids. Arriving in Chicago I went to meet Jenna, the short termer who was to travel with me. But the airline had bumped her to an earlier flight. God helped me find her. After her flight was loaded, I asked the agent if there was an empty seat that I could take instead of waiting two more hours for my scheduled flight. Yes, there was a seat, and it was very close to Jenna's! Praise God for His working! Thus we traveled to San Francisco together. God gave us another surprise when my sister Joan and her husband came to spend a couple hours with us while we awaited the trans-Pacific flight. The fifth flight of the trip landed us in Trat, Thailand, where Hubert gave us a happy welcome.

We visited the director and some of the staff at Trat Hospital since Koh Kong hospital sometimes refers patients to them, finished setting up our bank account in another town, and then walked across the border and through immigration into Cambodia. Hubert had done great, painting and setting up the house. Only a few piles of boxes of things remained for us to find places for, and more cleaning. We ate supper on our second-story patio watching the sunset over the estuary and mountains, feeling the lovely breeze from the water. God truly had watched over the ways of His saints.

My first Sunday back in Cambodia, July 4, 2004, was the first service of what would become Koh Kong Baptist Church. Hubert had walked around and invited neighbors during the previous weeks. Word spread around town. Chairs were set up in our house. At the 8 o'clock starting time, some children showed up, so Jenna taught a children's lesson and I interpreted. At 9 am some adults came, and Hubert started the worship service. By the end there were about thirty people in all. We praised God for this beginning.

Puch, a Christian neighbor girl, was among those present in the first service, and she continued to come. She said she had received Christ about a year before. She had recently come to Koh Kong. She asked to borrow a Bible and was excited to have a Bible study with me. However, after the second lesson, she returned the Bible. She was staying with our landlord and his family, and they refused to allow her to have a Bible in their house. They were afraid it would displease the spirits. She still had her songbook and sang from it at home for encouragement. But God worked, and about six weeks later, the landlord's wife started to study the Bible with me. She became so eager to learn, that when I finished teaching, she would read ahead right then to find out what happened next. It was delightful searching the Word together and eventually she prayed to receive Christ. However, after several months, she quit coming. Puch, meanwhile, moved back to her home province.

The second Sunday in August, a man named Tuen came to the service carrying his Bible. He was from a Baptist church in another province but had lived in Koh Kong for about five years. He longed for a Bible preaching church and had been praying for God to raise up a Baptist Church in Koh Kong. He returned the following week with his three children: two teenagers and a second-grade girl. His whole family, including his wife, Kenh, joined us for a meal after one service and were quite shy, but especially enjoyed our homemade bread. Bread was not sold in Koh Kong.

The older daughter, Pren, began helping me with the children's church. She and her brother, Petros, came for Bible Studies and piano lessons. Although most who came to the services were not yet Christians, God had provided this faithful core family for the church. Eventually Pren and later Petros taught the children's classes, and Tuen taught the adult Sunday School.

In November and December Tuen usually missed a service or two. Their house was on stilts over the water, and the estuary level was high that time of year. A few hours a day when the tide was in, their floor was under water, as well as the walkway leading to the house. Later God provided so they were able to rebuild their house higher.

Sunday schedule was very full. People arrived at 8:30 am for the morning service. Before and after lunch was visiting homes and having Bible studies or receiving visitors until children's church at 3 pm. The evening evangelistic service had different people than in the morning. These included Hubert's English class students and others. Often there were games after that service. One by one people turned to the Lord. God wove together the various aspects of ministry. A neighbor came for a medical consult at the house, brought by a little girl who came to children's church. It was like Naaman's servant girl in the Bible telling of the man of God. I asked the patient if he had heard of Jesus before. He said only from reading the tract that Hubert had given him a few weeks earlier. Some of the patients who listened to the gospel and read the tracts at the hospital, then came to church.

Petros witnessed to his friend and brought him to church. He also read the Bible to the blind neighbor who came faithfully and trusted in Christ. Later, we were able to get cassette players and cassettes of the Bible in Khmer for him and for people who never learned to read.

The wide estuary in front of our house was a beautiful place for the first baptismal service. After regular morning services, the church people walked together to the waterfront. Some of the evening service attenders met us there making eighteen in all. We climbed into Tuen's fishing boat, and he navigated a little way out. Near an island bordered with mangroves, he anchored in shallow clear water. Several of the people jumped into the water. Hubert spoke briefly and had Scripture read. He asked the candidates many questions about things that had been carefully discussed during baptismal classes. It was a testimony to the people witnessing the baptism. He then baptized them, and we all sang. People got back in the boat, and we returned home.

One Sunday evening I was especially missing my children and singing with them around the piano. I also missed singing with a larger group of Christians. Then God sent something special. Hubert and I were the only Christians along with six unsaved friends in that service. While we were singing, a bird right outside the front door, sang lustily with us. When our singing stopped, it also stopped. "Thank you, Lord Jesus, for that encouragement."

STARTING AT KOH KONG HOSPITAL

Koh Kong Hospital's complex of single-story buildings with each room opening to an outside sidewalk was typical of hospitals in tropical climates. It allowed for airflow in the sweltering heat. Some of the structures were fairly recent. Small plaques gave the name of which foreign organizations had funded its construction. A few crumbling wood wards bespoke eons of battles with termites and leaky roofs. There were bed frames and even a few mattresses. Woven straw mats brought by the patients were considered cooler and cleaner than using "public" bedding. Most of the occupants of the beds had a bag of intravenous (IV) solution and under their pillows, little bags of pills the nurse had given them that morning for the day. On any given morning, people gathered around the outpatient clinic room hoping to see a doctor and be given a prescription to fill at the pharmacy window nearby. It was not just a question of when a doctor might come, but if one would even show up.

Being a newbie to the system, the first job was to figure out how things worked and did not work, then dig in and help. Getting to know who was responsible for what in each department took quite a while. One of my first blunders was to urge for a cesarean section when the midwives asked me for help on a difficult delivery case, only to learn I had offended the head of the obstetrics department whose job it was to make that decision.

When the outpatient receptionist urged me to do consultations for the patients who had been waiting so long, I learned to graciously step in and help until a Khmer doctor arrived, then graciously slide out unless invited to stay and both of us see patients. Honesty in charting was sometimes an issue. One could only guess if the numbers written down for blood pressures, pulses, temperatures, and respiratory rates were actually measured or not. Thus, my doctor bag, always handy at my side, contained the essentials to check on the actual current vitals. If the pharmacy was out of a medicine that had been prescribed, the prescriber did not know that the patient never received it.

Over time, with much patience and perseverance, the Cambodian staff grew to understand that my role was to work shoulder to shoulder with them, helping them advance in their medical professions and improve the quality of care given to the sick. My prayer was that God would cause Koh Kong Hospital to succeed because of the presence there of a servant of God, just as He had prospered Potiphar because of Joseph.

Compassion was demonstrated as I cared for patients. When doctors were away for meetings, I filled in doing hospital rounds on the patients or outpatient consultations or night calls. Medical articles could be printed from the internet for physicians who understood enough English. Some information and forms that were in English, I was able to explain to staff who asked. Current treatment protocols could be shown to them from evidence-based research. The Cambodian physicians were responsible for patient care. God used several foreign organizations over the years that worked to upgrade the standards of the hospital and hold workers accountable.

Training Koh Kong doctors and nurses for the care of HIV/ AIDS patients was actively underway when I arrived in 2004. Often this entailed their going to Phnom Penh for a week at a time, thus explaining the paucity of staff onsite. Further training was provided by specialists coming from Brazil, England, Japan, and Canada at various times as the program developed. These graciously invested time to teach me as well.

Before treatment to reduce the HIV virus was available at our hospital, we concentrated on treating the opportunistic infections – infections that came because of the patient's decreased immunity. Spinal taps for cryptococcal meningitis along with IV meds wrapped in black plastic to protect from light were common. The tuberculosis (TB) ward was filled with patients coinfected with both HIV and TB, receiving directly observed therapy for two months before continuing treatment as outpatients. Emaciated patients from wasting syndrome were sad to watch.

Four months after AIDS care had begun at Koh Kong Hospital, the first medicines to attack the virus arrived. The first two patients to receive it were selected and watched for side effects. Eventually, all who needed it were provided the medicines, and many lives were saved.

Doctors and nurses from hospitals across the border in Thailand periodically came to visit and donate things to Koh Kong

Hospital. Occasionally, they gave their service and medicine as they did mobile clinics. One such clinic was held on the veranda of a mosque in the largest of the four districts of the town of Koh Kong. I enjoyed working with the Thai staff, some of whom I had repeated contact with.

The mobile clinic at the mosque stopped from 10:45 am to 1 pm because that was the time for the Muslim Friday meeting. During that time, we went to a veranda of a big house over the estuary to eat spicy Thai boxed lunches, enjoying the gentle breeze, and watching children in the water flying kites. People were meeting fishing boats coming in. God gave opportunity to talk again to two Thai doctors. The director had attended a Christian school as a child. The vice director was Catholic. I prayed the Lord would work in their hearts.

Another time the Thai team was doing consults outside in the Koh Kong hospital waiting area. Suddenly, lightning struck the hospital! I was at a consultation desk on the veranda. A radio antenna was next to a tree in the hospital courtyard by us. It was the target the lightning hit. The lightning traveled to the radio and blew it out! No more contacting distant health centers until it was repaired. A Cambodian doctor was sitting by the radio but was not injured. The lightning also followed a guy wire fastening the antenna to a low wall by me. Pieces of cement fell out from the wall. Another guy wire led to another veranda and a fire started there. It was quickly put out with an extinguisher.

Rain was blowing in hard. Consultations stopped and the crowds assessed the damage. It opened great opportunities to speak of life and death with the hospital staff and with a French-speaking patient there who had visited our church before. They were aware that death could have taken us all at that moment. But God had protected us.

As a missionary doctor, God wanted to use me foremost to get the gospel to people so they could be saved from eternal separation from God. He had placed me in medicine both to help the sick and suffering and to have opportunities to tell people about Christ. One day at the hospital, one of the nurses asked me for one of my books. I asked which one, the HIV book or an antibiotic book? "No," she said, "the one about Jesus." So, I gave her a tract and she sat right down and started reading it. Later we discussed it.

Often patients in the TB ward were happy to listen to Bible lessons, sometimes with brightly colored pictures. One lady in a TB ward asked me to visit her too. She was pregnant. She wanted tracts and to know more about Jesus. She used to wear a crucifix and felt it protected her. After she lost it, she felt she had more accidents, illnesses, and disappointments. We talked several times about the Lord. It was not a necklace that would protect, but God Himself. One day I asked if she was ready to receive Christ. She smiled and beamed. She had already talked with the Lord and believed in Jesus. She seemed so happy. After that, she enjoyed listening to cassettes of the New Testament since she could not read. When she was strong enough, she came to church frequently.

When visiting a lady in maternity who had had a D & C (procedure to stop hemorrhaging), she described how afraid she had been when she was bleeding. I explained to her about Christ. She said she had relatives who were Christians and had heard before. That day her heart was ready, and she asked Christ to save her!

A Cambodian physician who was an expert in HIV from Phnom Penh visited Koh Kong a few times. He shared his testimony of how God had saved him and used him to start two churches. When he was in Koh Kong for teaching about HIV, he came to prayer meeting at our house. He had gotten in trouble with the Ministry of Health (MOH) and with his French boss for witnessing at a hospital in

Phnom Penh. But in his private practice he witnessed freely. God was so gracious to me that Koh Kong Hospital did not object to my talking to people about the Lord. The staff openly said things about my faith in God, even though it was sometimes mocking. The vice director of the hospital set up a cabinet for reading materials for patients in the medicine ward. He asked if I would like to put Christian literature in it. Yes! What joy to watch the Lord working.

One October day, after the hospital work, a visiting British doctor who was Catholic, came home with me as she had done other times. We sat at the kitchen table and talked about God's Word. One question she had was, "On your death bed as you look back at your life, how will you know if you have been successful?" We looked at various Scriptures. John 4:34, "Jesus said to them, 'My food is to do the will of him who sent me and to accomplish his work.'" She had other questions about her life. Oh, that she would see her need for real life in Christ. Before she left a few months later, she said she was still thinking about what she had learned about the Lord Jesus.

Working as an interpreter for a visiting French dermatologist I learned more about dermatology. One of the days God gave a great opportunity to witness to her. God had been working in her heart. There were several house calls on foreigners from many countries living in Koh Kong. Some of the times I visited, they were willing to discuss about God, other times we only talked of other subjects.

When arriving at the hospital one morning, I was met by four Muslim ladies outside maternity. They were interested when I mentioned Jesus. They asked where and when we met to worship and asked for tracts! We talked a little while about what the tracts said. Another time, by the surgery building, one of the Muslim men asked what Christians believe. He told the other Muslim people around him, "We ought to listen to find out." What joy to explain what God says in His Word. After AIDS clinic another afternoon, the Muslim director of the hospital took me in her air-conditioned office. We studied a little English and a lot about the Lord. Obviously, it was God's doing! One day, when I did an ultrasound on a Muslim young lady, her mother surprised me, mentioning that I was a follower of Jesus and Jesus is good. I explained more about Jesus and gave them two tracts. I prayed God would keep working in their hearts.

Monday, July 4, 2005, I tried to reach the director of the District Health Office about my contract renewal to continue working at the hospital. I wanted to take the paperwork up to Phnom Penh that Thursday. The director said he was busy in meetings until Wednesday. People who were to write a support letter were in Phnom Penh but leaving soon for another province. Our internet was only intermittently connecting so I could not receive their letter electronically. It was time to watch what God would do.

On Wednesday, God showed His power. Signatures from three offices were obtained for the document. The support letter arrived in Koh Kong via a runner Wednesday night. Thursday, I traveled to Phnom Penh and handed them to the MOH. Monday evening when I got back to Koh Kong, the MOH called that my contract renewal had been approved! A couple weeks later I made the trip to Phnom Penh again to pick it up. It was amazing to see it all completed so fast – definitely God's doing. What a contrast to the first time getting approval to work in Koh Kong.

Many preparations were being made in town for a visit from the king of Cambodia in January 2006. The town was cleaned up and people spoke of it everywhere. It reminded me of our preparations for our great King coming. When the day came, people gathered in the square. The roads were blocked in the area where he was to arrive. After a brief wait, a soldier allowed me through the blocked road to get to the hospital. From there I had a great view of the two helicopters arriving, then the king's umbrella moving through the crowd as he shook hands, and then saw him mount the platform. I could faintly hear him giving a speech. When ceremonies ended, the king left, and the staff bustled to get back to their daily work. It will be different when King Jesus comes. The daily work we have been given now will be finished and all will be new. Jesus will reign forever.

IN THE HANDS OF KHMER ROUGE

LIFE camp was just about a week away. It was always a great occasion for Christians, mostly youth, to bring unsaved friends they had been witnessing to for an evangelistic outreach. When I invited Pren to go with me to Phnom Penh for the camp, she was excited. Her thoughts went immediately to her cousins in Phnom Penh that needed the Lord. Perhaps they would attend with her.

Tuesday, the departure day came and Pren arrived at our house along with her mother. However, she was now undecided whether to go or not. Her father had had bad dreams the night before about Pren going on the trip. Her parents left the decision up to her. So did I. I simply reminded her that she needed to do whatever she believed was God's will. She decided to cancel. For my part, I needed God's continued direction as well. Our daughter Hannah (in the States) had phoned to say that as she had been praying for this trip, she had great concern for my safety. My sister Sue e-mailed that she was praying especially for this trip. The camp planners were counting on my teaching and helping out. As I sought the Lord, God gave real peace to continue. "The eternal God is your dwelling place, and underneath are the everlasting arms" (Deuteronomy 33:27).

Hubert took me to the market to find transportation. God helped us find a pick-up truck with room in their front seat. After bargaining the price and waiting for other passengers, we took off. The mountains and forests were beautiful. The driver seemed interested when I talked about Christ to him. After the fourth ferry crossing, there was a stop at a juncture in the road for about an hour waiting in a shaded area and enjoying a slight breeze. Throughout the day a song came to me that I had frequently sung before in Central Africa, "Father, glorify Your name" (repeated once), "Father, glorify Your name in me. Whether in pleasure or in pain, o're my life I give You reign, Father, glorify Yourself in me." I prayed God would be glorified in my life, and in His planned time, be glorified in my death.

Mid-afternoon, it was a welcome sight to see two missionary friends coming outside just when we pulled up to the hotel where the camp was being held. Besides helping with set-up, God gave me good talks with my roommate Tida, the Cambodian girl from our Phnom Penh work, and time encouraging a short-term Filipino missionary considering career missions. We discussed following God's will. An American missionary came for a medical consult and sweet fellowship.

When the conference began on Wednesday, there were about ninety people from many provinces who had gathered. The program included English classes, sermons, skits, songs, videos, class presentations, picture taking, and games. Each Christian counselor was assigned one or two unsaved people to meet with during the buddy times. That was for answering questions, explaining, and finding out what difficulties people were having understanding the gospel. We pleaded with God to work in hearts. One of my counselees was a nineteen-year-old girl and the other was a forty-three-year-old mother of six whose husband had recently taken a second wife. Later a third young man asked to join our group. Many of the people listening had heard the way of salvation many times before the camp and had friends praying for them. By Thursday night, many people had made professions of faith. God was working.

The campers went to the waterpark the final day. As camp physician I saw three scrapes, one superficial cut, and someone with a headache. Tida was with me and most of the time we talked with staff and students from the LIFE camp. One girl who received Christ the night before said she was so happy that God saved her. A boy told me he would like to go to Koh Kong. I urged him to stay in his own province and witness to his family. Another student had been a Christian for nine months. He had many questions about baptism and other things. I was so grateful to God for the churches that could continue teaching God's Word to these young believers. After LIFE camp ended, there were a few hours to visit several other friends in Phnom Penh, some Christians and some not yet. The trip had certainly been worthwhile. I was so grateful to God for taking me there.

As I set out on Saturday's return trip to Koh Kong, Hannah, in the States, continued fervently praying. A motorcycle-taxi took me to the Phnom Penh market where I bargained for a seat in a small silver pick-up. It did not leave until 8 am so I studied and ate part of a roll for breakfast. There were three people in the tiny back seat of the cab, and the driver and I in the front. No one was very talkative. A heavy-set lady in the back only glared at me when I tried to converse. About a half hour into the trip, the driver was scanning for a radio station, and I heard preaching by a well-known American pastor. I asked him to let me listen to that program and he did. It was great hearing a sermon in English. It was about giving thanks even in difficult circumstances. After it finished, the radio returned to Khmer and announced a church in Phnom Penh. The driver changed the station.

During the next couple hours of the trip, I was memorizing Isaiah 12, especially enjoying, "Behold, God is my salvation; I will trust, and will not be afraid" (verse 2), and, "With joy you will draw water from the wells of salvation" (verse 3). The lush green scenery along the road going back was gorgeous. It had been a few months since I returned via the road route (usually taking the boat at Sihanoukville during the muddy rainy season). The final four hours of the route were through mountainous national forests with no houses except at the four river crossings.

Just past the first ferry crossing, the driver veered to the left side of the road and headed straight toward five people walking on the edge of the road! Two men had to leap into the ditch to escape being hit! The driver and the other passengers laughed about how frightened the pedestrians had looked. I wondered if the driver had consumed some alcohol with his rice dinner at the first ferry crossing.

The driver was more talkative from then on but very coarse. Sometimes I did not know if he was addressing me, or the guy in back, or nobody in particular. Then I caught bits of his crude conversation with one of the men in the back seat. They were talking about guns, seeing if the foreigner will look scared, throwing out my dead body in the woods, etc. They spoke of how Khmer Rouge killed foreigners, and they acclaimed bandits. They kept watching my reaction as they talked and sneered. They acted just like descriptions I had heard of Khmer Rouge. At the second ferry crossing, the driver talked disdainfully about the "white-skinned" people in another car. When I climbed back in the truck after crossing the river, he got in afterward and asked, "Where is that diarrhea?" then turned and saw I was in, and said, "Oh you're in already." I felt like I was surrounded by hostility, but never felt afraid. God's peace was great. I prayed that if they killed me, God would continue to give me His peace through it and get glory for Himself. When they did not get the reaction they expected from me, they let up threatening.

While waiting at the third ferry crossing, I tried to phone Hubert but did not have enough time left on my cell phone card. I took a picture of a cute little girl, actually to show the pick-up truck in the background. I figured if I did not get home and Hubert came looking for clues later, it might help to know the vehicle I had been in. We finally arrived in front of our house in Koh Kong. Hubert came to the truck to meet me and carry my suitcase. A couple motorcycle taxis also came up to see if there were passengers to take to the border. They saw I alone was getting out there and said, "Oh, it's the doctor!" The driver, not believing them, retorted, "She's not a doctor." Perhaps he was surprised to see I was established in the town. After unpacking a little, I went to the hospital to return an instrument that I had taken to get repaired in the capital. God allowed me to witness to a midwife and some patients. I thanked Him for the continued work He had for me to do in Koh Kong. Clearly, God had answered prayer and protected. His everlasting arms had surrounded me. And besides, He had given me His amazing peace the whole time.

THE BOAT THAT SANK

The Christians in Koh Kong Baptist Church were excited to hear that Dr. Anglea's Baptist Mid-Missions' medical team would be coming to Cambodia! The team's original plan was to serve in Sri Lanka, following up the Tsunami relief teams. But because of too much unrest in that country, the destination was changed to Koh Kong. We would watch for the great things God had prepared. The church prayed and considered how they could be involved with evangelism. Tuen recommended towns that needed medical care and the gospel. A list of medicines we would need to purchase in Phnom Penh was prepared. As I tried to email the list to the States for Dr. Anglea's input, the internet would not connect. It got late and we finally turned off the computer for the night. I prayed and turned it back on to try one more time. That time the email went out. Praise God for answering! In the morning, a reply was received with the additional information needed.

I traveled on *The Royal,* a big seventy-passenger boat that looked rather like a wingless airplane. Hubert rode his motorcycle to get it repaired in Phnom Penh. The sea was so calm that I was able to write down estimated quantities of medicines to buy and do some reading. Getting through port immigration was faster than usual and the motorcycle taxi helped me catch a bus to Phnom Penh that had already pulled out – so I had no waiting time. Memorizing verses from Psalm twenty-one was delightful as I enjoyed the Lord, my traveling companion throughout the eight-hour trip. "You make him glad with the joy of your presence. For the king trusts in the LORD, and through the steadfast love of the Most High he shall not be moved" (Psalm 21:6, 7).

The following day God helped me purchase medicines and line up interpreters for the medical team. As I took the bus and then the boat back to Koh Kong God helped with handling the three boxes of medicine plus my suitcase walking the plank to the boat. It stopped raining during the time we unloaded, keeping the baggage dry – an answer to prayer. About one hour after reaching home, it started to pour again.

Requesting official permission for the medical team was the next step. The director of the Health District was helpful in planning out destinations. Praise God he approved the island and mountain towns that Tuen had suggested. When one of the places had to be changed a couple days later, I was unable to reach the director for three days. People in the States prayed and that evening, he returned my phone call and approved the changed location. Two days later he had permission papers ready for us to take to each of the clinic sites.

November 21, 2005, Monday – the day for the arrival of the team! God gave great peace all day. I woke at 4:50 am to the sound of the aquarium pump making a noise like it was out of water. I hurried downstairs and found half of the living room floor covered with water (reminder of the floor covered with water in Phnom Penh when we had company there). The bottom of the aquarium had cracked again. I rescued the fish in the little remaining water and cleaned up the mess on the floor. Our friend phoned about 7 am that the medical team had just left on the bus from Bangkok to Trat. Hubert mowed the grass, changed the oil in his motorcycle, and then left about 10:15 am to meet the nine team members in Trat, Thailand. He arrived early afternoon precisely as they were getting off the bus. God's perfect timing. A truck brought them to the border where God helped them through knotty visa formalities. After the final five miles to our town, they got settled into rooms in a hotel and one couple at our home.

Tuesday began with formal introductions to the Health District office and a tour of the hospital. At our house, orientation included the visitors learning a few phrases in the Khmer language and planning for clinic flow. Medicines and supplies were sorted, and little packets of pills were prepared for easier dispensing at the clinics. Four Bible school students from Phnom Penh arrived to help with interpreting and evangelism.

With the Christians from Koh Kong, interpreters from Phnom Penh, and the US team, there were twenty-one of us in two vans that next morning. It took the drivers a bit to find the right road, but they got us to the water's edge. The transportation to cross the water to the town of Tuol Ta Ki was five small, low, wooden boats. One by one they were carefully loaded with supplies and people and pulled away from the bank. I arrived at the far side in the first boat to begin setting up and showing the way for the others coming. Boat two arrived. Boat three and four were almost across when they heard the four people in the last boat calling for help. Just as that boat's motor had accelerated the bow hit a small wave, which pulled it under the water. The driver and passengers were left treading water or clinging to boards and waving and calling. Dr. Anglea and Hubert knew how to swim, but the Cambodian doctor with them did not. The boat owner at the bank where they had embarked heard them and sent out yet another boat. They pulled the people out of the water. The supplies they were carrying were in zip-lock plastic bags and got retrieved from the water. Cameras and phones were damaged. We used damp medical forms all day.

People of the town invited the soaked people into their homes to dry off and offered them clothes to wear while theirs dried. Throughout the day, in the preaching and witnessing while caring for the sick, the boat that sank was talked about. "What if you had been in that boat and had drowned? Where would you spend eternity?" We thanked God for the rescue of all the people from the water and thanked Him for using the incident to help people in sin turn to Christ for rescue from everlasting punishment. We cared for about one hundred forty-five patients that day.

Our co-workers from Phnom Penh, the Freezes, joined us for the rest of the clinics. Thursday's clinic was set up under trees in Cham Yiem, a town by the Thai border. The shade from the hot sun was appreciated. Yellow tape marked off the waiting area and consultation area. A toddler with hot water burns was rushed to us for care in the middle of the day, occupying some of the staff while others continued seeing the long line of patients.

Evangelism at a Mobile Clinic

On Friday, fiberglass speed boats whizzed us about thirty-five minutes to an island town where we had done a mobile clinic one year before. We set up our clinic in a pharmacy/house with a large porch. Praise God for new Christians we met there this visit.

Koh Kapi was the island destination on Saturday. Again, we used speed boats. It took a while for the midwife there to find a key to an old unused health center building, and a bit of sweeping to make it usable. I had gotten to know her a little at Koh Kong Hospital when she did some maternity training there. Some of the team members were sick with flu so had to stay back at the hotel, but God still made the clinic flow smoothly. Returning home, we were grateful for raincoats when the downpour caught us in the open speed boats.

God used the team serving in a variety of ways in the Sunday services. Some preached, some taught Sunday School and some taught children's church. Several sang together for special music and shared testimonies. The Bible study in Kenh's home was delightful even though we got soaked in the rain going home. Praise God rain and oceans are warm and yet refreshing in the hot climate.

That night, Mike Freeze phoned from the hotel at 9 pm to say one of the two vans we had been renting was broken down and could not take us to Tema Bang in the morning. I phoned the other van driver and he said he'd try to find another. We prayed. The running van came about six in the morning as scheduled and then found another van while we waited. We did not get away until 7 am, but the delay allowed Tuen to join us again. Praise the Lord for the participation of Christians from Koh Kong throughout the week. The second van broke down on the road going up into the mountains prompting another prayer meeting. God answered again and the drivers got it fixed.

On arrival at the health post in Tema Bang, the health worker there asked me to see a pregnant lady with fever and trouble breathing. I started treatment immediately, then talked to her about the Lord. She was happy to hear about Jesus but did not make a commitment. The health worker used the radios between the health post and Koh Kong hospital to call for an ambulance. She was transferred to the hospital but died in the evening. Did she seek the Lord in time? Hubert and Tuen witnessed to people in the town while others witnessed at the clinic.

We left in time to be off the deeply rutted Tema Bang road before dark, but the main road we merged onto was muddy and slippery from recent rain and construction work. We were delayed three times by other vehicles stuck in mud. Michelle phoned when we were back in cell phone range and said she had supper ready for us all at home. Praise God for His encouraging servants ministering in many ways. We arrived home about 7:15 pm, thanking God for safety.

The sixth and final day of mobile clinics, we had eighteen team members in three speed boats. We went on the open ocean part of the way, then behind a long mountainous island. Dolphins and schools of small flying fish played beside us. On arrival at Koh Kapi, we hiked up the hill and set up the clinic. My first patient was a lady I had cared for before in Koh Kong and witnessed to back then. This day she prayed to receive Christ. Our totals for the six clinics were seven hundred seventy-seven patients cared for, many, many people who heard the gospel, and several decisions for Christ! God was working.

God continued to answer prayer as the team's time concluded. On December 4, 2005, four more Christians received baptism in the estuary. A boat took us out to a shallow enough place, and then it started to rain. Everyone got about as wet as those in the water. The following day, as I was riding my bike, a fifteen-year-old girl struck up a conversation with me. I witnessed to her and her friend, and the next day she came to the house and asked Christ to give her salvation. That same day, a young man, Lalin, who had been coming to church and to Bible studies asked the Lord to cleanse him from sin and give him eternal life. Three days later, an AIDS patient at the hospital said she wanted Christ as her Lord and Savior. Many Bible studies continued, some for new believers and some for people not yet born again. Hubert had an evangelistic Bible study that met three days a week. God was showing His love and grace.

God's people were praying for the 2005 Christmas celebration in Koh Kong. The Christmas eve church family dinner was a great blessing. Nineteen people, which included Lalin, the newest believer and also a few unsaved family members of other believers gathered around. We sang, ate, and shared testimonies and verses about what God had done. It was such a precious time of loving fellowship in the Lord. Our hearts were thrilled to see this body of believers that God brought to Himself and to each other.

CHAM YIEM

Across the toll bridge and nestled on the side of hills overlooking the ocean, about six miles northwest of the main town of Koh Kong, was the town of Cham Yiem. The name means "waiting and watching," which was an apt name for guarding a border check point into Thailand. After holding mobile medical clinics in Cham Yiem and witnessing to people along the dirt streets multiple times, a weekly children's Bible class was begun. At first there were up to forty children coming. Occasionally, adults stood on the outskirts, listened, and then walked on. The class met on the sidewalk in front of a candy store with a little roof overhang protecting from the burning sun and sudden rains. Several of the children sat on a low wooden bed-like platform about two feet high, a "kda" (It was a common piece of furniture in most Khmer homes used for sleeping or working or visiting.). Other children stood.

One Sunday afternoon when Pren and I went to teach, we learned that the father of one of our most faithful students had been murdered six days previously. Pren had witnessed to him, and I had witnessed to his wife many times. That day I talked with the widow while she was preparing food for a ceremony at the pagoda the following day. Over the course of a couple years, we had a good group for a while, learning the Bible lessons and verses and songs, but then those students would stop. The area was very Buddhist. Some parents refused to let their children continue when they understood that we were teaching that Jesus is the only way to God. Yet the Lord brought others to hear. One young teen girl that received Christ moved away soon after.

There was a new chapter in the story of God's work in Cham Yiem. One day at the hospital, I was talking to a little girl who was a patient, and her father, about the gospel. The father's face lit up. He shared his testimony of when he received Christ while in a refugee camp during the time of the Khmer Rouge. Since coming to Cham Yiem, he could not find a church. He was right, Cham Yiem did not have any. But I told him of Koh Kong Baptist Church in Koh Kong, and of the children's Bible class in Cham Yiem. The next Sunday he brought five children to the class. He said it would be good if we could meet in a building. Later, he phoned that he had found a large house we could use for free to teach in. It was in the small village of Kong Nong down the road from Cham Yiem. That village had about twenty-five houses, one of which was his house. He wanted his neighbors to hear. So, God worked that a second class was begun near Cham Yiem. The new one met at 2:45 pm and the original one at 3:45 pm Sunday afternoons.

The youth from Koh Kong Baptist Church faithfully taught God's Word and poured into the lives of the families of these two towns. Eventually, the class in Cham Yiem proper was stopped. In Kong Nong, the house to meet in was no longer offered, but there was a kda under a tree at the entrance to the town which became our meeting place. Sometimes, when we arrived for class, we went around to homes to call the children to come. One mother told us that her son loved to sing songs praising the name of Jesus. Another time, Lalin went to the swimming hole to call the boys to come. The class became too large to study all together, so it was divided with the older children meeting a little way off from the younger ones. Since we were meeting outside, distractions during the lessons were common, including dogs fighting, and once a child was stung by a scorpion. The students prized the handcrafts each week and worked diligently. Over the years of teaching in Kong Nong, God worked in the hearts of several of the children.

When it was time to leave for furlough, four of the Koh Kong young people spent an evening at the ocean with us. A little pond nearby had paddle boats which we rode until it started to rain. We walked and talked and made memories. Lalin drew in the sand a picture of Christ returning in the clouds. What blessed hope.

Chapter 7

Koh Kong 2007-2011

*Consecrate yourselves, for tomorrow the Lord will
do wonders among you.*
Joshua 3:5

THE GROWING CHURCH

God continued to build His church in Koh Kong. Lalin had continued teaching Bible studies while we were away for furlough. Tuen preached on Sundays. Upon our return, the meetings were moved back to our home to have more space than at the home of one of the believers where they had been meeting. New people came from Hubert's English classes, from the hospital, and from other towns. God kept giving opportunities to teach Bible classes. The joy of the Cambodian Christians learning to teach Bible lessons to the children was exciting to see. Short termers teaching God's Word was an encouragement to the church as well.

A Sunday afternoon Bible study continued at Kenh's house. One visit, filthy water from the high tide stirred up garbage floating under the complex of houses on stilts. It covered the wooden catwalks. Kenh provided clean water from their big clay pot to wash my feet. After class, I walked back to the shore where my bicycle was parked. Just at that moment, a lady was trying to "borrow" my bike but could not get the kickstand up. "Thank you, Lord, for making the kickstand stick." I was happy to take my bike and ride home. A couple weeks later, walking back on the same catwalks, now at lower tide, a Cambodian girl ahead of me slipped off the boards. I helped her back up. Another time Kenh herself fell from the rickety walks. We thanked God each time we safely traversed those precarious pathways.

God gave encounters with a new group of people when Hubert was asked to teach English to the governor of our province and the general of the military. Late September, lessons began in the governor's office each morning at 7 am. That led to Hubert teaching several officials, some of them at their homes. After some years, when the governor was transferred to a position in Phnom Penh, he requested a teacher like Hubert to continue teaching English to him. God provided another missionary to hold out the light to him there.

On the Cambodian calendar, dates of holidays were printed in red. But December 25 was black like ordinary days. Koh Kong had no malls with Christmas music. No colored lights and beautiful decorations. Most people had no concept of snow in a land averaging eighty-six degrees Fahrenheit. One little restaurant put up a scraggly Christmas tree for the few tourists who passed through. Some English classes had Christmas parties and talked about Santa Claus. It was part of learning about other cultures. In a Buddhist and Muslim community there was no interest in giving attention to Christ and the commemoration of His coming to earth to die for us over 2,000 years ago.

But for the believers, it was a different story. Children and teens from two families in the church helped us decorate our house. We had a brightly lit Christmas tree with an angel on top. Bells, stars, little wreaths, and other decorations were hung from the security bars in the windows. A little first-grader delightedly punched out figures for the Christmas story from a bulletin board kit I had found in a missionary cupboard on furlough. After placing each figure, she would call, "Auntie, look!" Christmas cards from years before were taped up and down the banister. Most of our new cards arrived after Christmas.

The young people got together extra times to practice special songs to offer praise to God. Youth and adults were digging into the book of Acts preparing for the Christmas Bible quiz. A big Christmas party/hamburger fry was being held for outreach to unsaved students in Hubert's English classes. But the highlight was the Christmas meal with the people of the church. Before eating, there was singing. After the meal was a time for reflection on things God had done the past year in our individual lives and in our church. Glory and praise were given to His great name. And yes, there was time on Sunday, just before Christmas to quietly read the Christmas story and sing Christmas songs in gratitude to God for descending to earth, becoming man, and dwelling among us. With it was the anticipation of His coming again – perhaps in the arriving new year 2008.

God used Petros to witness to his high school friend, Wichet. When Wichet professed faith in Christ, his mother kicked him out of the house. He was permitted to return home and eat with his family again by renouncing Christ. However, God did not give up on him. After two years, Wichet turned to the Lord and his life beamed with evidence that he was born again. God then used Wichet to lead his mother, Wi, to Christ. Wi had a lot of questions at first about the trinity, why a sacrifice was needed for sin, and many other things. She avidly read through a sketch picture book of the Bible as well as read the Scriptures. Her witness to people at mobile medical clinics was strong and clear, explaining why following the true God is right rather than worshiping at ancestor altars. Her husband threatened to divorce her if she continued to follow Christ and attend church. God answered prayer and her husband stayed another six years before leaving her.

The church studied doctrines of Scripture for the church doctrinal statement and church covenant. That was followed by making a church constitution. July 13, 2008, Koh Kong Baptist Church officially organized with nine charter members. It was a time of joy and unity as they promised to pray for each other. About six weeks later, in answer to prayer, God moved our Buddhist landlady to offer to ask the police for permission to put up a sign for the church. A sign was made in Phnom Penh. Displaying it on our gate in Koh Kong was an invitation to all to come. Sunday morning attendance rose to twenty-seven and the evening around eleven – many of them youth, different from the morning families. To train leaders for the church, Hubert taught an Old Testament survey course three days a week with six of the Christian young people. After that, they studied more doctrine, and then other Bible topics, like a Bible Institute. It was wonderful to see their eagerness to learn and diligence in doing assigned homework. Two of the young men who were interested in becoming pastors were taught preaching.

A tall antenna stood at the edge of the estuary beaming FM radio waves throughout Koh Kong province and into Thailand. Early October 2008, when Hubert talked with the local FM radio station, they were favorable toward a weekly fifteen-minute program teaching the Bible. We prayed God would use this "Bible Study Hour" to get the gospel to a wide area. In January 2009, recording, and re-recording the first programs began. But when the first CD was taken to the radio station, they rejected it, stating we had to get permission from the local Department of Religion. That office required us to have a church permit before allowing the radio program.

So, pursuit of permission for Koh Kong Baptist Church began. Our local Department of Religion required any religious group regularly meeting to have a permit, unlike some others in Phnom Penh that only required it of larger groups. The permit needed to be obtained through the national Ministry of Religions and Cults (MORC) in Phnom Penh, but they hadn't issued any in recent years. There followed months of praying, visiting offices, and waiting. In May, the Phnom Penh MORC finally had the applications available, and Hubert picked up the form and got the first of many stamps and signatures required. However, within a couple weeks, the MORC put out different forms. We were thankful that in that short period of time we had obtained initial papers which were allowed to be exchanged for the new application. Of course, we had to start over getting stamps and signatures from various offices.

We continued to ask people to pray for the proper papers and proper signatures to have the church legal and to enable us to begin the radio program. Eleven church members signed and put their thumbprints on the page listing members. Throughout June and July, the stack of forms was completed multiple times trying to satisfy the various offices. In August, Hubert got signatures from one more of the offices in Koh Kong, but the following office seemed to want a large bribe. They demanded an additional paper, and it would need signatures all over again from all the previous levels. It seemed an impossible situation. But God could not be stopped. Hubert took the papers to the governor, his English student and friend, who was happy to help. His office got the required signatures from the lesser offices and then the last one on the list, the governor's own signature. Hubert picked up the completed application papers on September 1, 2009, and the next day we took them to Phnom Penh.

The account in Mark 5 of Jesus telling Jarius not to fear but believe, and then demonstrating his power by restoring life, was my devotions that next morning. About the same hour, Hubert was trying to turn in the completed church permit application to MORC, but the office refused it. We went back together in the afternoon, and I prayed that as Jesus had raised Jarius' daughter to life, He would use His power and make the office accept the paperwork. God answered! They took the papers. Next, we prayed the permit would soon be granted.

Waiting teaches patience. Often there would be several months seeing no one turn to Christ, but then there were times of great harvest. One short-term missionary couple lived and worked with us and the Freezes for four months while their church in Cleveland was praying. It was amazing to see five decisions for Christ in one week! The first was a patient at the hospital. The second was a young man at church on Sunday. Monday a fifteen-year-old student prayed asking Jesus to save him. Tuesday the wife of one of the church members made a profession of faith. Wednesday the mother of one of the believers at church trusted in the Lord. They were all people that we had witnessed to for a long time. The angels rejoiced and so did we.

Seeing God use so many of His people in teaching His Word brought us joy. One day, Petros joined me and helped teach a Bible lesson at the hospital TB ward. A new believer at the hospital encouraged another patient to read the Bible. At McKong hamburger shop, which Lalin ran, Lalin taught a lesson from Matthew to some of his workers. Back at our house, our short-termer taught a new believer, while his wife witnessed to the neighbor girl. Hubert visited Nok Siem, the father of one of his English students to help him know more of Christ. Another lady in the church expressed concern for her nephew's salvation.

LEKANA

Among the children laughing, running, and skating in front of our house was Lekana. When she and her friends reached high school, they would pop by during a free hour between classes and play our Blokus game or do puzzles. They also tackled learning proper English language pronunciation, comprehension, and much more in Hubert's daily English classes. Sunday evenings found them singing in English and listening to messages in both English and Khmer explaining about the true and living God. Visiting her family at their home several times, God allowed us to witness to her parents and sisters. At times they seemed interested, other times not. Lekana clearly was not.

But God was working in Lekana's heart. Gradually after hearing the gospel many times over several years, she began discussing with us about the Lord, getting her questions answered. When we asked her if she wanted to receive Christ, she replied, "After my sister's wedding." True to her word, three days after the wedding, she walked into our home and said, "I'm ready." She wanted to become a new person in Christ. Praise God for saving her. Her life burst with joy. Yet, she feared a strong reaction from her parents and rejection from her friends. At first, she did not want to tell them. But God gave her courage to tell her father and he responded that she had made the right decision. She was surprised and relieved. It was some time later when she told her mother and met an angry response. But God guarded her and gave grace needed. Eventually, she told her friends, and they remained her friends. Lekana was a diligent student as she came daily to study God's Word. She was excited about her new life in Christ and loved God's Word speaking to her heart. "Therefore, if anyone is in Christ, he is a new creation" (2 Corinthians 5:17).

Lekana was eager to be baptized. It was decided to have the baptismal service at the shore of the estuary rather than take a boat out to the center where the water was cleaner. The church people and some of her friends came on motorcycles and bicycles to watch. Three monkeys peered down from the trees. What Pastor Hubert discovered once in the water, was that it was a narrow strip of waist deep water and then a drop-off behind them. God protected and the baptism was safely performed.

Teaching English

MORE OUTREACHES

Boating up that same estuary another day, God answered prayer and made the wind calm so we could travel safely to the island town of Kau Pao. On arrival, we walked through the length of the town meeting people. Most of the men were gone to places of work since it was late morning. Women sat down in groups to listen as we shared with them the gospel message and gave them tracts. For most of them, it was the first time they had heard about the true God. We were thrilled to see God cause them to listen so well. We anticipated returning to that town again to water the seed planted, perhaps also bringing a Christian video and a mobile medical clinic. We asked God's people to pray for wisdom and fruit. Returning home was a relaxing ride in the fishing boat, passing sand-dredging boats and mangroves. The boat driver rigged up a cloth on poles to provide shade from the sun high overhead. The sunbeams scattered sparkles across the water reminding us again of God's promises.

The children in Kong Nong, the border town, were excited to prepare the 2009 Christmas program. For several weeks they practiced acting out the nativity story. Wi used her seamstress skills for the Lord in making Christmas play costumes. She went with us to Kong Nong and measured each of the children who had a part. She also shared her testimony with ladies in the town, relating how God saved her and could save them. In less than a week, she had all ten costumes completed and the children eagerly had their dress rehearsal.

On the Sunday before Christmas, Hubert and Lalin transported ten Kong Nong children and youth to the church in Koh Kong. Lekana and another young lady served them rice with meat for breakfast since most of them had not eaten before coming. About forty people enjoyed the Christmas service. After the songs and sermon, Wi and another lady helped the children with their costumes and the curtains (sheets over a wire strung across the room). The play was eagerly presented even though the actors often had their backs to the audience and only the listeners in the front rows could hear. At the completion, the children faced the audience, recited Psalm twenty-three and salvation verses, and sang so sweetly. At 3 pm, some of the church youth and I went to Kong Nong and helped as the same cast performed the Christmas play there for their own town. We prayed God would help people to understand God's love and plan of redemption. Riding back home on our motorcycles sometime later, God gave us a big beautiful double rainbow. Crossing the mile-long bridge over the estuary, it looked like the ends of the rainbow were on each side of us, plunging into the water. We passed under it and looked back, but it had vanished.

One and a half years after the radio station had put a hold on airing our Bible Study program, Hubert visited them again. New people had replaced the previous staff. They were satisfied that the church permit application had been approved by the local offices, even though Phnom Penh MORC still had not issued the actual permit. Work on preparing programs resumed. Lalin helped Hubert translate them into Khmer and then read them into a microphone wired to the computer. A little tweaking with the recording program on the computer made them ready to burn onto a CD. April 29, 2010, a contract with the radio station was signed!

Three days later we huddled by our tiny battery-run radio, since our electricity was off, and heard the first program airing! A neighbor listened with us. Each week, Hubert delivered a CD to the station. The following day, God's message was heralded to the mountains and islands of southwestern Cambodia and to the Cambodians across the border in Thailand. We heard that many people were listening.

Later, the Christians prepared a seven-act play about four Cambodians who, one by one, came to know the Lord. Many questions Cambodians have about Christianity were answered in it. While practicing one day before recording, we could hear a monk chanting loudly over a speaker at a funeral a block away. I prayed that sound would not get on the recording. Just as they began to record, the chanting stopped! The radio play was aired at a different time than the ongoing chronological Bible study. Our landlord told me that once when he heard me listening to the play, he tuned in at his house also.

The Koh Kong Department of Religion started pressing us for the church permit that Phnom Penh MORC still had not issued. The local office then required us to submit to them a quarterly report of our weekly attendance, how many men and how many women, and what the sermons were about. Hubert gave them the Bible reference that he preached on for each sermon, and the statistics. We prayed God would give us favor in their eyes, since they had authority to shut down churches. Praise God that over the ensuing years, they were satisfied with our faithful compliance.

We finally heard through missionaries in the capital that the Phnom Penh MORC was looking at our church permit application. They required more photos. Lalin made the trip to the capital to provide those. The next month they requested a service fee before proceeding. The church sent funds with Tuen who went to meet with them. And again, we waited for the permit.

Making roads in Koh Kong usually meant laying down split bamboo for reinforcement and then pouring cement from buckets as it was mixed on site. Cement trucks were only for big cities. We were delighted that we would soon have a paved road, but right in front of our house, where the church met, the pour was slated for Sunday morning! We prayed God would help people be able to get in and out of the gate for church. God sent rain so the cement crew stopped until later in the day. God's people worshiped together as scheduled.

TEMA BANG

In the mountain town of Tema Bang about two hours away we did door-to-door evangelism many times and then began weekly trips to teach the few Christians. Hubert would take one of the young men of the church to teach a children's class. Sometimes, many children gathered for the Bible lessons. Other times, they were busy with their families, planting peanuts or harvesting bananas. The motorcycle took spills a few times on the rugged terrain, but God protected everyone from serious injury. The beautiful rivers and streams were occasionally picnic spots. In the rainy season it was muddy and slippery, and the streams were harder to ford. Upon returning home one trip, the motorcycle clutch handle broke off right in our yard. God had guarded that it did not happen while up on the mountain roads.

A Ferry Crossing

One Sunday after the morning church service in Koh Kong ended, one of the Christians from the mountain town arrived. She had traveled to the town of Koh Kong that morning. We had a good Bible lesson together. She said her life had changed when she received the Lord. She was gentle instead of gruff. Neighbors criticized her for following Christ. She said her husband believed in Christ before he died. She had been blessed with ten children but five died of malaria and dengue fever. She asked if Christians eat pork and how they are buried, because her neighbors had told her they were thrown in the river. We prayed that God would cause visitors to catch a vision of the need and return to concentrate on reaching the island and mountain towns.

Mobile medical clinics were held in the area towns several times. One of those times, Hubert went around town inviting people to see a gospel video. When it got dark, we set it up in a building that had electricity. Only about twenty people came and most left before the end, but we were grateful to God that the equipment worked, and the DVD did not quit part way through. The speakers were loud enough in spite of music coming from other establishments. Many people were praying.

There was one restaurant in town. The owner invited us to spend the night in her home. She gave us two bedrooms with beds and nets. Once tucked under the mosquito net, I saw a spotted twelve-inch Tokay Gecko adhering high on the wooden wall beside me. It was good to know this nocturnal hunter would be after the unwanted insects and mice, but I prayed his loud Tokay call and strong bite would not interrupt our sleep. God faithfully protected us. In the morning we began the drive home, stopping to be led by a guide through the woods to a large, majestic hidden waterfall. What an awesome creation of our great God. Perhaps a deterrent to many people making the hike were the leaches that hitched a ride back with some of our group.

Some Christian motorcycle riders from the States came to have an outreach to the mountains. The teams loaded the motorcycles with equipment and supplies for working and staying a few nights in villages, including mosquito nets and a portable water filter. In spite of falls, the heat, a fallen tree blocking the road, a snake, and other surprises, over thirty watched the gospel videos in one town, over sixty people in a second town, and over one hundred in the farthest town. Most of the people in that town had never heard the gospel. They practiced Satan worship. There were many opportunities for witnessing one-on-one also. While the men were traveling, God blessed a special four-day ladies Bible study we held in Koh Kong.

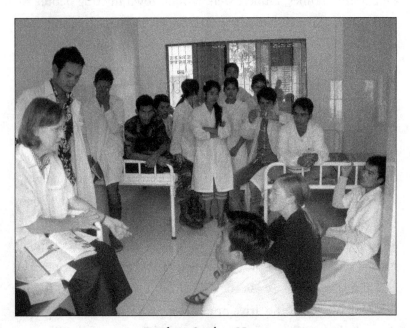

Teaching Student Nurses

For a few months the Sunday trips to Tema Bang were discontinued, but then God brought Sam. Sam was bitten by a snake and was rushed from Tema Bang to the hospital in Koh Kong. There he received care including anti-venom. During his recovery in the hospital, he heard of salvation through Christ several times. He repented and opened his heart to the Lord Jesus. When he went back home, Hubert and Lalin started weekly trips to Tema Bang again to teach him more of God's Word. They also taught the children. Many times, they witnessed to other people around, but drunkenness was a real problem and people would laugh at them. One man, in particular, Van, Sam's cousin, would call to Hubert and mock him in front of others. Hubert hoped he would not meet him again. But one day Hubert met him and saw he was sober. As they talked Van said he had never learned anything about Christ before and wanted to listen.

The next time Van met Hubert, he invited him to his house and showed him his banana farm. He said he would like to study God's Word weekly. After studying a few weeks, Van turned to the Lord for salvation. Saturday mornings my sisters in the USA, and I in Koh Kong, met and prayed together over the internet. That day we were praying for Hubert and Lalin while they were teaching Van. Van quit drinking alcohol and was eager to learn about the Lord. He was only semiliterate so appreciated hearing cassettes of the New Testament and listening to our radio Bible study. Lalin continued to teach him.

MEDICAL WORK IN KOH KONG

Medical missions is an exciting calling! The Lord allows His servants to introduce people to the God of the universe, their Creator, to teach His infallible Word day after day, and to care for people with medical needs. There is great variety in the individuals one meets from high status to low and all sorts of characters. The diverse medical needs presented are definitely interesting and challenging. Every activity, each day, needed to be saturated with prayer.

God taught me that when I prayed before procedures such as lumbar punctures and abscess aspirations, they went smoother.

When patients heard me pray, it helped them know God was there. Depending on the Lord, He helped me interpreting ultrasounds and X-rays. One day, nearly all the ultrasounds were abnormal, including a molar pregnancy (a tumor), a mass and blood clot between the liver and diaphragm, a suprapubic tumor with necrosis, and others. Abnormal X-rays that day were a patient with dextrocardia (the heart in the right side of the chest instead of the left) and another with pneumothorax (air between the chest wall and the lungs).

Among some of the AIDS patients, a patient's mother said her daughter had no more hope. When I explained real hope that is in Jesus Christ, a girl in another bed asked me to help her pray and receive Christ. She had tears in her eyes. She had heard of Christ before in Phnom Penh. Another day, I heard patients calling another patient "Kon Preah" – "Child of God," because she had started recovering after I prayed with her. I am glad they saw it was God who healed, but sadly she and her family did not repent and ask God to bring them into His family.

One patient who was studying the Bible with me was putting her Gospel of John under her pillow to keep from having night-mares. I suppose it replaced a knife or scissors the Khmer often put under the pillow of sick people or new babies to try to keep away evil spirits. More praying and teaching were needed. The Bible is not a good luck charm. Assisting the birth of new babies takes patience and waiting but at the right time, the infant arrives.

Watching Cambodians being born into God's family also takes time and patience, but it is thrilling to see the new life.

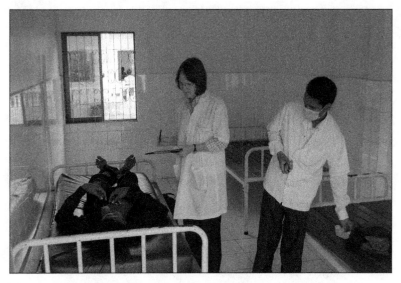

Admitting a new patient at Koh Kong Hospital

One of the trips escorting patients overland to Thailand was for a small child with hemorrhagic dengue fever. Because his platelet count was getting so low, a short-termer, Elizabeth Morrison, and I went with the child and his mother to Klang Yai Hospital, in a coastal town across the border. God helped us find meals in town to take back for the mother in spite of our not speaking Thai language. The child's aunt arrived in a couple of days to take over care of the patient and his mother. He recovered fine and returned home.

Walking on a pier between boats and buildings in Klang Yai, Elizabeth and I watched mudskippers, which are amphibious fish. Lots of them wiggled in the mud under houses on stilts. Using their pectoral fins and pelvic fins to walk on land looked so amusing, resembling having front legs but dragging back legs. The dorsal fin on their back would alternately fan up very big, or fold down. They could be out of water for extended periods of time and were quite active in the mud at low tide. In the water, they swam like fish.

Our next trip to Thailand, three weeks later, was to meet an American pharmacy student coming to work with us. The motorcycle taxis we had asked to take us to the border at 10 am did not show up. So we walked a bit and found others. Our first stop was Klang Yai Hospital again to check on a different patient that had been transferred from our Koh Kong hospital. The Lord helped us find him. He was in a ward and his attending doctor was at his bedside right at that moment! We were able to discuss the labs, X-rays, and plans.

Later, walking in town after a stop at the bank, Elizabeth's shoe broke, making it difficult to walk. In answer to prayer, a short distance further a shoe-repairman had set up business on the sidewalk; God's doing. I never saw him there any other time.

We took a van from Klang Yai to Trat, then God provided a pick-up-truck-taxi to take us the forty-five minutes to the rural airport. But we were disappointed that the pick-up did not agree to wait for the plane and take us back. Since there were only two flights a day, there was little transportation available. When the student arrived, God provided a ride back to town in a nice van that kept the luggage dry. It was much better than the truck we had ridden in to the airport. God's ways are always better than our own.

At home in Koh Kong, we sometimes ate supper on the second-floor porch to enjoy the evening cooler air outside. One day our two American students met a French girl in town who had just arrived to volunteer at an orphanage. We invited her to join us for supper, along with Lalin and Pren. That made three languages among seven people. Hubert and I kept switching between French, Cambodian, and English, depending who we were talking to or interpreting for. It was a lot of fun. God allowed us to witness to the French girl a little and invite her to church. We prayed He would draw her to Himself.

Those short-term students participated in many ministries. In three days of mobile medical clinics in remote towns we treated about 364 patients. The patients, along with family members who brought them, heard the gospel presented and received tracts. God showed He was in control. Even though it was the rainy season, the rains did not interfere with our travel or with people coming to the clinics. God helped us cross rivers on broken bridges, ford others, get through mud holes, edge through a herd of cows on a narrow road, and get around fallen trees.

We were able to show a DVD of the story of Noah in one town where we spent the night, sleeping in the health post. Down the road from the health post a bridge had recently washed away. When the local midwife went home, she walked through the waist-deep river, holding a rope tied from bank to bank to steady herself from the fast-flowing current, and with the other hand steadied a bundle on her head.

Some of the Cambodian hospital staff and Christians from the church participated in each of the clinics. God allowed us to have good talks about the claims of Christ with a couple of the Cambodian doctors who went with us even though at one point we were surrounded by lots of big mosquitoes. We prayed for God's continued work in hearts. Some of the people from one of those towns came to our home later to discuss further about the Lord. Working together at the hospital and meeting people in our home and theirs, hearts bonded. The love of Christ was seen. On the morning of their departure, several people came and sat with the two short-termers. Hospital staff and people from the church comprised a group of seventeen people at the border to say good-bye to them. There were hugs and tears. I accompanied them to Trat, and the next morning they flew out on the 9 am flight.

On one of my on-call days at the hospital, Hubert took me at 7:30 am with my blanket, pillow, etc. which I tucked in the ultrasound room for use in the evening. The on-call doctor was responsible for all emergencies and admissions for the next twenty-four hours, and then worked a regular day after that. It was a windy and rainy morning, so the hospital was not very busy. But in the afternoon, there were several patients who came. Among those admitted was a sixty-five-year-old lady with an epigastric mass, dyspnea, and cardiac irregularity. Another was a sixty-five-year-old man with urinary retention. Then there was a lady eight months pregnant who had vertigo. A couple of children with pneumonia were pretty sick on the ward. God showed His sufficiency to help me caring for patients.

Hubert brought lunch and supper and we ate together. There was time to talk and pray with a Christian patient from a far island. I made a note to bring her a Bible the following day. She said hers back home was worn out. It was interesting to watch life at the hospital after hours. The hospital did not get quiet until 10 pm. God allowed me to get quite a bit of sleep that night. The nurse called me a couple times and a patient's family once. Breakfast in the morning was a little granola I had brought with me. Then there were the next day's inpatient rounds and outpatients to see. Just after 11 am I walked home. It was nice to be home, fix lunch, fold clothes, and teach the children's lesson to Pren and Lalin, to prepare them to teach on Sunday. At 2 pm I went back to the hospital until 4:45 pm. The outpatient receptionist asked for a clock for her department, which led to a trip to the market to purchase one.

Then I visited two Khmer ladies at a facility that helped rescue girls twelve to twenty-two years old who had been raped or were victims of trafficking. One of the ladies working was a Khmer Christian who had recently come to Koh Kong. After that she started coming to church. A few days later she brought a mother and baby to our house for a medical consult for the child's cough. Earlier, the parents had been caught by the police trying to sell the baby. Occasionally, people imprisoned for that offense were brought to the hospital for care, wearing prison uniforms.

About that time, Sen, a patient who had received Christ about three years earlier and then moved to Phnom Penh, moved back to Koh Kong. She had been hospitalized three times in the previous month and was not doing well. That day when I saw her, she was crying in pain. I was alone with her in the ultrasound room and asked her more about her past. She had shared bits of her story before. She said she was sold into the sex trade at the age of six, being an orphan. It was in a town in the northwest of Cambodia, and she knew the person who sold her. Someone bought her freedom when she was thirteen-years-old but she was recaptured at four-teen. She escaped at about sixteen when a foreigner helped her. I first met her at eighteen-years-old, alone in the world and suffering from AIDS and TB.

The hospital was out of all analgesics stronger than an anti-inflammatory medicine, so I went and searched the three pharmacies in town and brought her something to help ease the pain. I read Scripture with her, and we prayed together again. She died about 4 am the next morning. I saw the hospital workers carrying out the body. I was sad. How alone she was. But I knew God had saved her and she had moved into the joyful presence of Christ in heaven.

Construction of several new hospital buildings and remodeling of the old ones began November 28, 2007. Within a few weeks a bulldozer was shoving chunks of old foundation around right in front of the out-patient consultation room. The windows and doors were open, and it provided a great view of the activity. However, it was challenging to hear patients' heart and lung sounds with my stethoscope. About one hundred laborers came from provinces all over Cambodia. We prayed for a way to witness to them and began by talking about the Lord to a few families of the workers who were camped on the hospital grounds.

Koh Kong Hospital Buildings

Then I asked the director of the health district if we could show a Christian video. He consented on condition that we also show a health video he would provide. On the chosen date, when it got dark, we set up the computer and projector for the two DVDs. While a malaria presentation was running, we walked around inviting construction workers and patients to come. While the gospel DVD was showing, people came and went, with perhaps fifty seeing parts of it. Two-thirds of the way through, the DVD quit. Hubert and Lalin talked to the listeners about God's offer of salvation. In spite of the small turn-out and the DVD stopping, we prayed God would use it according to His plan. After one year of building, the hospital staff began to move into the beautiful new complex of twelve buildings.

They were connected with covered sidewalks to protect from rain and sun. New landscaping brightened the grounds. It was sad to see the hospital staff all seated on a mat for a Buddhist ceremony of dedication with offerings to spirits.

One morning in mid-2008, I took Hubert the twenty minutes to the Thai border before it opened at 7 am. He was to travel to Bangkok to meet two more short-termers. When I got home, I saw his backpack still at home. He had grabbed the wrong one – the one with tools for his motorcycle. Since there was no way to reach him, I went ahead to the hospital and did an ultrasound for a mother in labor. A few patients later, I got a call from Hubert. He had returned to the border and used someone's phone when he discovered the backpack mix-up. He asked me to bring the right one to him. At the same moment, I was asked to start the outpatient consultations since there was no other doctor around to do it. I went home and engaged a motorcycle-taxi to take Hubert's backpack to him and bring back the one with tools. Returning to the hospital I finished helping a child with anemia get on her way to Phnom Penh, helped a patient with a neck mass, and turned the outpatient clinic over to a Cambodian doctor who arrived. During lunch break I prepared guest rooms in our home. The following afternoon Hubert returned with two new short-termers.

Another on-call night at the hospital God was my help. One of the patients was brought having tried to commit suicide by eating pesticide. She had symptoms of organophosphate poisoning, like I had seen in Africa twenty-five years earlier. I could not find enough atropine at the hospital to treat her, but her husband went to a pharmacy in town and bought some. She responded to high doses and later went home fine.

A month before the January 2008 medical team arrived, God clearly worked that I was able to meet the right people in the

Provincial Health Department (PHD) and they quickly agreed to my request for the mobile clinic sites and processed the papers! A couple of weeks later found me in Phnom Penh borrowing fifteen life vests and four air mattresses from another missionary (After the boat sinking two years previously, we used life vests each boat trip.). At the open market I got big clean empty fish food sacks for transporting the life vests. After purchasing them I noticed a peculiar odor of fish food. I hoped that would not permeate the life vests. I bought other supplies and medicines for the clinics and sent the shipment via a pick-up truck going to Koh Kong, then traveled myself the following day.

Like many previous times, on the day of the team's arrival, the morning started with water spraying in the bathroom from a leak. God was reminding us of our need to depend on Him in everything. Hubert got the problem hose replaced before crossing the border to Thailand to meet the guests arriving from the States. Over the next ten days, we saw God provide for every detail.

Mobile clinics were held in four towns. The first one, Cham Yiem, was near where we had weekly children's Bible classes. The Sunday after the clinic, some of the ladies expressed appreciation for the relief they had gotten from their medical treatments and were attentive as the Word of God was taught.

The second town was on an island in the mangrove swamps. Mangrove trees grow in saltwater in tropical coastal areas and have numerous buttress roots. Tuen's slow fishing boat and one speed boat transported our team of sixteen people through dolphin territory in the ocean. The third site was in the mountains. Although we had to wait for a pile of sand in the road to be leveled, we thanked God that the road was being repaired right then and most of the rivers and streams had bridges that time. There was a crowd waiting for us.

The fourth town was only accessible by four-wheeled vehicle in the dry season when the big river near it was low enough to ford. God provided vehicles for us to borrow and drive ourselves for that trip. The "mayor's office" building, a rickety wooden building on stilts, containing only a rough table and a couple chairs in it, was designated by the village chief for our use. After cleaning it, we set up our clinic and began. The gospel was presented in preaching and witnessing during the medical clinics, and a Christian DVD was shown after dark. The men on our team camped in that building that night, and the ladies were in a house.

The next morning, we held clinic again, with people arriving from towns further away. Then we packed up, thanked the chief, and signed his registry. God had sent a nice rain in the night to settle the dust, but it also raised the level of the river a little. When fording the river to go back home, both vehicles had trouble going up the steep sandy bank on the other side. We tried many things for a long time with a few of the people from town assisting. Finally, in answer to prayer, the first truck made it up and pulled the second with a borrowed long rope. Further along the road, a freshly fallen tree barricaded the way. We prayed and God helped us get around it. It was great to see again the Cambodian Christians from Koh Kong church excited to serve the Lord in outreach together with the Christians from the USA.

God orchestrates every situation. One of the things the team left with us was a recent article on AIDS medications. I took it to the AIDS clinic a few days after the team's departure. Right at that moment, one of the Cambodian doctors was seeing a patient that needed to start on a medicine that was new to us. The article supplied the dosing information needed.

On another occasion, three patients were admitted to the hospital at night with pufferfish intoxication. Some of their friends who had consumed the poisonous fish did not live to make it to the hospital and one died right after arrival. All pufferfish have pointed spines and most live in tropical, salty water. Trained chefs can cut these fish in a way to avoid the poison or people can eat the non-poisonous varieties of pufferfish. Thankfully our admitted patients survived and hopefully avoided those fish after that.

The hospital staff really appreciated a visiting internist from Virginia who taught on rounds and lectured late mornings and late afternoons. One of the patients who came while he was there had burns from contact with a live power line. An eighteen-year-old boy had an unusual skin disorder. A prisoner had Meniere disease. One of the days of the specialist's visit a clinic was held at a health center along the main road about one-and-a-half hours away. More than one hundred patients were cared for. Tuen gave the devotional in the morning and Lalin in the afternoon. There was very little rain until on the way home, when it poured. Praise the Lord for answering the prayers of many people for that ministry

Another time, a patient whom God had saved was getting worse. I sat with him, read Scripture with him, and prayed. In the afternoon he was a little better, but at midnight the Lord took him to his celestial home. I thanked God for salvation He gives. At times the hospital was bustling with action, but then there were times one could sit and talk with people unrushed. Sometimes opportunities open while sitting and waiting which cannot happen while we are running.

KIM

Kim's house was on stilts over the water, with their little fiberglass speedboat parked by the back door. Her husband's occupation was taxiing people in his boat. Their son studied English with Hubert.

Kim's husband took her to Phnom Penh and to Vietnam trying to get help for her progressive neurologic illness, but the diagnosis and recommendations were the same as the American specialists that I contacted. She felt frustrated that the treatments could not reverse her disease and she kept returning to traditional remedies, which were equally ineffective. As her ability to walk decreased, she was embarrassed to leave her house and have the neighbors see her.

As Kim studied God's Word with me, she understood Jesus could help her on her journey. She made a profession of faith but later said she could not give up all other gods. She admitted she had only tried to become a Christian to see if that would heal her. She returned to spirit worship. Christians from the church urged her to truly turn to Christ. Wi had much compassion for Kim, their sons were school friends, and she did a great job explaining God's Word to her.

After I had been teaching her for one and a half years, her husband brought her to church. He carried her from their motorcycle to a chair inside. It was her only time to make it out to church. Her husband usually worked on Sundays, and she would not let anyone else lift her. Kim told Lalin that she wanted to follow Christ, this time for real. I was disappointed that after the service some of the Christians talked more about her physical health and their suggested remedies than about her spiritual health and encouragement in Christ and His Word.

Kim's family dog liked only the family, so if Kim was home alone, it was difficult to get past the dog. When the dog had puppies, we especially appreciated Kim's daughter restraining the dog and holding its mouth shut as we walked past. Visits to her home continued and she affirmed that she sincerely trusted in the Lord. Christ had come into her life to reside. Each week she wanted to send her offering to the Lord back to church. She asked for a songbook.

She listened to J. Vernon McGee's "Through the Bible" in Khmer on the radio. Hubert bought a wheelchair in Phnom Penh for the church to have if she returned. I enjoyed teaching her. Each time a group from church went to visit her, we would sit on the wood floor around where she lay on her mat, singing together, and taking turns teaching. She grew in her understanding and God was blessing.

KLEN

Klen, his wife, and small child, lived on an island a couple of hours away by boat. That is, until Klen became a paraplegic, possibly from TB of the spine, and sought medical care in Vietnam and then in Koh Kong. His wife continued her job back on the island, while his mother and sister provided his care. While at Koh Kong hospital they were all interested in hearing the accounts from the Bible that I related to them. After a time, Klen asked the Lord to be his Savior. His sister said that from that time on his countenance was changed. While his eyesight was affected by meningitis, he asked his sister to read to him from the book of John. His mother said she wanted to believe in God so He would heal her son. I explained what true repentance and faith are. Lalin took over teaching Bible lessons to Klen.

When Klen left the hospital, we continued teaching him. He rented a small dark room made of sheet metal. In front of his room was someone selling four-foot-long blocks of ice. Some customers would purchase only a portion and have it chopped up. So the seller sawed off a piece and dropped it in an ice crusher. The noise of that machine forced us to stop and wait before we could hear to continue the Bible studies or visit. Klen loved singing songs about the Lord, so we brought our songbooks when we visited. It encouraged my heart to praise God together. Across the street was a Muslim mosque. Their loudspeakers with the loud prolonged calls to prayer also made it difficult to hear one another. But we rejoiced that God now had His witness right in the middle of the Muslim section of town. Klen rejoiced to be able to testify of Christ to neighbors who visited him. He listened to cassettes of the New Testament. He longed to be able to sit up so he could go to church. After some time, the Lord gave Klen the strength to sit in a wheelchair and gave improved eyesight. He used his hands to repair cellphones.

One day when we visited, his wife had come. She wanted a divorce. Another man had offered to marry her and support her. Klen reminded her that marriage vows are for life. A few weeks later, Klen was sad because his wife had left, taking their four-year-old son. But he read his Bible and sought the Lord through the heartache. After a couple months, Klen and his brother started their own telephone and electronics repair shop. He lived in the back of that shop.

One Sunday in January 2011, three men arrived at church on a motorcycle. The middle one was Klen, being supported by his brother sitting behind and their assistant driving. He enjoyed the fellowship with the body of Christ. They came again three weeks later. Those were his only two times of attending church. He did not have enough strength. Most of the time he could not sit up but continued to serve customers from his bed. God gave him joy. He was encouraged by regular visits and Bible studies. God gave him opportunities to continue to witness to his family and friends.

DR. ANGLEA'S 2010 MOBILE CLINICS

Hubert and I explored the district of Tuol Ta Ki, where one boat sank going to our 2005 clinic. We found more small towns where roads ended at the water, and a newly constructed sandy road to drive to the main town. We would not have to use boats to cross to it! To get permission for the American medical team arriving on January 18, 2010, Hubert and Lalin went to several selected towns and received eager affirmative responses. But asking for a new location, the larger town of Andoung Tuk, along the main road to Phnom Penh, resulted in a rebuff. They were in a different district than ours and that district health office would only grant permission if I went through the PHD. We continued to pray for God's guidance. After several letters, phone calls and visits to the PHD and district offices, the PHD gave me a letter stating I was restricted to taking medical teams to hospitals and to towns that have health centers. It was a disappointment to no longer be permitted to go to the further destinations which had no regular health care. But God did open the way for us to serve in the larger town of Andoung Tuk and other places in that district. His ways are always better than ours.

Wi had said that she could only participate in the mobile clinics if her grandchild was born before the dates of the clinics. She wanted to be with her daughter at the delivery. Sunday the 17th I went to Wi's house after church about 10 am and verified her daughter was in labor. I met them at the hospital at 4:30 pm, then after the evening service went back and assisted the delivery of her grandchild. How exciting! What a clear work of God to have such good timing for the arrival, ten days before the baby's due date, and three days before the clinics started. Wi could share the gospel at the clinics.

Monday the medical team from the States arrived. Tuesday Hubert and some of the men went to Trapeang Rung to show a video but had trouble with the equipment so had to stop and come home. Wednesday and Thursday clinics were held in that same town. Besides seeing decisions for salvation, we met a Christian patient whom I knew from before. She wanted to have a Bible study.

Friday most of the guys went in Tuen's boat to Koh Paoh and showed a video. This time the equipment worked. We thanked the Lord. The return boat trip was in the dark.

At the Cham Yiem clinic, Wi joined the team for witnessing. Again, there were decisions for Christ. Sunday a baptismal service was held for some new believers that had been studying God's Word for months at our church. We went out in Tuen's boat. Before reaching the chosen sandy spot, I saw a water snake. Most of the water snakes in the Bay of Thailand are poisonous. Praise God for His protection.

A couple of days later found us in Andoung Tuk, for which permission had been so difficult. Hubert went by motorcycle, but it broke down again so he had to push it, on mountain roads until he could get a truck to bring it back. He prepared supper for us. At Andoung Tuk people came from distant towns around. There were lots of people! We had to limit the numbers we handed out to patients. It was good they had a health center there to provide care to those exceeding the number we could see. For most of the people it was their first time to hear the gospel and they listened attentively. We praised God for opening this town to hear His good news. After the team flew back to America, a new Bible study was begun in one town and some new believers came to the existing Bible study in another. In Heaven we will see the full results.

DAILY HAPPENINGS AT KOH KONG HOSPITAL

The Lord continued to bless with awareness of His love and presence. One day in late February was difficult because of three deaths. One AIDS patient who had repeatedly rejected the gospel died during morning rounds. I saw her breathe her last. I hate death. It is part of the curse. A sixty-two-year-old patient from the prison, who said he believed in Christ, died in the evening. The third was a baby who died during birth. When I went home from maternity, I had trouble sleeping the rest of the night. I had put my wedding ring and diamond ring with my watch in my pocket when I put on gloves in the delivery room. In the night, I thought of them. They were not in the pocket or my purse. Only the watch was in the purse. In the morning, I found the rings in the office at home with the gate keys. Clearly, God had protected the rings when I pulled the keys out of my pocket in the dark outside by the gate. God watched over me and my things. A missionary patient phoned to thank me for the medical care I had given, and report God had answered prayer and healed her. How encouraging to see God restore health, such a contrast to events the previous day.

May Day Holiday had only on-call staff, so I checked on some of the patients. A comatose three-year-old malaria patient was in the pediatric ward and His father caring for him had a fever. God helped me find the hospital lab technician to do a malaria test. When it was positive, I took medicine to the father. The following day the three-year-old child died. His eleven-year-old sister was alone with him at the time. I held my arm around her as she cried until her father came.

Whether malaria, pneumonia, strokes, or dermatology, the need for more teaching was always present. Christians were praying for the October medical team of four Christian doctors coming from the States to teach. As we asked the Lord to use it to bring Cambodian doctors to Christ, we also asked God to give permission from the PHD for their coming. The PHD decided my own permission to work in the country needed to be renewed with Phnom Penh MOH before they would authorize further visitors. So we were back to submitting letters and a new contract with the hospital and then the PHD. The hospital director was very helpful in writing a cover letter and making changes a few times on the contract over the course of a month, until the PHD accepted them. When things were all arranged for my trip to Phnom Penh to submit the papers to the MOH, the director said they really needed me to fill in at the AIDS clinic that next day. I asked if she or one of the other doctors going to PP could take the PHD letters to the MOH and save me the trip. She agreed and I was delighted. God had worked in the whole process.

One June day was very busy at the hospital with calls from multiple directions. One ultrasound showed a ten-centimeter ovarian tumor. Another patient's ultrasound revealed ascites and cirrhosis (liver problems). In a pregnant lady, the midwives could not hear a fetal heartbeat. But we were happy the ultrasound showed a healthy live baby. The outpatient department doctor left for Phnom Penh late morning, so I did outpatient consults the rest of the morning. One man said he had right lower quadrant belly pain. He had localized tenderness and his ultrasound showed signs suggesting acute appendicitis. While trying to find someone in the surgery department to admit that patient, another patient arrived with attempted suicide – taking an overdose of medicine. Being lunch break already, most of the staff was gone. I phoned a nurse who worked in the medicine department and she and her nurse husband came. He took care of the appendix patient and she got help and did a gastric lavage for the overdose. I eventually got home for a late lunch. The appendix patient got his surgery that evening. God gave opportunity for his wife and her sister to hear the gospel.

While in Phnom Penh to pick up my permission papers from the MOH, they sent word that one paper was not correct. Since I did not have my computer or printer with me on the trip, I went to missionary friends and used theirs to make a corrected letter. When I resubmitted that to the MOH they accepted it and assured me the permission had been granted. They would phone me in Koh

Kong when the papers were ready to be picked up. A couple weeks later Hubert took a bus up to the capital and got them. It was now mid-August.

With my permission to work in Koh Kong in hand, I asked PHD about the team coming in October. That request had been on hold since May. The office came up with additional requirements: copies of their medical school diplomas and curricula vitae plus a letter concerning finances for their time with us. They said it would all need to be submitted to Phnom Penh MOH and since it would take time, maybe consider waiting another year for them to come. But I emailed the participants asking for their documents. I was discouraged with the continual roadblocks. I needed wisdom from God to know the right channels to pursue in processing the request. I was able to prepare more papers and meet the helpful director of the district office about the October team. He said he would discuss it with PHD. Praise the Lord, within three weeks we had received all four of the curricula vitae and diploma copies from the October conference speakers, so I phoned the district director. But he was away in Phnom Penh.

The following day, while doing rounds at the pediatric department I got a call from the district director that he was back in Koh Kong, and I was to meet him right then. He had signed the letter of request for the team coming and told me to take it to PHD for their signatures. I took it there, a man signed it, but then said to show it to the PHD director's office. It sat there another week. Then I went to their office at God's prompting late morning. They said to return at 3 pm. Then they signed, stamped, and gave it to me. The district office and hospital director continued to help with getting invitations to health care providers in health centers all over the province and finalizing the lecture schedule. I reserved rooms at our neighbor's guest house for the visiting lecturers coming. By

God's power all was accomplished in time. The two-day conference went well. During the noon lunches God gave opportunities to share the gospel as well as several other times. I met many of the attendees other times throughout the years as part of the tapestry God was weaving.

LIFE IN KOH KONG

The beautiful low mountains in Koh Kong province with clouds nestled in the valleys, and sunrise colors stretching across the horizon were constant reminders that our help comes from the Lord. "I lift up my eyes to the hills" (Psalm 121:1). The western sky also proclaimed God's glory as the sun sank into the ocean. Incoming waves hit against the cement wall at the edge of a park, then receded to clash with the next waves arriving, spraying up like sounding cymbals. At night, lightning flashed magnificent light displays.

At 3 am one could get another view of the clouds on the mountains. Hubert tried traveling to Phnom Penh on his motorcycle very early to arrive in time to have the full day for his tasks there. However, maneuvering the inclines and curves through fog and darkness made for slow travel. He arrived on the yonder side of the mountains in time for sunrise over rice fields – a great photo opportunity.

Bicycling out of the town for relaxation and exercise led to discovering new places. It could also bring surprises. After going out about a half hour, one of our bikes had a flat tire. It took over an hour to walk it back home. Hubert made it to the Bible class he was teaching that Saturday afternoon while I took the crippled bike to a neighborhood repairman. After the repairman finished putting on a new tire and tube, he asked several good questions about Christians.

God had appointed that time to share with him, his wife, and his assistant. God works all things together for good.

Improving the road through the mountains meant years of mud, dynamite, and maneuvering around work crews. When four big bridges began to be built, bus companies foresaw business. Ferries were too small to carry buses, but the buses could do relays. Passengers disembarked, crossed the water on ferries along with their baggage, then walked up to the next waiting bus. For the rough road, old buses were practical if not dependable. When the bridges and road were finished, the ride was much smoother, usually with only one bus the whole trip from Phnom Penh to Koh Kong.

However, on one trip, we took a bus line scheduled to leave the capital at 9:20 am. By 10:30 am it was still waiting for some shipments to arrive and was picking up people to sit on stools in the aisle until it was full. The right side of the bus was definitely the right side that day, as the left side had the sun streaming in the windows and the air conditioner dripping on the passengers. About an hour before Koh Kong city, the bus broke down. The driver and his assistant got the leaky water hose re-taped and refilled with water and we rolled for another twenty minutes. That time it was not repairable on site, and we had to wait for a different bus to come. Everything and everybody got transferred to the "new" bus and it then towed the old bus – a rather slow way to travel through mountains. When bus DVD players were broken, we were very happy, for their entertainment included movies that were indecent and had foul language. In later years, they got buses that were more reliable and stopped showing DVDs.

In March and April, the daily temperatures were steadily above 100° F, hitting 106° F in May. That was when heat rash was rather itchy. Evenings brought welcome relief with cooler air, if you were outside. City water and rainwater tanks tended to run out those months. We prayed for rain. One friend had an open well by her house, so once she took our laundry to it, drew water, and washed it there for us. When the rain came, even a half inch collected from the roof and running in large hoses to our 1000-liter reserve tank could fill it half full, provided the hoses did not fall out. Then from June to November, rainy season was in full force: four inches one day, six inches another, and more. The rain gauge could only hold five inches, so sometimes it had to be emptied and the amount entered in the logbook, ready to collect more to complete the twenty-four-hour reading. Laundry on clotheslines took several days to get dry even though it was under a roof.

Comforting a friend at the death of a loved one is important. The grandmother of one of the Christian young men from the next town, Ba Klong, died. Four of the other young people from the church asked me to accompany them to his town. If we could have left at 7 am, if the speedboat would have taken us promptly to his town, if,...then perhaps I could have gone with them and yet gotten to the airport in Trat, Thailand, when another short-termer was arriving at 3:30 pm. However, we did not leave the house until 7:45 am, walked to the boat docks, and began bargaining with the boats. At that point, a storm arose and lots of whitecaps appeared, closing that route. Boat taxis were aware of the near drowning victims we treated at the hospital, and those who did not make it to help. So, they exercised caution. The four young people rode bicycles the long way around, across two bridges, through the rain, wind, and mud – an all-day trip. I headed for the border, grateful for a good raincoat.

The van on the Thai side was delayed waiting for the wind to calm down. When it went to its first stop, the town of Klang Yai, I was able to visit the bank and post office. It took the post office worker a long time to figure out how to send two birthday cards to the States, but I was grateful the van waited. By noon we were in

Trat. After some errands there, a pick-up truck taxi took me to the airport forty-five minutes away. When the plane did not arrive, I inquired at the ticket office. They informed me that the flight had been cancelled and to wait for the 5:30 pm flight. The taxi agreed to wait the two hours since returning to the town and back to the airport would consume one and a half hours. I was grateful to God for the ultrasound book I had brought along to use the time studying. Our visitor arrived fine, but it was too late to get back across the border before it closed for the night. Our phone at home was out, but I was able to reach Lalin's cellphone, and he notified Hubert of our delay. We had a restful night at a simple hotel in Trat and went home in the morning.

Three people made decisions for Christ during the time that the short-termer worked with us. She taught well-prepared lessons on the attributes of God. She got to watch surgery and dressing changes and did vital signs in the outpatient clinic. She interacted a lot with three French medical students and another French girl volunteering at the orphanage in town. She went to homes of Cambodian friends and talked with many at our home. One of the French girls came to stay with us a few days before our visitor left. She accompanied us on the trip back to Trat airport to see our visitor off. With delays getting vans for the multiple legs of the trip, I was praying the whole trip that we would make it in time for her 6:30 pm flight. God answered. We arrived at the airport just at 6 pm. The plane left early – 6:15 pm – and she was on it.

A visit from our daughter Cherith, son-in-law Jonathan, and their three precious children was a great treat before Christmas 2010. It was Hubert's first time to meet our fourteen-month-old grandson Josiah. The general who studied English with Hubert loaned us his car for taking the family around. When we arrived home in Koh Kong with them, the neighbor's wedding party filled the street and our yard. They graciously moved chairs and tables for us to get the vehicle into our garage. A bigger challenge was the loud music until 11:20 pm. We thanked the Lord that we were able to sleep a little off and on and that the singing was pleasant enough outside of the volume. But our guests got no sleep until all was quiet. About a month later, when they Skyped us from the other side of the world, we told them we could hear loud music coming from a different neighbor's party. Cherith told seven-year-old Adrianna what we had just said and asked, "Do you know what that means?" Adrianna nodded and answered, "Yes, it means you can't sleep." They prayed for us. God answered. We drifted off to sleep in spite of the noise. God showed His loving care.

In preparation for Hubert's English class party, Pren and Lalin helped me make about one hundred twenty rolls. When Petros arrived, we had a Bible study at the kitchen table while watching the oven. The oven was small and could accommodate only pans smaller than 9 x 13. I moved the rack higher and lower to get the rolls evenly browned. In the afternoon we made a big pot of au gratin potatoes and manioc chips. Three other girls came just before 4 pm. They sliced tomatoes, formed hamburgers, and prepared toppings. Hubert and some students grilled the burgers. I wondered if we would have lots of left-over food. But at 4:30 pm students started arriving until we had about forty people. It was a fun time as Hubert led games for them and one young man shared his testimony of salvation. After the party, I swept through the house and set up chairs for the next morning's Sunday service.

We had been praying for God's provision to replace the leaky house of Bani, the sight-impaired man in our church. His father was a builder. When the new house was finally done, we went to visit. Steps led up to the entrance door since the house was high on stilts. Praise God for a roof that did not leak! But rain blew in the unfinished window openings until shutters were added. Light peeped through holes in the used sheet metal which were the exterior walls of the single room home. I asked if they would use their old house next to it for storage. They laughed. "What would we put in it?" Yeah, sometimes I ask dumb questions.

Underneath the house, crickets chirped in their screened cages. There were special dishes for incubating the eggs. They showed me how to tell which were female crickets. Stones in the water dishes kept the insects out of the water. They were raised to sell at the market, as many people found crickets very tasty.

The day before the church Christmas dinner, Bani's wife brought one of their few chickens. They were delighted to be able to contribute to the meal. They must have killed and cleaned it the night before, for red ants covered the scrawny chicken in a plastic bag. I put it in a basin of water, cleaned it up, and boiled it. Added to some other chicken and rice, it made a delicious dish.

Bani memorized some of the passages for the Christmas Bible memory contest. One of the other members had recorded them for him. God provided audio Khmer Bibles for Bani, first on cassettes and later on a little radio with a USB. We were so grateful to God for providing those. God blessed them with two sons. They led him to his customers for whom he sharpened knives.

Shoes waiting outside our door could conceal any kind of critter. As I slipped my foot into my flip-flop, skin made contact with a red centipede. Naturally, the centipede retaliated with a bite into the top of my foot. Speaking from experience, it was as painful as a scorpion sting. There were two little puncture marks with swelling and redness around the site. I used ice and elevation, then tried soaking it, but finally needed to leave for the afternoon work at the clinic. A nurse at the hospital injected the area with lidocaine, which numbed it for about twenty minutes. God helped me through the rest of the day and gave me sleep at night. Word spread and the next day many of the hospital staff asked how I was. I appreciated the concern of my co-workers, and God using even that to strengthen relationships with the staff.

For about five years, Hubert witnessed to Nok Siem, whose daughter was in his English class. I treated him for various medical problems and his health improved by God's mercy, for which he was very grateful. He had been unable to work for several years. Hubert invited him to church several times, encouraging him to commit to coming for at least a month, which he did, but afterwards stopped.

On one visit to Nok Siem's house, Hubert asked him what it was that was keeping him from turning to Christ. He pointed over his shoulder to an altar. "That," he said. He was afraid if he turned to Christ and gave up worshipping his ancestors at the household altar, their spirits would become angry and cause him harm. He was also afraid that his friends in the area, all Buddhists, would reproach him for turning away from the Cambodian religion. Finally, he began coming to church regularly again. Several times Hubert asked him if he desired to trust in Christ and be saved. He would answer that he needed to learn more. Finally, one Sunday in September 2009, when asked he replied that he had recently trusted in Christ to save him and had given up ancestor worship. Praise God for rescuing him from darkness. When his friends questioned him about it, he told them he could no longer follow Buddhism or spirit worship since now he had Christ.

A fruit dish on our table tangibly reminded us of Cambodian friends God had brought into our lives. There were mangos from N's mother (from their farm), mangos from S's mother (from their farm, and mangos from L's mother (she brought them from another province). It was definitely mango season. We thanked God for the eternal fruit He gave in Koh Kong and prayed for more. As we left for furlough on June 20, 2011, sixteen people saw us off. There were gifts, a bouquet of roses, lots of hugs, good-byes, and some tears. God would care for His work, and we looked forward to returning in ten months.

CHAPTER 8

KOH KONG 2012 – 2016

*I will instruct you and teach you
in the way you should go.*
Psalm 32:8

2012 VICTORIES

A glorious sunrise welcomed us back to Cambodia in May 2012! Hubert had arrived the month before and painted the whole inside of our rented house, then unpacked our things that had been stored away. After preparing our duplex in Michigan to rent out, my sister Sue and I flew to Cambodia visiting Davar and family in Canada, and Hadessah in China on the way.

Getting extended Cambodian visas and buying medicines for mobile clinics kept us in Phnom Penh for a couple of days. We loaded tuk-tuks with our luggage and purchases but found at the bus station that it was only a nineteen-passenger van instead of a big bus going to Koh Kong. They could not fit our twenty-four pieces on – including our new washing machine purchased in Phnom Penh. Hubert, who met us in Phnom Penh, unsuccessfully checked three markets where trucks leave to carry things to the provinces. The bus company agreed to keep six boxes and the washing machine and send them the next day on the big bus. They managed to get the rest stacked beside us in the back of the van. God had solved the dilemma as He is so good at doing.

About halfway home, news reached us that the only road to Koh Kong was blocked by demonstrators. What was God going to do? Police directed traffic to detour through a muddy, bumpy road of the sugar plantation and sugar mill, which was a treat to see so closely. On arriving home, a lady from the church was waiting for me to check her two boys. One had a fractured olecranon (in his elbow) and the other had diarrhea. It made me feel welcomed back, so did the tropical night sky ablaze with stars and the southern cross. God gave His peace and joy.

Several new doctors and nurses just out of training joined the staff at Koh Kong Hospital. That gave new opportunities to teach and encourage. An epidemic of hand foot and mouth disease was in full swing at the hospital clinic, with many children showing up with vesicles on palms, soles, and inside their mouths. Some were admitted because of not being able to eat. Fortunately, the timing was different than the annual months of the pediatric department surge in census from dengue fever cases.

DR. ANGLEA'S TEAM

THE TIME SO MANY THINGS WENT WRONG

Before our return to Koh Kong, permission had been granted via emails for the next medical team. Their arrival was scheduled soon after ours. Now visiting the district health office in person, we were informed that no gatherings were allowed right before the national elections. What was God going to do? We juggled the dates to have all four mobile clinics during the second week of the team's visit.

Hubert left home at 7 am to meet the team at 11:30 am in Trat, Thailand. However, they had gotten an earlier bus than planned and arrived at 10:45 am. Someone from the bus station found Hubert at the big store and told him his visitors were waiting at the bus station. He arranged a van and a pick-up and got them from Trat to the border. They ate dinner at an ocean front restaurant at the border. Tuk-tuks (three-wheeled motor vehicles used as taxis) had been arranged to meet them at the restaurant at 2 pm to bring them to Koh Kong. But the main tuk-tuk showed up empty at our home in Koh Kong at 2:30 pm. Hubert had to find other transportation to bring them the five miles. We thanked God for their safe arrival to serve God with us for ten days.

On Saturday, one of the men went with Hubert to some of the towns to let them know the team was coming. Lalin and his father took them in their fishing boat to Koh Pao, an hour away. Coming back the engine stopped. They had only one paddle, so they used boards along with the paddle. Throughout the team's days there, I had a boil on my back, blisters on my feet, and other health issues, plus lost lots of information on my cellphone – all reminders of how helpless I am, and how I need to rely on God. And God was sufficient, with His strong arms upholding.

About twenty of us went in a thirty-foot fishing boat to Koh Pao and experienced rain on and off. It was a unique view of the landscape along the banks through the rain. On arrival, we were directed to an empty building over the water. We set up our clinic but lacked chairs or tables. Lalin negotiated to use the school. It had two rooms, much larger, and tables and benches. So, we moved over there and set up again. The children did not mind getting out of school early. The clinic went smoothly in spite of the rain. People with eye infections, skin disorders, headaches, urine infections, and many more problems were cared for. One lady made a profession of faith, and many heard the way of salvation.

The next couple of days' clinics went well. Then the last day we took two vans plus Hubert's motorcycle to Chumka Cheik. Heavy tropical rains were brief but frequent as we traveled making the road muddy and slippery. At times, we had to get out and wade across streams while the van forded. It took three hours to go a distance usually covered in one and a half hours. By the time we arrived at a river on the Chumka Cheik road, it was too swollen to safely ford. Reluctantly, we turned back. Word was sent to the people waiting for us. There was no health care in that town.

We took time to eat lunch before one van full of people went to see a waterfall. The falls were so full and overflowing, we could not walk down to a viewpoint to see it well. As for the other van, I had sent my house key with one of the young men but forgot to give him the gate key. They managed to climb over the high gate, but could not get the trunks of supplies in, nor take bicycles or motorcycles out until the rest of us arrived. We finally all got in, unpacked and repacked and the next day they departed for the States. God had taken care of us all. He had used the team in getting His Word to surrounding towns, in spite of the challenges.

About a week later, Lalin and his father took us in their boat back to Koh Pao to follow up on the lady who had made a decision for Christ at that mobile clinic. God answered prayer for the wind and waves to calm down so we could safely go. The people at Koh Pao knew her and pointed the way to her town on the other side of the estuary. On arrival at a house there, the people pointed to a path. We hiked a long time, crossed a stream, and finally arrived at some scattered houses. One was hers. She was happy she had made peace with God and was on her way to heaven. We encouraged her in her new faith and gave her a Bible. She said it would be difficult to read the Bible, due to her poor vision. God had answered prayer to let us meet her again. Over the next year we returned several times, once hiking to find where she was gathering grass to make brooms to sell, and another time I experienced heat exhaustion. But God faithfully protected us.

Hospital Permission

A new term in Cambodia meant new permission to work as a doctor, since approvals were for specified time periods. I wrote a request, got help translating it into Khmer, and took it to the hospital administration for a support letter. The hospital was helpful in providing that and even sent my request to the MOH via one of the Cambodian doctors going to Phnom Penh so that I could stay in Koh Kong and help at the hospital. Four days later, in the middle of doing rounds on patients, PHD phoned asking me to see them. They received word from the MOH that my request to work should clear PHD in Koh Kong first. This seemed like déjà vu – the same issue as ten years previously. Within days of arrival back in town, I had met with PHD, and they wanted me to get MOH approval first. God would need to accomplish this again. Within a few days, PHD gave me my request letter stamped with their approval and a cover letter from them to complete the packet to take to MOH. Hubert and I went to Phnom Penh by bus. At the MOH many of the staff had changed since my first request years earlier. The lady I met was very nice, but she said it was unusual for their office to approve an individual rather than an organization. She did not know if my permission to work would be granted or not. What was God going to do?

The next morning, Hubert went back and forth to the printer a couple of times trying to get his books printed. It seemed like many defeats all morning. The Israelite army in Judges 20 had advanced at God's command but met defeat a few times before God gave them the victory. The optometrist could not find the new lenses for glasses that Hubert had ordered the previous month. The pharmacy did not have one of the medicines I wanted for patients. I could not find used curtains for Lalin for his shop. The police stopped us for the rented motorcycle's light being on. We could not figure out how to turn it off. After a while the policeman let us go.

Then God began showing victories again. After a search, we found a new Christian bookstore and got some literature. The optometrist phoned that they found Hubert's lenses and we went and got them. The printer phoned that the literature was ready, and Hubert picked those up, though still not exactly right. Even the MOH phoned that my permission letter was ready, and the office worker met me at a big market to give it to me, since it was after her office had closed! We ordered new curtains for McKong, Lalin's shop. God had surmounted every obstacle!

In addition, a girl who worked at the guest house where we stayed told me that after she read the tract I had given her some time before, she began to think about Christ. She received God's gift of salvation and was attending church regularly. On another occasion, a Russian girl who worked in Thailand met me at the same guest house as we had arranged. We talked for one and a half hours, much of the time about the Lord. She could not see that she was lost in sin. She had just spent the previous month in a Buddhist monastery in Thailand seeking peace, but not finding it. God calls people to come to Him. Some receive Him, many reject Him. It is a privilege to serve the King, and we must leave the results with Him!

2013 REJOICING

Two men from the audio-visual department of Baptist Mid-Missions came to video some of God's work in Cambodia. We met them in Bangkok on the Friday night of their arrival. However, their luggage with their equipment did not arrive with them! The airline expected it would come on the Saturday night flight. Hubert and I went ahead and traveled back to Koh Kong on Saturday. The missionaries in Bangkok took them to the airport that night and they intercepted their bags with expensive equipment as another passenger was walking away with them! A van was found to drive them through the night to Cambodia. Hubert met them at the border when it opened at 7 am. They arrived at our house at 7:50 am and were standing behind the cameras ready to shoot before 8 am when the Sunday morning service began. They had had little sleep and little food but were serving the Lord. Praise God for His enabling His servants!

During the crew's days in Cambodia, they videotaped interviews with Cambodian Christians and with missionaries, along with footage of Bible studies, English classes, hospital work, and outreaches in other cities where our mission was working. We prayed God would use the finished video to help people give thanks to God for His working, pray for God's work in Cambodia, and challenge Christians to serve Him.

In March 2013, Hubert and Lalin went by motorcycle to a mountain village where they had never gone before. After getting permission from the head of the village to show a video that night, they went from house to house passing out tracts and sharing the gospel. As far as they knew, they were the first to talk to people in that village about Christ. Several people asked questions about the literature they received. Hubert had forgotten to bring a sheet to be a screen for the video. They drove into the neighboring town, about twenty minutes away, to buy one, only to find there were none available.

They returned to the village and set up the projector and speakers and were surprised to find nearly one hundred people present. The sun had just begun to set when the head of the village told them that they also needed to get permission to show the video from the district leader in another town. They rode again to that village and found the man they needed. He knew them and quickly wrote and signed a letter which they brought back to the village where the video was to be shown.

At first, the video was not very clear projecting onto the wooden doors of a house. But then a man came with a sheet of his own for them to use. After the video, Lalin preached and many people asked very good questions about Christ and salvation. They planned to return the next dry season, between December and February, and stay a little longer. They praised the Lord for safety on the road and for His marvelous care.

THE REST OF KLEN'S STORY

Klen, who was paraplegic, continued to enjoy visits from Christians as he lay on his hard wooden bed. It was encouraging to us as we all sang together and studied the Word of God. I continued to give him medical care, visiting his home often. On rare occasions, he was delighted when his ex-wife brought their little son to visit him. We continued to witness to his mother and siblings. In early January 2013, we were happy when Klen and his sister showed up for Sunday School.

But two months later Klen was hospitalized. Christians from the church held a worship service in his hospital room. I spent hours sitting with him and his family, expecting he was soon to leave to go to his heavenly home. The morning of March 19, 2013, Klen entered the presence of the Lord. While he was singing and leaping and praising God in Glory, we were looking for a burial plot. This was the first funeral for Koh Kong Baptist Church. Tuen and Kenh knew of a tiny "Christian cemetery" and were able to secure a place. Muslims had their own cemetery and Buddhists had theirs at their temples. Lalin, Hubert, Kenh, and I visited the homes of each of our church members to tell them of Klen's homegoing and about the funeral services.

A tent was set up at Klen's house and a few neighbors stopped by to comfort the family. A loudspeaker played Christian music and Scripture reading throughout the day. The Muslim neighborhood heard. Via our blog, God's people were urged to pray for God's glory through this Christian funeral. Two services were held there at Klen's home, one in the afternoon and another in the evening. The next morning, we gathered very early. Klen's brothers and friends built a simple wooden casket and dug the grave. We had about nine people from our church and a few others came. Tuen led yet another service and Hubert preached. The procession to the cemetery used a borrowed pick-up truck carrying the casket and family, followed by the rest of us on motorcycles. Klen's little dog followed more than halfway to the cemetery.

Once at the cemetery, we had prayer and the burial. It was so peaceful. One of the relatives asked afterward if he could have a funeral like that. Someone explained that it was knowing Christ and having assurance of heaven that made it so different. The Buddhist funerals were to chase away evil spirits and were eerie and scary. Here there was such a spirit of love and unity among the people in the church, and love poured out to Klen's family. The gospel was clearly presented. God was glorified.

Six months after the funeral, I had a bad headache and considered not going out, but Lalin and I did go to Kim's and then the home of Klen's mother and sister for our ongoing Bible studies. That day, Klen's sister Chan asked the Lord to save her. She continued to study the Bible with us for six weeks more until she and her husband moved to the mountains for his work. When she periodically visited back in Koh Kong, she loved studying the Bible together and coming to church.

One of those times, a couple years later, God clearly orchestrated our rendezvous. I had gone to visit someone else, but that person wasn't home. So I went a little farther to visit Chan and Klen's mother and ask her about Chan, who then lived far away in another province with her husband and child. Her mother said she had arrived in town two days before and was leaving the next day. I had to wait for her for about fifty minutes, but it was a golden time to talk with other family members. It was a happy meeting when Chan came. She said she read her Bible a lot and prayed but there was no church anywhere near her. We had only a brief visit, but it was a beautiful gift from God.

ANSWERS TO PRAYER

The Christians saw God's care in many ways. When grass fires were encroaching on Tuen's orchard, God sent rain at the right moment and put out the fires. We prayed for more customers for Lalin's shop and God sent them. God was helping Hubert writing theology and Christian life books for Cambodian Christians. Easter Sunday God gave orange daylilies blooming in front of our wall and a dazzling sunrise. The handbell special number beautifully helped celebrate the day, and the Sunday afternoon service at Kim's house was blessed.

Occasionally, Lalin brought us fresh fish that he and his father had caught, and often our landlady cleaned them for me when she saw how slow I was at that job. On a day when the restaurant next to our house played their music louder than usual, I prayed that God would cause them to turn down the volume at our bedtime. God granted the request. Renewal of the church permit this time took only three months! What a great God we serve!

Clearly, there was continual need to rely on the Lord to enable for the work He had given. One day at the hospital, of twelve ultrasounds done, many of them were abnormal: a tumor in the uterus, an unborn baby with anencephaly (most of the brain absent), a twin pregnancy with preeclampsia (mother with hypertension and organ dysfunction), a patient with an abnormal kidney and a bladder mass, a dyspneic child with hepatomegaly and plural effusion (hard to breathe, large liver, and fluid around the lungs), and a patient with liver cirrhosis and abundant ascites (fluid in the abdomen). Another patient had situs inversus (her abdominal organs as liver and appendix, and thoracic organs, her heart and lungs, were on the reverse side of normal). She also had hydronephrosis (large kidney) probably from her kidney stone. Another day, one interesting ultrasound showed a big worm, probably Ascaris, caught in the neck of the gallbladder. Its long tail was wiggling around in the bile.

Soon after lecturing to the hospital staff on anxiety and depression disorders, a patient was helped by the information shared. When aid organizations from various countries sent workers for some months, it was an opportunity for input into their lives. They helped with improving record keeping, sanitation, continuing education, and more.

I was saddened one day as I did an ultrasound for a pregnant lady. Surrounded by amniotic fluid was a still, lifeless baby. I felt like I was looking into a somber tomb. The patient's husband was far away, she was lonely, and she had AIDS. She was wife number six, and he was still trying to produce a son. She also had signs suggestive of coagulopathy (blood clotting problems).

In May, a man came to the hospital from Trapeang Rung, a town on the main road, about an hour away from Koh Kong. He had been bitten by a snake (probably a cobra) and his leg was very large. He was given anti-venom and the swelling slowly decreased. When the gospel was presented to him, he was eager to hear. Two days later he turned to Christ to save him. He was very grateful to know his sins were forgiven and he wanted to begin Bible studies. He read the Bible and literature given to him. When he was discharged, Hubert and Lalin went weekly to teach him. Three other people from his neighborhood joined in that study. We had presented the gospel many times before in that town but knew of no other Christians there.

The brother of one of the students coming to church was hospitalized with dengue fever. When we visited him, his mother said she wanted him to attend the church services so he would have a good life like his sister, and not run around with bad friends. God worked, and a couple weeks later the sister made a profession of faith in Christ and eagerly studied the Scriptures in spite of her father's opposition. Eventually, the brother also turned to the Lord for salvation. Unfortunately, their parents rejected the message of eternal life.

RAIN

Rain is a wonderful gift from the Lord, especially during the dry season. Heavy but short tropical showers were interspersed with sunshine popping out to start drying up the ground. One morning we woke to a big puddle in our main room from rain following the ham radio antenna cable in via the window. Being experienced in puddles in the house, we got it cleaned up fine, and changed the angle of the cable.

Collecting rainwater to supply households was very common. But when dry season came, it was nice to have city water. However, the city's reserve was a lake that depended on rain, so it often ran out. When city water pressure was low, we juggled buckets to collect water during its intermittent flow and poured it into our house water tank. Then when the rains came again, we got twenty-two and a half inches in six days. That nicely dropped our temperatures down into the eighty's. The yearly average rainfall for Koh Kong was over thirteen feet per year. The record twenty-four-hour collection in our rain gauge was fourteen and a half inches, and it continued another one and a half inches in the next three hours. That flooded main street and our neighbor's house for a few hours until it ran off into the estuary, but our house was dry. God shows us His loving care.

God allowed us to enjoy more of His creation out in the open on our fortieth wedding anniversary trip to Khao Yai National Park in Thailand. Deer and monkeys played next to our lunch table near the visitor center. After a day of hiking and resultant aching legs, we invested the next morning sitting by a stream and watching colorful birds, kingfishers, red-billed blue magpie, sambar deer, barking deer, rhesus macaque, hornbills, Chinese pone heron, more monkeys, and two water monitors. We were glad the two large lizards were on the opposite side of the stream. I did not want to be too close to their whip like tails, sharp claws, or sharp teeth. They were about half the size of a huge Komodo Dragon I had seen in Sri Lanka.

A British family offered us a ride to a gorgeous high waterfall. It had a history of elephants falling over it more than once. Hubert ran races with their six-year-old on the one-kilometer hike down from the main road. We appreciated the cold of the mountains and the heavy blankets to sleep under in the cabin at night.

2014 GRATEFUL

Another trip into Thailand found us in a van from the border to Trat talking with a Muslim lady from Koh Kong. She asked if I remembered her. She was wearing a full black Muslim burka. I did not recognize her eyes and voice. She said she appreciated my doing an ultrasound on her two years previously and helping her during her surgery. "Thank you, Lord."

God helped with getting the district health office permission and a doctor and pharmacist from the hospital for a mobile clinic in the mountain town beyond Araing. The chief had asked us before to visit that town. The hospital also offered one of their ambulances and a driver, who also worked in the lab. Hubert and Lalin went by motorcycle up to the village and got permission from three different authorities there.

On the day of the trip, God brought the team to our house by 6 am. In answer to prayer, Wichet, who thought he might not get there in time, was the first to arrive. The driver drove well, except he drove fast and did not have the four-wheel drive-in place at Araing River. He said he lacked a wrench for it. Hubert drove his motorcycle and took one rider. Lalin helped direct the way for the ambulance. Some of the team got carsick, but only one vomited. After that, the front seat was reserved for that person. We all tried to keep looking forward and holding on tightly not to be bounced out of our seats. We arrived just after 9 am.

A room was provided for us, and our first task was to get rid of the ants on the two wooden bed frames with slats. A teacher tried burning the ants. I sprayed myself with repellent when I felt ants in many places on my body. Fortunately, they were not in over-whelming quantities nor biting too hard. Hubert went and bought cans of insecticide which worked to make the beds useable for patients to sit on for consultations.

Lalin preached before the morning and the afternoon sessions. We saw patients from 10-12 am, then 1-3 pm. Five Christians from Koh Kong church did one-on-one witnessing while the Cambodian doctor and I did consults. We saw one hundred five patients. The Pharmacist ran our pharmacy well and the lab tech/driver assisted him. Someone in the village chief's house made a good meal for us with the ingredients we had brought. We left shortly after 3 pm.

The vehicle had trouble getting up the far bank of the river, like the last time that we took vehicles to cross that river for a clinic. Many things were tried. Gradually, men of the town gathered to help. They tried pulling with a garden tractor. Finally, a couple of men directed the driver to go back across the river, turn around again and come on a slightly different path over the submerged rocks. That time there was success in getting up the bank.

Hubert was worried about reaching the newly paved road before dark since his headlight was not good to see the ruts and holes in the mud road. We had lost one and a half hours at the river. God answered prayer to get us out of the river and reach the paved road before total darkness. The vehicle arrived home at 7:15 pm and the motorcycle at 7:30 pm. The next day many at the hospital were excited about the adventures the day before and wanted to see pictures. We prayed God would give eternal fruit from the day's work for Him, both in the mountain town and in the lives of the hospital staff. Several months later, there was trouble with some foreigners in that area over logging, and we were no longer allowed to go there. Praise God for getting us in during the window of opportunity.

THE REST OF KIM'S STORY

Kim's physical health slowly declined, but her desire for spiritual things was steady. At first, her husband would listen as we taught Bible lessons, but later we seldom saw him. In July 2012 we were surprised to see her standing propped by a window with her wheelchair behind her. After that, she was only sitting, and later only lying on a mat on the wooden floor as she grew weaker. In one of the regular Sunday afternoon visits with a small group from the church, the study was on Stephen's death in the book of Acts. She was especially interested, probably anticipating seeing the Lord in heaven. The Christians encouraged her, sang, prayed with her, and studied God's Word. Then a Sunday came when Wi told us in church that Kim had slipped into heaven Saturday night, March 15, 2014. Some of us went to Kim's house and found Buddhist rituals already in process. Her husband said a couple times that Kim had requested a Christian funeral, but his relatives insisted on a Buddhist one. It was a sad time, yet we were grateful to God for taking his child home to heaven with him.

SPECIAL PEOPLE AND TIMES

Four days before Kim's homegoing, one of the AIDS patients who had asked Christ to save her just one week previous to that, quietly slipped into the arms of Jesus. A patient admitted to the TB ward reminded me that she herself had become a child of God during her previous admission. Since that time, she had such joy and peace, was reading her Bible, and was telling others about Christ! Praise God for His rescuing people!

We were praying God would give our church more families. Most of the believers were the only person in their families who had been saved. We kept praying for the spouses and children of the married ones and the parents and siblings of the singles to receive the Lord. God brought us a family in a different way. At the hospital, I met a young lady whose father was a monk. The father was receiving care as a patient and listened as I shared the gospel and a Gospel of John with his daughter. The daughter started coming to church with her husband and two young children. Hubert soon began weekly Bible studies in their home. After several weeks, the husband trusted in Christ at church after the Sunday School lesson. The following Friday, during the Bible study in their home, the wife did as well. God had answered prayer to have another Christian family in the church.

Tuen, Kenh, and Sipa took the church youth on an outing to their orchard about an hour away. The sky was partly cloudy, and the water smooth at high tide so the boat maneuvered the short cut, a channel that had been cut through the mangrove forest. The picnic meal as we sat on mats near the shelter in the orchard included rice and pork "take-out boxes" that had been provided by one of the mothers, bread and jam, and fresh jack fruit and mangos. Kenh gave me a delicious, juicy, yellow, tree-ripened mango, while the others got their preference of hard green ones. We sat and relaxed, then walked through the orchard. Lots of big red ants under some of the trees kept me hopping and slapping a bit.

When the boat had gone about half-way home, Tuen stopped for the kids to all swim. They laughed as they threw mud at each other. We got back before 4 pm but everyone had to get showers at their houses before the youth meeting. Later, they Skyped New York to chat with one of the girls who had come as a short-termer. After supper, Hubert and I picked the fruit pieces out of the big jackfruit Tuen and Kenh had given us, a very sticky job. Lalin gave us the tip that cooking oil gets it off the hands. The next day we made jackfruit bread and jackfruit smoothies.

Life in Christ has so many blessings. It also has trials. A week later, part of Tuen and Kenh's orchard was burned again by a neighbor who hated Christians. But God made the wind blow a second fire toward the first fire, thus containing it. He cares for His children. Tuen and Kenh invited the church people to their rebuilt, higher house over the water in the town of Koh Kong for a housewarming. We prayed together thanking the Lord and asking Him to bless. Then they served soft drinks and cookies. It was so beautiful compared to the worldly drinking parties of neighbors' housewarmings.

Many of the patients who turned to Christ while at the hospital were from a great distance away. They had no churches to attend. One such lady had begun her walk with the Lord after her cesarean section. She returned to the hospital seven months later. She said her husband had recently also believed on the Lord. Another patient came specifically to see me at the outpatient clinic to tell me of his joy in his new life in Christ. He had turned to Christ about two weeks earlier when hospitalized for hepatitis. He was thanking God for restored health too.

But there were other kinds of patients. A foreigner came to the hospital early afternoon one day and spoke in French about God. He claimed to be a prophet, telling people the judgement was coming in one year – April 2015. That same day, a French Cambodian visited the house during the 5 pm Bible study. The subject of the day was cults. The visitor was Mormon. What a timely application of the lesson. We prayed for the false teachers to repent and for the true Christians to stand firm for the truth of God.

The Cambodian believers are continually challenged by the Buddhist culture surrounding them. During Cambodian New Year, one of the youth carefully stayed away from her home for a day. She took Hubert's practice TOEFL test (a standardized English test) in the morning, then helped him translating early afternoon, then went to the hospital with me the rest of the afternoon, until time for the 5 pm Bible study together. Praise the Lord for making this way of escape for her from the Buddhist ceremonies going on at her house all day. Her mother had approved her plan.

The following Saturday, Wichet spent the day with us. He had come back to the province during the holiday break from university in Phnom Penh. On this particular day, his father was surrounded with drinking buddies. His step-father did not want him home with his mother. He savored being in a Christian home. He discussed issues with Hubert, then baked bread and cookies with me. His girlfriend had recently broken up with him. He really wanted God's leading in his life decisions. God did lead him later to a lovely Christian wife, a good job in Phnom Penh, and a church in which to serve the Lord.

God showered many little gifts on me during the two-week trip to the CMDA-CME conference in Athens, Greece, April 22 – May 10, 2014. I had attended this excellent medical conference for medical missionaries every two years, but this time it was held in a different country than before. At the border leaving Koh Kong, Lekana's father was the immigration police who stamped my passport. One of the van service workers on the Thai side expressed appreciation for an ultrasound done for his wife sometime before.

After flying from Bangkok to Dubai, United Arab Emirates, the next gift was at boarding when the flight attendant said, "Congratulations, you have been moved to business class!" The tender beef and warmed mixed nuts and other Middle Eastern cuisine were exceptional. Having room to stretch out was so nice. A smaller plane made the hop from Athens to Thessaloniki. When my suitcase did not appear on the belt with the others, God answered prayer and the claims desk clerk said to look in the next room. It had come in as international arrival.

The "Footsteps of the Apostles" tour began that evening at a beautiful hotel. Many of the fellow tour members were missionaries or presenters I knew from previous conferences. The following day the tour buses took us to Neapolis where Paul and his companions had first entered Europe by ship about two thousand years ago. We followed the old Roman Via Egnatia, a road constructed in the second century BC. At Philippi, the river believed to be where Lydia and friends met, was a perfect spot for sitting and reading the account from Acts 16. Walking in the archeological site of old Philippi, we could envision the demon possessed slave girl following Paul and Silas, and God's power poured out to rescue her. Then we stood on the probable spot where officials arrested and beat those early missionaries. Exploring the theatre where Christians were martyred was sobering. After seeing the Agora (central public square) and other antiquities in Thessalonica (now Thessaloniki), it was on to Berea where Paul taught in the synagogue and the believers searched the Scriptures daily, then helped him escape, via a long journey through mountain passes down to Athens.

The grave of Philip the Second, father of Alexander the Great, in Vergina, displayed many treasures. Among those was Philip II's dazzling gold diadem, shaped like intricate fine branches and leaves. Our tour guide, a Greek Bible College professor, explained diadems and crowns in history and in Scripture signifying victories and awards. Athens was rich with ancient history of philosophers, democracy, Paul's sermon on Mars Hill, and much more. The following weekend our destination was Corinth, crossing the deep Corinthian canal to reach the archeological site. There was so much evidence in stone for skeptics of Scripture.

The medical conference, on an Aegean Sea island outside of Athens, had a gorgeous view of mountains and superb Greek food. My roommate, Joy Hart, served as a missionary physician in Chad, and had helped at Ippy, CAR, back when she was a student. We shared stories of what God had done and enjoyed walks together. Several pre-conference courses were offered, from which I had chosen Trauma Assessment and Resuscitation. It was excellent and I thanked God for helping me prepare for it during the months leading up to the course. I used that information many times in Cambodia.

Subsequent days were filled with a great variety of lectures from experts in their field who also had overseas experience and loved God. The content of most talks was so applicable to the practice of missionary medicine. Others informed us of new things happening in medicine which we needed to know, especially upon our return to the States. Prayer times, preaching the Word, and hearing reports of God's work in medical missions in so many places were so encouraging. Truly God had poured out blessings in abundance preparing me to reenter His work in Koh Kong.

In June, Hubert went to the US Embassy to apply for a new passport. The photos he presented were not accepted, so he had to leave and reenter two more times until he had one that was right. He still had time to pick up new glasses, grab lunch and catch the bus to Koh Kong. Three weeks later, Thursday, June 26, 2014, I went back to Phnom Penh. God helped in getting a tuk-tuk to the hotel, in getting a rental motorcycle at the hotel quickly, in finding parking at the US embassy, and walking out with Hubert's passport about five minutes later. The paperwork I had taken to allow me to pick it up was all in order. I took the passport to the travel agent to get a Cambodian visa. She said it usually takes four working days. I prayed it would be only three days so I could return to Koh Kong on Tuesday but was happy to do whatever God had planned.

Monday, I changed my bus ticket from Tuesday to Wednesday since the visa had not yet arrived. Tuesday was a quiet day, waiting for the call that the visa was ready. Late afternoon I went to check on it and was told – not until Wednesday. I was disappointed because I also needed to get it to the Chinese embassy for a visa for our trip to China. But God had a special purpose which I did not want to miss.

Wednesday morning was a lovely time with the Lord as I again waited in the hotel. About 8:45 am I got a call that the Cambodian visa was ready! I hurried to pick it up, photocopy the new passport and visa, and head to the Chinese embassy. God helped me find parking and cross the busy street. The man at the counter said I needed a copy of Hadessah's passport and visa as well, since she was inviting us to visit her. I went back to the hotel and then to an internet café where I phoned Hadessah in China. She sent the document by email, which I was able to receive at the café and put on a flash drive. I took that to a photocopy shop to print out.

Then I drove back to the Chinese embassy, stopping for gas when I saw the tank was on empty, and got there by 11 am, thirty minutes before they closed for the day. They accepted everything and said to pick up completed visas on Monday! I was able to catch the 1 pm van that day from Phnom Penh to Koh Kong! There was plenty of room for my baggage. The ride was good. I enjoyed the Lord and His creation. The van delivered me to our house at 6:20 pm Wednesday. What an amazing God! A week later Hubert picked up our passports with their new Chinese visas. In August, we had a wonderful ten days visiting Hadessah.

In October 2014, a husband and wife team from the USA arrived in Koh Kong at 10 in the morning. At 11 am they taught the first session on protecting unborn babies, to some people from the church and students from Hubert's English classes. In the afternoon, they taught at the hospital 2:30 pm – 4 pm to the nurses, midwives, and doctors. We prayed the lives of babies would be saved and some of the people who heard the presentations would find salvation in Christ. The presenters had travel fatigue and jet lag during their less than twenty-four hours with us, but served God. The next day I took them back to Trat.

Koh Kong hospital did not do abortions, but midwives did them at their private clinics. Later, the obstetrics doctor said that after seeing the DVD showing dismemberment abortions, she would never do an abortion. The visitors gave me a set of fetal models (like little dolls) made to the true size and weight of babies in the womb at different months of development. I used them many times when talking to patients after doing their obstetric ultrasounds, especially for the mothers considering termination of their pregnancy.

On October 24, 2014, Hans phoned from Michigan announcing the birth of our new grandson, Peter! A few hours later I was present at the birth of another of Wi's grandsons in Koh Kong. How special for grandmothers to celebrate together! The next day, when I visited Wi with her grandchild and the parents, Wi related that when she had stepped out of the room, the baby's great-grandmother had tied a piece of red yarn on the baby's wrist for protection from evil spirits. The baby cried and cried. When the great-grandmother left the room, Wi cut off the yarn. The baby became immediately quiet and slept peacefully the rest of the night. Wi knew that protection came only from God.

God arranges networks of people. Hubert and I needed to check out the town of Sipat for possibly having a mobile clinic there the following January. It was in the next health district, but now the PHD had approved me to work anywhere in the province. Lalin had a friend who loaned us his pick-up that Hubert could drive up to the mountain town. When we turned off the main road, we chose roads following the telephone line to know where to go. There were five forks in the road, connecting fields in this agricultural region. At one point the road was blocked by a tree but there was a motor-cycle ahead of us and we followed him, finding the detour. God's provision. When we reached a big river, there was no driver for the car ferry. So, we parked the pick-up and crossed on the pedestrian/motorcycle ferry.

Walking in and around the main town, we saw perfume trees, sugar cane fields, rubber trees, a waterfall, rapids, and many gorgeous flowers. Tourism was developing there. We found the health center and talked with a midwife, with the director, and with a peace corps volunteer. The director was the man Hubert had met on a bus, who had encouraged him to visit Sipat. We checked guest houses and found them very basic and without electricity. One of the ladies at the restaurant recognized me and said years ago she had visited our house with Pren. Hubert met a man who asked if he knew Lalin. They used to be neighbors. God opened the way for a mobile clinic to be held there the following January. One patient arrived late morning carried on the back of his younger teenage sister. They were orphans. The severe weakness in his legs and arms was probably Guillain-Barré syndrome. They saw no way to get to a place with advanced supportive care, and the sister carried him away.

2015 PEACE

A newborn at the hospital had developed signs of sepsis (infection) four hours after birth. The parents wanted him transferred to Phnom Penh, but the hospital felt he was too unstable. The next day they said there was no doctor available to accompany the patient in the ambulance, and how would the baby be kept warm. I volunteered to go and urged that the infant be placed skin to skin with its mother for warmth, kangaroo style. We took off. The father followed the ambulance in his car. Just out of Koh Kong city, the midwife realized she had forgotten the transfer papers. The ambulance stopped and the driver asked the father to go back to the hospital for them. I prayed we would have the paperwork needed to admit the patient on arrival. The ambulance then proceeded at high speed. The father retrieved the paperwork and caught up with us!

It was a record time for the ambulance: three hours and ten minutes to go 186 miles – the last being in city traffic! Praise God that it was the first day of Chinese New Year, so traffic was not as heavy as usual. Many city dwellers were gone to the provinces. The pediatric hospital began the needed care and forty minutes later the midwife and I headed for the exit. As we left, the parents thanked us profusely. It took us four hours and fifteen minutes to return as we stopped for supper halfway. I had expected to get home in the middle of the night, but we made it by 8:15 pm. We did not see any wildlife in the darkness through the mountains the last couple hours of the trip. The baby made a good recovery.

One busy day at the hospital began at 4:30 am with a call to go do an ultrasound for a trauma victim. He had a knife wound with internal bleeding. He was taken to surgery, and they sutured his lacerated liver.

A couple of weeks later, Lekana joined me at Koh Kong hospital during her break from medical school in Phnom Penh. The staff was always happy to have medical students. That day I assisted on two cesarean section operations. The first baby had fetal hydrops which I had seen on the ultrasound. It did not survive. The seventeen-year-old mother lived in Thailand but had been sent across the border to Koh Kong for care because she was from Cambodia.

During her hospital stay, she made a profession of faith, so Hubert and I later visited her in Thailand several times for discipleship.

"The water ate my leg" was the complaint of a fisherman with chronic kidney disease who arrived with one huge leg. It resembled elephantiasis from filaria I had seen in Africa. Searching the UpToDate medical program on my phone led to the diagnosis of marine lymphangitis. The leg was definitely infected. After many days of treatment as an inpatient, he finally recovered.

MORE WATER CHALLENGES

The 2015 rainy season was late in starting. City water was off for some time, then when it came on, we had trouble filtering drinking water due to the slime. Sometimes we strained the water through a pillowcase before using it for laundry. About a week later, it was rainy all day. The evening was cool and nice for sleeping. It was nice to have plenty of rain for the laundry but hard for the clothes to dry.

Two days later, Hubert had to fix the water pump for our rainwater system. Praise God he found the part he needed in Koh Kong. In the past, we would have had to get it in Phnom Penh or Thailand. Two days after that, the guest bathroom toilet started leaking, so Hubert and I worked together much of the afternoon fixing that. And yet a couple days later, our water saga continued, repairing the toilet fixtures in the guest bathroom again. The city water intermittently sent high pressure which the weak plumbing could not handle. Next, water leaked through the ceiling from the upstairs bathroom like a couple of years previously. Then in September, a single day registered 8.9 inches of rain plus wind. The result was some wet tables and papers at the hospital since the medicine ward nurses' station was both a room and a place to write on the veranda.

LEAVING THIS EARTH

Monday, November 9, Cambodian Independence Day, I was hoping for the day off along with the rest of the staff but knew that the visiting French doctors would need interpreters. Lots of patients were waiting for them. I helped with completing forms and interpreting. We stopped at noon, and I went to join all the hospital staff who had come in and were waiting at the emergency department for patients from a bus rollover in the mountains. Someone bought all the doctors sugar cane juice while we were waiting for the ambulances since we were missing lunch. A few minutes later ambulances started arriving. In all, thirteen victims arrived. The first had lost a lot of blood from a traumatic amputation. There were lots of head injuries, several fractures, a probable hemothorax (blood in the chest), and many other injuries. Patients got cared for. Some were intubated but neither the emergency department nor the intensive care unit had ventilators, so friends manually squeezed Ambu bags to assist breathing. Four patients were transferred to Phnom Penh. Two patients died at the accident scene and two more in the hospital. The patients were all workers for one company. High officials and newsmen came. What a reminder of how suddenly without warning the end of life on earth can arrive. People need to be ready to meet God.

It was a big step forward when the hospital initiated their electronic medical records system. The paper charts now were filed and retrievable for continuity of care. The computer listed diagnosis codes and patient names and numbers, so the staff learned to look up and chart the codes. Staff and patients were running back and forth to get things in place and flowing. Patients carried their charts to the cashier's room, now computerized, where the records were filed. We were grateful to have better records to assist in patient treatment.

On a Saturday Skype visit and prayer time with my sisters, I learned my step-mother's health was declining more. She was ninety-one years old and had gastric cancer. What comfort to know the day of her homegoing was planned by God. He would orchestrate if I could attend the funeral and He would take care of the work in Koh Kong. Emails kept us informed of Mother's condition. I anticipated a call at any time.

God sent Hadessah to celebrate Christmas with us as well as be a comfort to me during the time of Mother's departure. After phoning my step-sister, Noreen, and praying, I believed God would have me go ahead and book tickets to fly to Michigan to be there for the funeral. I made arrangements for teachers in the various classes while I would be away and told the hospital director my plans. Late that evening was a special time talking and praying with Hadessah. Tuesday, December 29 Hans phoned at 1:30 pm telling us Mom had just peacefully stepped into glory.

The next morning Hubert and Hadessah saw me off on a van to Phnom Penh. Many people were praying, and God gave strength for the trip plus he gave opportunities to share the gospel with fellow passengers on the various flights. The reading light did not work, and no one was seated by me in the fourteen-and-a-half-hour flight from Doha to Philadelphia. The cabin was kept dark except for meals. It gave good time for prayer, and rest, and thinking of happy memories of Mom. After nearly twenty-four hours of darkness, it was nice to see a glorious sunrise above the clouds just before landing through the solid layer of low clouds. It reminded me that our lives are by faith and not by sight. Beyond this life, Christians will see Christ and the splendor of heaven. January 2, 2016, was the funeral with all ten children and most of their spouses present.

God had worked things out that I could be part of the celebration of her life, lived for the Lord. After four more days enjoying stateside friends and family, I traveled back to Cambodia.

2016 FINISHING IN CAMBODIA

Our February – March 2016 prayer letter reported:

> We are thankful that our church here voted to call a Cambodian Pastor, Mr. Lalin. He is a young man we led to the Lord over ten years ago and we have taught and discipled him since then. A second deacon was voted in as well and a new member added. The church is now autonomous. We will remain here for a short time in only an advisory position. Please pray for the church to joyfully follow God's leading in everything. Lalin has a real pastor's heart. He loves people, visits the members of the church, and prays for them. He is good at preaching, and teaching from small children to adults. He has been teaching discipleship courses for a long time. He is also humble and a hard worker. He has an ice cream shop/business which can supplement his small salary from the church. It also makes him well-known all over town. Please pray that if it pleases the Lord, God would bless the shop so that it can continue, and yet allow Lalin the time he needs for pastoral responsibilities. We are anticipating leaving for furlough this coming July. We do not expect to return to Koh Kong. We

do not know yet what ministry the Lord has for us
after furlough.

On June 19, 2016, the church began meeting in Lalin's shop
instead of our house. It was so nice for the church to have a
bigger space.

The CMDA conference in April 2016 was again in Athens,
Greece, and again God blessed richly through it. On one of the
flights returning, while over Saudi Arabia approaching Doha, Qatar,
the plane went into a holding pattern. The map on the screen in
front of my seat showed the plane circled the airport twice. Looking
straight out the window, it looked like the bright white half-moon
glided past us, and a little later, glided past again. When the plane
landed, I looked up to see the moon fixed high in the sky and yellow
through the sand suspended in the desert air. The moon hadn't
changed. My view of it had. God never changes. May we get to
know Him ever more clearly as we watch Him work in diverse ways.

God gave me a friendship with a pharmacist in Koh Kong
whom I visited sometimes at her pharmacy. It was raining lightly
on one visit. She had lots of questions about Christianity. We visited for over an hour, although there were a few interruptions for
her to wait on customers who weren't stopped by the rain. God was
blessing so much. A couple days later, even though the hospital work
was quite busy both morning and afternoon, God gave great peace.
I was able to teach on the Good Shepherd at 11:15 am at the house
and give a piano lesson at noon. At 5 pm was a discipleship lesson on
Elisha with a student. He was delighted to learn stories he had never
heard before that showed God's power. I loved the work God gave.

PHD asked for a paper summarizing my work in Cambodia
that they could keep for the record. They offered to prepare a letter
of recommendation for me. It was a good note to finish on. The

Buddhist hospital administrator mentioned that I was earning lots of merit with God by my service to people at the hospital. He said God was pleased with me because He gave me good health. I tried to explain to him again that only the work and merits of Christ given to me by grace count for salvation from sin. God had blessed me with health to do the tasks He had for me. People have such a hard time understanding. Only God can give sight to the spiritually blind. When the hospital director was discussing with me a patient who had advanced hepatocellular carcinoma (liver cancer), we talked about palliative care. He suggested I talk to the patient about Christ. It was amazing to hear this Buddhist person admit that hope is found in the Lord Jesus and no other.

In May and June, five short-termers from the USA worked with us. Specialty clinics at the hospital in the morning drew many people as specialized care for patients was provided. Point-of-care teaching was valuable for the staff. Various Christians from the church talked with patients one-on-one about Christ as they waited. Afternoons were lectures for the staff with practical medical information in dermatology and neurology. The last couple of weeks at the hospital were busy. Three Bible studies a day continued at home and packing got sandwiched in.

It was good news that a missionary family was led by the Lord to transfer from another country to work in Cambodia! They graciously agreed to accept our household items, which was God's provision for them and for us preparing to leave in July. We joined our co-workers from two other towns to meet the new family at Phnom Penh airport, then celebrated their arrival over lunch. Hubert and I took the afternoon bus back to Koh Kong, arriving about 7:30 pm to a dark house with no electricity, and it was raining. We learned from our landlord that a storm the day before had caused damage to wires going to the house's meter. The electric company said they could not put up new wires until the rain stopped. But it was rainy season in Koh Kong, where it rained almost every day!

Wednesday, day three of lots of rain, the moving truck scheduled to come at 7 am was waiting to come until the rain stopped. Meanwhile, a crew of friends was standing, waiting at our house, eager to load. After phone calls, the truck came and was able to back under the awning. The truck bed had sides, but no top, so a tarp was placed across the top. One of the church men did great at organizing and packing things in the truck. Many hands helped. By 9:30 am everything was loaded in spite of two inches of rain in two hours. More tarps were tied over everything. God worked and the truck delivered its load about 8 pm to the new missionaries in Phnom Penh, with everything dry!

Lalin brought over his nice two-burner counter-top gas stove for us to cook on. The house looked rather bare. We were grateful for some furniture from the landlord. He also strung an extension cord from his house to ours, so our kitchen had a light bulb. Without electricity, we could not pump rainwater into the house system but there was a good supply of city water. Hubert washed clothes by hand, but they took a week to dry. One bedroom's ceiling was leaking again. God protected and not much got wet of our stack of things there to pack for the USA. The tiles in the middle upstairs room buckled and cracked from the humidity. Without electricity to charge the cellphone, run the computers or connect with the internet we had to take them to Lalin's to charge. The lesson for the Ladies' Sunday School class that week was on contentment. Our little ice box with blue ice from Lalin's shop's freezer was working well since we no longer had a fridge (or oven, or microwave, or washer, etc.). We slept well in the cool evenings as the rain continued. God continually showered us with the blessings of seeing His enabling us and meeting every need.

On my last day working at Koh Kong Referral Hospital, in the morning staff meeting, the hospital director gave a speech of appreciation for my years of volunteer service with them. I thanked the hospital and staff and told of Christ once more. Many photos were taken. That evening there was a farewell dinner at a restaurant. They graciously presented me with a staff photo taken in 2010, and a painting. I loved the special people I worked with day after day for so long. But my heart ached knowing most of them were still on their way to eternity without Christ. The new buildings functioned well. Rooms and the grounds were cleaner. There was new equipment. The staff gave good medical care and showed compassion. Record keeping was updated. The government commending Koh Kong Provincial Referral Hospital for having become one of the best provincial hospitals in Cambodia was because of what God had done.

The next Sunday was sunny all day! It was nice to have lower humidity and things drying. In the morning service, there was a young lady visiting for the first time. She wanted to know how to have her sins forgiven. She also wondered if she could do something for her deceased mother. It was wonderful to watch Wi and Kenh answering her questions. No, it was too late to help her deceased mother. But God offered forgiveness to the living who would believe in Him. A baptismal service was held the next Lord's Day for a young lady we had been discipling for some time. The church would remain. God's people could continue teaching His Word in Koh Kong. People we had talked with knew they could go to the church for answers from God's Word.

Our Phnom Penh missionary friends had a special farewell for us during their Fourth of July celebration. We met with many Cambodian friends in Phnom Penh to say goodbye, pray together, and admonish them to faithfully follow the Lord. God would be present with them.

When we returned to Koh Kong, we whittled down our possessions to one check-in bag apiece plus carry-ons to take with us back to the States. The electricity was finally restored to our house after ten days being off. Electric lights seemed so bright compared to the candles we had been using. Throughout the last week, visitors were stopping by to say thank you and good-bye, and we visited many friends. Bible studies continued. God answered prayer for the paperwork to get done for the sale of both motorcycles.

The final Sunday, my Sunday School lesson to the ladies was on Hebrews 12 – looking unto Jesus. What a reminder to them and to us for the days ahead. One of the ladies brought a cake she had beautifully decorated showing Jesus the Good Shepherd. The evening service was packed with about sixty-one people. At the end, the church surprised us with a ten-minute video of God's working through us in Koh Kong which a missionary friend had helped them put together. Then there was a meal that several people had helped to prepare. Lots of pictures were taken, lots of hugs, some tears. Several people came that had not come to church for years – still unsaved. The mother of two of the youth came and helped. She was so grateful for her two children following Christ. I longed for her to follow Christ also. We thanked God for what He had done.

Tuesday morning we closed the suitcases and cleared the last things out of the cupboards. Friends came to say good-bye, some tearful that they might never see us again. About 10 am many others came – church people and friends, and an Australian man asking for a medical consult. The retired hospital director and her husband drove up and loaded our bags into their nice car. I rode with them, and Hubert drove our little motorcycle to the border to deliver to the buyer. We delivered two spare tires for the big Honda as well.

One mother in her car, a couple of hospital vehicles, and several motorcycles followed us to the border. It was Lekana's father who stamped our passports for departure. We took pictures and said goodbye to our hospital friends. The church people walked with us to the Thai border and waited there for the pick-up taxi to leave. We thanked God for our Cambodian friends.

On arrival in Klang Yai we left most of our bags at the van station and walked to the bank. But it was closed for a holiday. We decided to spend the night and talk to the bank in the morning, trusting God to get us to our afternoon flight in Bangkok on time. We had a relaxing afternoon watching mudskippers by the docks. We were waiting at the bank when it opened at 8:30 am and made it to Bangkok airport two hours ahead of our flight's departure. Check-in went smoothly. There were no lines in security nor in passport control. We were able to sleep a bit on the five-and-a-half-hour flight to Abu Dhabi, the capital of UAE. A six-hour flight took us to Paris where we took the train to Bordeaux to begin a wonderful month with Jonathan and Cherith and family. They were missionaries there. Eventful travel kept us depending on the Lord, who faithfully helped us make all our flights, including changing planes in Iceland, and on to Michigan, August 17, 2016.

Reporting to our churches in the USA the next year, we were delighted to tell what God had done in the lovely, rainy land of Cambodia. Numerous people had heard the good news of Jesus Christ. God had rescued many individuals, giving them eternal life. People had grown in the knowledge of God and His Word. Cambodians were teaching others. The sick had received care. We had seen God powerfully work. The Lord had kept His promise, "I am with you always" (Matthew 28:20).

CONCLUSION

God delights to show us his power! What joy to watch His victories over the challenges! He is more than able to care for us wherever He leads. Entrusting our lives to Him and following the path He has chosen for us leads to knowing Him more and seeing His marvelous working. In response we praise Him. The Lord does not just send us to serve Him; He takes us there, with His precious presence continually with us.

As God reminded the Israelites throughout Deuteronomy about His presence with them and tender care for their every need, so we need to recall God's faithfulness in the past. We have not only seen Him work in the big picture over the years, leading and letting us serve, but also in the daily challenges. Our lives will bring glory to God as we truly let Him take us anywhere He chooses, and do anything He wants through us. God's ways are so much better than our choices. There will be tests of our faith to strengthen us, and lessons to humble us. Among many other things, language learning was humbling. "That he might humble you and test you, to do you good in the end" (Deuteronomy 8:16).

The first step is being sure you have received salvation from sin. Do you truly have Christ living in you? In each of the countries God took us to, we saw people repent and believe in Jesus to cleanse them from sin and give them eternal life. Their lives were changed by the power of God. They are rejoicing on their way to heaven.

From that point, one continues to study the Bible, the Word of God, and obey what it says. Through it we know God and His ways. Be regular and active in a church that teaches God's Word well. The Lord promises to be with His own and guide as we walk with Him by faith. "I will instruct you and teach you in the way you should go; I will counsel you with my eye upon you" (Psalm 32:8).

Someday, in heaven, we will be gathered with the "great multitude that no one could number, from every nation, from all tribes and peoples and languages, standing before the throne and before the Lamb, clothed in white robes ... crying out with a loud voice, 'Salvation belongs to our God who sits on the throne, and to the Lamb!'" (Revelation 7:9-10).

About the Author

God saved Mary Broeckert at the age of 7 and called her to serve Him as a missionary doctor at the age of 11. Her pre-professional studies were at Grand Valley State University, and her M.D. from Michigan State University. After linguistic training and French language study, she and her husband, Hubert Broeckert, M.Div., with their four young children left for the Sahara dessert. Then the Lord moved their family, now including a fifth child, to the grasslands of Africa to work in Baptist Mid-Mission's hospital at Ippy, Central African Republic. God enabled her in the medical and surgical duties of the hospital as well as in teaching, administration, construction of new buildings, and outreach to remote mission clinics. Later, the Lord took the Broeckerts to Cambodia in Southeast Asia where Dr. Mary cared for patients together with the Cambodian medical staff of a government provincial hospital.

Although now retired from active missionary service, God continues to use Dr. Mary in various ministries of her local church, on medical mission trips, in Women's Missionary Union, and in the Christian Medical and Dental Association. She also enjoys playing piano, hiking, and scrapbooking. She would be delighted to hear from you concerning your relationship with God or about is leading you in missions. Her email is PresentandPowerful@ gmail.com.